Andrew Glassner's Notebook

RECREATIONAL
COMPUTER
GRAPHICS

THE MORGAN KAUFMANN SERIES IN COMPUTER GRAPHICS AND GEOMETRIC MODELING

Series Editor, Brian A. Barsky

Andrew Glassner's Notebook: Recreational Computer Graphics
Andrew S. Glassner

Curves and Surfaces in Geometric Modeling: Theory and Algorithms
Jean Gallier

Warping and Morphing of Graphical Objects
Jonas Gomes, Lucia Darsa, Bruno Costa, and Luis Velho

Jim Blinn's Corner: Dirty Pixels
Jim Blinn

Rendering with Radiance: The Art and Science of Lighting Visualization
Greg Ward Larson and Rob Shakespeare

Introduction to Implicit Surfaces
Edited by Jules Bloomenthal

Jim Blinn's Corner: A Trip Down the Graphics Pipeline
Jim Blinn

Interactive Curves and Surfaces: A Multimedia Tutorial on CAGD
Alyn Rockwood and Peter Chambers

Wavelets for Computer Graphics: Theory and Applications
Eric J. Stollnitz, Tony D. DeRose, and David H. Salesin

Principles of Digital Image Synthesis
Andrew S. Glassner

Radiosity & Global Illumination
François X. Sillion and Claude Puech

Knotty: A B-Spline Visualization Program
Jonathan Yen

User Interface Management Systems: Models and Algorithms
Dan R. Olsen, Jr.

Making Them Move: Mechanics, Control, and Animation of Articulated Figures
Edited by Norman I. Badler, Brian A. Barsky, and David Zeltzer

Geometric and Solid Modeling: An Introduction
Christoph M. Hoffmann

An Introduction to Splines for Use in Computer Graphics and Geometric Modeling
Richard H. Bartels, John C. Beatty, and Brian A. Barsky

Andrew Glassner's Notebook

RECREATIONAL
COMPUTER
GRAPHICS

Andrew S. Glassner

Morgan Kaufmann Publishers
San Francisco, California

Senior Editor   Diane D. Cerra
Director of Production and Manufacturing   Yonie Overton
Production Editors   Julie Pabst/Cheri Palmer
Editorial Coordinator   Belinda Breyer
Cover and Text Design   Ross Carron Design
Copyeditor   Julie Pabst
Proofreader   Ken DellaPenta
Composition and Illustration   Technologies 'N Typography
Indexer   Steve Rath
Printer   Courier Corporation

Morgan Kaufmann Publishers
Editorial and Sales Office
340 Pine Street, Sixth Floor
San Francisco, CA 94104-3205
USA
Telephone   415 / 392-2665
Facsimile   415 / 982-2665
Email   mkp@mkp.com
WWW   *http://www.mkp.com*
Order toll free   800 / 745-7323

Library of Congress Cataloging-in-Publication Data

Glassner, Andrew S.
    Andrew Glassner's notebook : recreational computer graphics /
Andrew S. Glassner
      p.   cm.
    ISBN 1-55860-598-3
    1. Computer graphics.   I. Title.
    T385 .G578 1999
    006.6—dc21   99-28111
                                                           CIP

To the memory of
Leo Hershdorfer,
uncle and inspiration

Contents

Preface

This book is about having fun with computer graphics.

In 1996 I started writing a regular column called *Andrew Glassner's Notebook* for the bimonthly magazine *IEEE Computer Graphics & Applications.* I thought it would be fun to come up with interesting and entertaining topics and write about them. I was right! But what I didn't expect was how absorbing the process would be. Generally I start each column with a vague idea or an interesting little fact, and by the time I'm done I'm half-convinced that there's an entire lifetime of investigation lurking behind the subject. Writing each column has been like opening a new door. In reading this book, a compilation of the columns, I hope you'll experience the same feelings of pleasure and discovery that I found in each one.

In the Beginning

The origins of this book trace back to the 1995 annual Siggraph conference, when Bert Herzog, then Editor-in-Chief of *CG&A,* spoke to me about writing a column for the magazine. My first thought was that it would be superfluous—Jim Blinn had been writing a very popular and highly respected column for *CG&A* for several years. But perhaps my approach to graphics might be sufficiently different from Jim's that my column could make a contribution. On the strength of that possibility, I agreed to write a first column on spec for Bert, and he could judge whether or not he wanted to pursue it. I had no idea what I would write about, or where column ideas came from, or how I would write a column even if I had an idea.

At the time I was working at Xerox PARC in Palo Alto, California, at the northern end of Silicon Valley. A couple of months after my conversation with Bert I accepted a new position at Microsoft Research, near Seattle. A wise friend counseled me to take some time off between jobs, and I embarked on a three-month hiking and camping trip through the national parks in southwest Utah.

One day while driving across the New Mexico desert I saw an astounding sight: what looked like a herd of enormous satellite dishes spread out over an acre or two of land. I followed a few dirt roads toward them and found myself at a national radiotelescope facility called (appropriately enough) the Very Large Array. The VLA is made up of 27 dishes, each with a diameter of 82 feet. They are equally divided over three railroad tracks, each 10 miles long, arranged in a Y formation. The dishes can be moved along the tracks—I happened to catch them at a time when they were close together. All of those eyes looking skyward were an inspiring sight.

Touring the visitors' center I read about some of the VLA researchers' recent work. They had captured an image of a group of stars moving faster, it seemed, than the speed of light. They eventually figured out that the stars weren't breaking the law; it was an illusion resulting from a very specific and tricky bit of geometry involving the Earth and the stars. Wow—light, geometry, science—it all sounded like a column! Out there in the desert, I wrote my first column for Bert. I'd been reading some Sherlock Holmes stories at the time, so for fun I adopted Sir Conan Doyle's style for the column. When I finally made my way to Seattle and got settled, I finished the column and sent it in. I'd had fun writing it, and Bert liked it, so we had a match and a column was born.

That column was never published. I wanted to start with something more specifically related to graphics and instead wrote a new column describing solar halos. That column was printed in January 1996, and it's the first half of Chapter 1 of this book. I should probably revise and use the faster-than-light column. Otherwise, the floppy disk format it's saved on will become obsolete and unreadable!

Many Columns, One Book

The halo column, like several others that came after, was too long for a single issue, so I split it into two pieces that ran in successive issues of the magazine. Making a two-part column work is a tricky job, because I can't assume that a reader of one part has read (or will read) the other part. So each half has to be somewhat self-contained, yet they need to be cumulative. I'm happy to say that when we put this book together, I took the opportunity to merge each pair of columns into a single whole.

I also dug into my correspondence and notes to improve each column. Of course, I first attacked all the errors I was aware of and addressed them. Sometimes this meant simply fixing a typo, but in some cases it meant adding new text or figures. I believe that the columns, printed here as chapters, are free of all preexisting errors. I hope I haven't added many new ones! If you should find one, please send an email describing the error to *glassner@mkp.com*. I will post any errata for the book on my Web page at *http://www.research.microsoft.com/glassner/*. There you also can find notes and errata on the original columns, as well as online files and animations.

Then I went back over my original drafts to look at material that didn't make it into the magazine because of space considerations. In some of the chapters I've been able to restore entire sections that were reduced or even eliminated. In others I've added material that I ran across or thought of after the columns were originally published. I hope that this new material will interest people who read the columns when they first appeared.

Theme and Variation

I still don't know where ideas come from, but looking back over this collection a recurring theme stands out: patterns. There are patterns in the geometry, in the figures, and even in the occasional wordplay in the text. I know that patterns of all types have always fascinated me, and I have found that other people share my appreciation and enjoyment of new patterns.

My theory for this is that patterns have a special quality that is resonant with the human spirit. We are creatures of the world, after all, and respond to aspects of the world that seem to connect with something of how we're built. We clearly aren't random beings—our bodies are the result of engineering of breathtaking scale and complexity. But we also don't have the rigid, static structure of a quartz crystal. Rather, we're somewhere in between structure and randomness.

And that's where patterns are. A chaotic bashing of piano keys is unattractive to most of us, because it's too random to hold our interest: there's nothing to latch onto and examine. And a structured running of the scales also fails to inspire, because the precise and expected nature of the sequence is simply boring after a while. But when the piano keys follow a prescription laid down by J. S. Bach, something emerges: patterns of melody, rhythm, and harmony grab our attention and reward it. A Bach invention has surprises, but it has security. We are delighted and comforted at the same time by Bach's beautiful manipulation of musical patterns.

There are patterns everywhere, occupying the sweet spot between chaos and order. There are patterns in the fall of raindrops in a puddle, the sounds of our friends' voices, and the way they walk across a room. We see structure in the shapes of clouds, we hear words in the wind, and we make sense of the world around us by understanding the patterns it contains.

Along the Path

You may have noticed that there are a few chapters in this book about building real, physical models. That may seem unusual for a book about computer graphics—after all, where's the computer? My reason for writing about physical models is that I've found that they are a terrific way of building up the mental muscles involved in imagining and visualizing other 3D shapes, including those that can only exist inside a computer. Although I'd heard other people describe the power of 3D models for building up an internal intuition, I didn't realize it myself until a vacation to New Zealand several years ago.

A friend suggested I visit the town of Wanaka, where I would find a large hedge maze. It wasn't hard to find—it was a very big maze. In fact, the sign out front proclaimed it was the largest 3D maze in the world, with "1½ km of confusing passageways including 200 metres of overhead paths & gentle stairways." Of course, I paid my admission and entered.

The maze was a dense nest of corridors that were just wide enough for two people to pass if both folks turned sideways. The walls were made of tall wooden partitions that were too high to see over, but every now and then I found myself climbing a staircase and then walking across a bridge—these bridges were what made it 3D. Each bridge was like a two-lane road with a big wooden wall in the middle. As you traveled over the bridge you could look down over the side nearest you and see some of the maze below.

The maze was a huge rectangle, and in each corner there was a colored flag. The stated goal was to find each flag, then make your way to the center where a shop was located. There were emergency exits every now and then that you could scoot through if you wanted to give up.

When I first went into the maze, I walked around at random for a while, enjoying the novelty of the experience. But then I decided to actually try to solve the maze and find the flags. My first idea was to use a trick that lots of early maze-searching robots used, called the Right-Hand Rule. You put your right hand on one of the walls and simply walk along, always keeping your hand touching the wall. If the maze doesn't violate a few specific rules, you're guaranteed to eventually visit the entire maze.

I remember putting my hand out but then feeling a little embarrassed—it seemed ridiculous that a human being, enjoying a warm sunny day in a beautiful place, faced with a unique and challenging puzzle, should reduce the whole experience to an algorithm. Surely there was a better way!

I wandered around, looking for visual cues, but the maze was pretty uniform: dirt and grass below and wooden walls to the sides. At one point I found myself on one of the bridges, with a bird's-eye view of about half the maze. Aha! I pulled out a pen and paper and started to draw as much of the maze as I could see. But then again, I stopped about as soon as I'd begun. First, it would take forever to draw this big maze. Second, even if I did draw the whole thing, then I would have succeeded only in reducing this one-of-a-kind experience down to the solution of a paper maze, which hardly seemed fitting.

I resolved to approach this maze as it deserved: an experience for my mind and body to solve together. Standing at a four-way intersection, I took a few breaths, calmed my mind, and then carefully looked at the space around me. On the wooden partitions I saw weather marks and peeling paint in interesting shapes. On the ground I saw rocks and small tufts of grass. I couldn't have articulated everything that I noticed, but I took in the details that made up this particular spot.

Then I started to walk, slowly, staying alert, looking at everything, following a corridor as it twisted and turned. Eventually I hit a dead end, and I turned around. When I returned to the intersection, I recognized it, and I turned to the left. That corridor branched and I took one of the branches at random, and when it turned into a dead end I came back and took another new branch, and so on. Even when I was several branches deep into my search, I was always able to unwind to the next appropriate spot and head off into a new direction, because I always recognized each intersection and remembered the paths I'd taken before.

Without intending to, I found myself walking faster, and eventually I found the red flag. I was feeling great, and I decided to go around the maze clockwise and find the next corner. I zigged and zagged and before long I found the next flag, and then the next, and the next, all in clockwise order! Then I made my way to the entrance to the shop in the middle. They were serving lunch, and I rewarded myself with a sandwich and tea.

I thought about my experience. The trick to success didn't come from reducing the maze to an algorithm or to a diagram, but from engaging with it with mind and body. Just by walking and paying attention I was implicitly building up an internal image of the maze, part mental picture and part muscle memory. Add in the bridges and ramps and the maze sections under them and it was a pretty complicated 3D structure. But I navigated it with surprising confidence—I probably retraced my steps a couple of times, but not very many. I didn't understand the maze intellectually, but I understood it intuitively.

This experience taught me the value of directly experiencing 3D things with the mind and body together. I started to take advantage of opportunities to hold and examine 3D models, and I even tried my hand at building a few. Each time I felt that I gained a stronger appreciation of how things work in three dimensions and improved the ability of my mind's eye to imagine new 3D shapes and how they related.

Some of the chapters in this book describe how to make 3D models that are fun to build, beautiful to look at, and instructive to hold and examine. Each one has taught me something more about the subtle patterns of space. If you choose to build one or more I hope they offer you your own version of a rewarding experience.

About the Math

Some of the chapters in this book have a bunch of math. If that's not your thing, don't worry—you can skip right over it while reading the text and still follow what's going on. I've included the math because it's such an economical and precise language: in a mathematical formula you can summarize a few paragraphs of text exactly and compactly.

Writing out equations is actually a relatively recent phenomenon, given how long people have been thinking about the world. It's a specialized kind of notation, like the black dots on horizontal lines that we use today for music. And the notation changes over time—even musical notation is changing with the arrival of synthesizers and computers that are able to create sonic effects that dots and lines just can't capture.

The math in this book is largely provided to nail down details. I have worked very hard to make sure that the things I say are correct, but the math is there if you want to check for yourself and work along with the development.

I know some people who are able to read text and math together: they start at the beginning of a chapter, and devour the equations as they appear just as though they were text. This has always seemed like a remarkable skill to me. Generally, I find that the attitude required to analyze, interpret, and internalize a mathematical equation is very different from the attitude I take when reading something new for the first time. I find that reading math goes well with an analytical, step-by-step approach where I dot every i and cross every t. In contrast, reading about a new topic goes well with an open, free-associating kind of thought, where I try to hook into the author's message and see how well it fits with my own view of things. Switching back and forth every few lines is tough, and it interrupts both processes.

My approach when looking at a paper or chapter with math is to read it through once, kind of glancing at the math and maybe trying to get an overall feeling for it, but not worrying about it if that doesn't come. Then once I know what's being discussed, and I know the flow of the discussion, I might go back and look over the math again, burrowing into details here and there.

If you're not comfortable with math, you might want to try this kind of approach. Sometimes the math is easier to understand when there's context. If it's still tricky, and you want to get the details, I recommend getting together with a friend. Sharing insights is rewarding and a lot more fun than working alone and banging your head against the wall.

Tools

I believe that your tools influence your work, so I try to use good tools.

Generally each column begins with a few dozen pages of scratch paper. I print out a lot of stuff during the day, and anything that I print single-sided I save and then use the blank side for scratch. I fill the pages with notes, pictures, sketches, snippets of math, doodles, page numbers in reference books, and other bits and pieces of information that I make up or find as I explore a topic.

Once I have a big collection of bits, I sit down and try to get the big picture. Sometimes the point of a column is one or more big results, then I try to find an interesting and straightforward path to those results. Sometimes the point is to visit a bunch of interesting places along the way. Then I try to sequence those so that they start somewhere engaging and build from there. Generally I do this by scribbling big numbers on the various pages and writing pointers on yellow Post-its that I tack on here and there. I'll do this a few times until the structure makes sense to me, and then I run through the column in my head, jotting down rough sketches for the figures. So far, it's all pencil and paper.

Then I sit down at the computer and start writing the text, usually adding and removing figure references along the way. Then I make roughs of the figures, which usually invites new questions, which I then address in the text, sometimes requiring new figures, and around it goes. It's sort of like writing the lyrics and music for a song at the same time, each influencing the other. When I finally have both words and pictures roughly in place, I start editing.

The process requires an extra step when there's programming involved. Once I have the rough draft, I then write the code to make the images. Of course, I always expect it to take an afternoon, and it usually takes days to get the pictures just the way I want them.

When it's time to edit, I usually find that I've got about three to four times more material than I can actually fit into a column. The editing process forces me to choose what to keep, focus it, and tighten up the entire presentation. By the time I'm done I've usually rewritten the column two or three times. Editing is sort of like debugging, where you're trying to understand how the pieces you're working with interrelate and trying to make sure that the connections between those pieces are well formed.

The text for each chapter was composed with Microsoft Word. For some drafts of the more math-heavy chapters, I wrote LaTeX source in Word, typeset it with miktex, and then used Ghostscript for previewing. (Morgan Kaufmann used Corel's Ventura Publisher for the book's final composition.)

I created all of the figures in this book using software tools. Most of the line art was drawn with Adobe Illustrator or imported into that program for annotation and cleaning up. To create the starting versions, I used Geometer's Sketchpad from Key Curriculum Press for some of the more geometric figures, Wolfram Research's Mathematica for the plots and graphs, and sometimes my own programs that created PostScript files directly.

Similarly, almost all the raster figures passed through Adobe Photoshop at some point. Many were made directly in Photoshop, while others started out as the result of direct programming. I used MetaCreation's Painter to draw some of the color art and Kinetix's 3D Studio Max to build and render the 3D images. The photographs were taken with a Kodak DC120 digital camera.

When I needed to write programs, either to collect data or to create figures, I used Microsoft Visual Basic and Visual C++ on my PC, or vi and cc on a Silicon Graphics Indigo2 Extreme. I used geomview from the University of Minnesota Geometry Center as my interactive viewing tool for 3D objects on the SGI.

When including math, it's important to get all the details right. I double-checked most of my calculations using the symbolic and numerical tools in Mathematica and some of the geometry using Geometer's Sketchpad.

Acknowledgments

It gives me great pleasure to thank the many people that have helped me create this book. It began with Bert Herzog, Editor-in-Chief at *IEEE Computer Graphics & Applications*. It must be a scary thing to turn over to someone else several precious pages in every issue of your magazine. I appreciate the trust that opportunity represents—thank you, Bert. The staff at *CG&A* have been a pleasure to work with, and I thank Managing Editor Nancy Hays and her talented editorial staff: Robin Baldwin, Joe Daigle, Anne Lear, Alkenia Winston, Linda World, and Robin Yeary.

Several people have helped me with various columns and/or spotted errors or oversights after publication, which I have corrected in these pages.

For their help I thank Ronen Barzel, Paul Besl, Jim Blinn, Jules Bloomenthal, Bobby Bodenheimer, Marco Corvi, Maarten van Dantzich, Lakshmi Dasari, John Dill, Jim Kajiya, David Kurlander, Brian Mirtich, Nathan Myhrvold, Michael Newman, Paul Nicholls, Dan Robbins, Alvy Ray Smith, David Walton, and Geoff Wyvill. Special thanks to Eric Haines, who possesses the remarkable skill of being able to spot a good idea hiding inside a crummy one.

Microsoft Research has generously allowed me the time to develop and write these columns as part of my job. For their support at MSR I'd like to thank Michael Cohen, Jim Kajiya, Dan Ling, Rick Rashid, and Curtis Wong, as well as my colleagues in the Graphics Research Group and my new colleagues in the Next Media Group.

The friendly and creative staff at Morgan Kaufmann made the production of this book a pleasure. Thank you, Mike Morgan, Diane Cerra, and Cheri Palmer. A special thank you to Julie Pabst for organizing the project and producing a handsome result on a tight schedule.

Onward!

Writing this column is a rewarding experience. It gives me the opportunity to focus in on some interesting subjects, learn a lot about them, and then try to communicate some of the highlights in an informative and entertaining way.

I've had a lot of fun writing these columns. I hope you have a lot of fun reading them!

Andrew Glassner
Kirkland, Washington

Solar Halos and Sun Dogs

ANDREW GLASSNER'S NOTEBOOK
January & March 1996

If you walk outside on a sunny winter day when there is moisture in the air, you may notice a bright circle surrounding the sun, as in Figure 1.1a. This is a *solar halo:* it has a sharp inner edge that is located about 22 degrees away from the center of the sun and then fades out. This is shown diagrammatically in Figure 1.1b. Sometimes only fragments of the halo are visible, just as sometimes you only see an arc of a rainbow.

I live in the Seattle area, where I have frequently seen small pieces of the 22-degree halo off to the sides of the sun, as in Figure 1.2. Called *parhelia* (and informally referred to as "sun dogs"), these small fragments of bright color seem to just hang in the sky, acting as ornaments to the sun. Also visible in Figure 1.2 is the *upper tangent arc,* so named because it is tangent to the top of the 22-degree halo. As the sun rises, this upper arc wraps around and ultimately joins the *lower tangent arc* to form the *circumscribed halo,* which is visible in Figure 1.3. Finally, on rare occasions you can see a dim, large 46-degree halo centered at the sun.

If you look at the sky closely, you can see some color effects in these phenomena. But they aren't rainbows, which are created when sunlight passes through droplets of water suspended in the air (rainbows are produced by an entirely different process).

Figure 1.1
(a) The solar halo is a bright circle surrounding the sun. (Photo by Robert Greenler.) **(b)** Viewing the 22-degree solar halo.

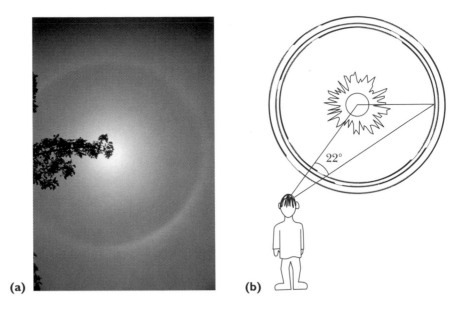
(a)   **(b)**

Figure 1.2
Sun dogs, or parhelia, are small pieces of the solar halo seen off to the sides of the sun. Here the sun dog appears on the horizon, to the right of the sun. The 22-degree halo and upper tangent arc are also visible. (Photo by A. James Mallmann.)

A single, simple mechanism is responsible for the solar halos, sun dogs, tangent arcs, and other phenomena mentioned above. Although people have been drawing and hypothesizing about solar halos and sun dogs and such for many years, the pioneer who developed a solid quantitative demonstration of their origins is Robert Greenler, a professor of physics at the University of Wisconsin–Milwaukee. He and his colleagues started publishing the results of their investigations in the 1970s, and he has recently

Figure 1.3
The circumscribed halo occurs when the upper tangent arc (also visible in Figure 1.2) wraps around the sun and ultimately joins the lower tangent arc. You can see it most clearly in this figure at the left and right sides of the 22-degree halo. (Photo by Robert Greenler.)

written a lovely book summarizing his work (see the Further Reading section). In this chapter, I will present the essence of Greenler's elegant approach and then show how I generalized the idea to produce full-color simulations.

Sunlight and Ice

Greenler's basic hypothesis is that solar displays arise from the interaction of sunlight with a cloud of simple ice particles. We're all familiar with the tendency of ice to crystallize in six-sided prisms: the intricate sixfold symmetry of snowflakes is famous. But the humbler hexagonal prism, shown in Figure 1.4, is all we need to bring about the effects discussed above. Actually, we will find it useful to distinguish two forms of the crystal: the *plate* (in Figure 1.4a) and the *pencil* (in Figure 1.4b). I consider a crystal to be in the pencil form when the ratio of length to radius exceeds about 2. I chose this number because it seems to distinguish different effects neatly; we'll see why a bit later in the chapter. Greenler's hypothesis was that all the solar phenomena we have mentioned are due strictly to light reflecting off of and refracting through these little hexagonal ice crystals as they take on different shapes and orientations.

To duplicate Greenler's results, we need to make a bunch of simplifying assumptions. We'll relax these later, but a simple model is often a good starting place. There's a famous physics joke that makes lighthearted fun of this desire for simplicity.

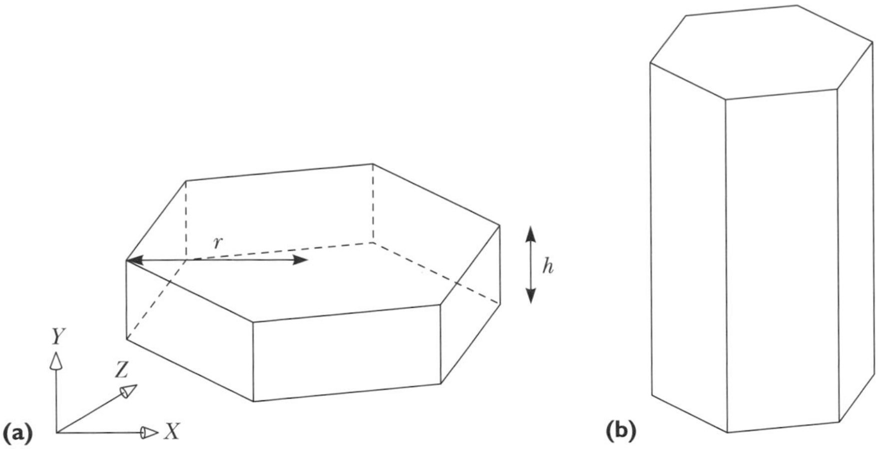

Figure 1.4
Hexagonal ice crystals can take two forms.
(a) The plate.
(b) The pencil.

The story goes that the rich owner of a horse-racing track wants to get even richer (imagine that), and so he calls the dean of the local university. "Dean," he says, "I want faster, stronger horses so I can run more races every day. How do I get them?" The dean suggests that the owner give the university three grants—one each to the biology, mechanical engineering, and physics departments—and let each department work for six months to come up with proposals. Whichever proposal the owner likes best he can pursue by writing another, bigger grant to the university. The owner agrees and writes three big checks.

Six months later, the dean shows up at the owner's door with three professors, one from each department, who have come to show their work. They retire to the drawing room, and the biology professor goes first. "Clearly horses are biological creatures," he begins, "so I have made a comparative study of nutrition, exercise, and psychological care. Certain approaches improve performance, such as . . ." and he proceeds to show a sequence of slides to make his case.

When he's done, the mechanical engineer stands up. "To my mind," he says, "a horse is clearly a mechanical structure. The issue here is to examine the stresses and impacts on the horse, and replace the weakest and limiting joints with man-made synthetics. Over the last six months, I have taken X-rays of horses after they've run and created these interactive computer simulations to study their bones and muscles." He then proceeds to show a series of slides and computer results.

When he has finished, the physicist stands up. "Horses are much too complicated to study all at once," he says. "So I've spent the last six months finding the optimal running patterns for a spherical horse."

Clearly the physicist's sort of simplification can lead to a problem that doesn't reveal anything in the long run. But used with restraint, simplifications let us begin our attack on a problem and, if they're well chosen, let us focus on the most important aspects of the problem first, leaving details for later. We will follow that course here.

First, we will ignore reflection altogether and consider only light that travels through the body of the crystal. Second, we will ignore all energy effects that could serve to diminish the energy of the light as it interacts with the crystal. That means we'll ignore Lambert's law where the light strikes the crystal, Fresnel's law both where the light enters and leaves the crystal, absorption within the crystal, and polarization. Third, we will ignore all but first-order effects; that is, we will pretend that a given ray of light leaves the sun, interacts with exactly one crystal, and then reaches our eye without ever interacting with another crystal. Finally, we will assume a thermally uniform and empty atmosphere, where light travels in straight lines and is never scattered or absorbed by airborne particles. With these simplifications, we can begin to make our first approximation to the solar halo.

Building a Solar Halo

We'll begin by studying plate crystals with a thickness-to-radius ratio of about 1.5. We'll assume that they're uniformly distributed in a cloud between where we're standing and the sun, and that the wind is kicking up, so they're all tumbled every which way. What would we see if we looked at the sun through a cloud of these crystals?

The most straightforward approach might be to build a 3D model of one crystal, instance it a few hundreds of thousands of times throughout the cloud, and then ray-trace the model. This probably would work and lead to a picture, but it would be very slow. When Greenler first studied this problem in the '70s, computers were much slower than they are now, so he was forced to find a more efficient approach. Greenler invented a technique that is so elegant, I will make it our starting point too.

Greenler's idea was to model a single prototype crystal and then give it a random orientation. He found where the crystal had to be in space to refract light back into our eye from that orientation, and he marked that

Figure 1.5
To see light leaving
a crystal, we must
be looking at the
crystal along the
direction of the
outgoing light.

Figure 1.6
The result of the
simulation for
40,000 light rays,
crystals with a
thickness-to-
radius ratio of 1.5,
and the sun at the
horizon.

direction as the source of light energy. Then he returned to the prototype crystal to pick a new random orientation and a new position. In other words, we follow the process backward: we assert where the light leaves a given crystal, and then we decide where in the sky it would have to be located in order for us to have seen that light. Let's look at this in a bit more detail.

First we build a prism with hexagonal top and bottom faces and rectangular sides. I chose to build mine in a left-handed coordinate system, as in Figure 1.4a. To simulate the effect of wind, we rotate this crystal around all three axes into a random orientation. Then we create a ray of light that starts at the sun and ultimately strikes this crystal, and follow the ray forward as it refracts upon entering the ice and refracts again when leaving. If we're to see this outgoing light, then we must be looking at the crystal along the direction of the outgoing light, as shown in Figure 1.5. In other words, the final exit direction is a source of light energy. So we add into an accumulating image a little bit of light coming from that direction. This approach shares a common spirit with Turner Whitted's seminal 1980 paper on ray tracing, where he suggested following rays backward from the eye into the scene.

Figure 1.6 shows the result of this simulation for 40,000 light rays, crystals with a thickness-to-radius ratio of 1.5, and a sun at the horizon (so technically we would not be able to see the lower half of the figure). My simulations are made with a viewing angle of 180 degrees, so the entire visible hemisphere is projected into the image (like photographing the world reflected by a shiny sphere, as in Figure 1.3). In this figure, we can see energy from both the 22-degree halo and the 46-degree halo, and they both have the correct form: an abrupt inner edge at the correct angle, trailing off to the outside.

PATHS TO ENLIGHTENMENT

Each ray can take one of five different paths through the crystal. Each dot of Figure 1.6 is color-coded to show which path was taken by its corresponding ray. The five different types of transmission paths through the crystal are illustrated in Figure 1.7; I call the top and bottom hexagons the *lids* and the six rectangular faces the *sides*. If the light enters through a lid, it can come out through the other lid (so I call this type of path LL) or through a side (LS). If it enters a side, it can come out through a "direct neighbor," that is, a side directly adjacent to the one it entered (SD); a "far neighbor," which is next to a direct neighbor (SF); or through the opposite side (SO). These are bidirectional paths—transport from a side to a face is indistinguishable from light going from a face to a side. In the simulations, I have color-coded the path taken by each ray: LL is red, LS is cyan, SD is green, SF is yellow, and SO is magenta.

Let's think about what these paths represent. Light following an LL path enters a lid, refracts, strikes the other lid, refracts again, and exits in the same direction as it entered. In general, anytime light enters a medium bounded by two parallel flat faces, its exit direction is parallel to its entry direction. So if we are looking directly at the sun, we would expect all of the LL rays to land right on top of one another, in the center of the sun. In Figure 1.6, all LL paths have been plotted in red, and they do indeed all land in the center. The same analysis holds for the SO paths, since again we have a ray entering and leaving through parallel faces; the red dot in Figure 1.6 represents them as well.

Paths connecting neighbor sides (SD) can't occur in this kind of crystal. To prove that to yourself, assume an index of refraction of 1.33 for ice and consider the fact that in order to exit through a direct neighbor, the

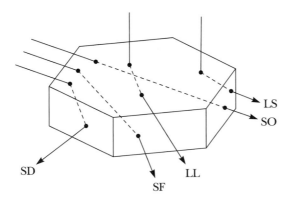

Figure 1.7
The five different transmission paths that can be followed by light as it passes through the crystal.

Figure 1.8
The results of sending 20,000 rays through a crystal cloud for different sizes of randomly oriented plate crystals and different elevations of the sun.
(a) The sun at 0 degrees above the horizon.
(b) At 30 degrees
(c) At 60 degrees. In the graphs, the thin solid line represents LL paths, the thin dashed line LS paths, the thick solid line SF paths, and the thick dashed line SO paths.

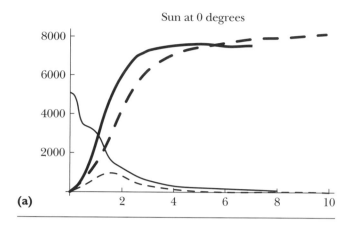

(a)

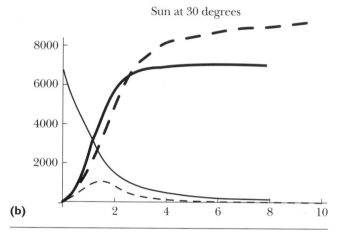

(b)

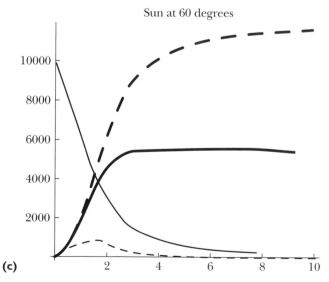

(c)

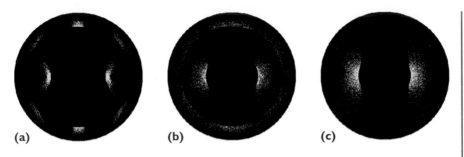

(a) (b) (c)

Figure 1.9
Orientation of the crystals is restricted to ±7 degrees on the X and Z axes.
(a) The yellow arcs at the left and right are sun dogs.
(b) The X and Z rotations have been extended to 20 degrees in either direction, resulting in more complete halos.
(c) Enlarging the crystals to a ratio of 6 causes the number of rays contributing to the 46-degree halo to drop dramatically.

transmitted ray must make an angle of greater than 60 degrees with the normal of the incident face (if that doesn't do the trick, think about the critical angle at an air-ice interface). Basically the geometry and physics just don't let light make that much of a turn. So LL and SO paths are all the same and SD paths can't happen, leaving just LS and SF. And as we can see from Figure 1.6, it does seem that the LS paths (in cyan) are responsible for the 46-degree halo, and the SF paths (in yellow) build the 22-degree halo.

The 46-degree halo in Figure 1.6 seems less densely populated than the 22-degree halo. In fact, it's far less common to see the larger halo, and that's probably because it's dimmer. How much dimmer, though? Keeping in mind that we have decided to ignore energy effects, we can still learn something just by considering how many rays take each of the possible paths. Figure 1.8 shows the results of sending 20,000 rays through a crystal cloud for different sizes of randomly oriented crystals and different elevations of the sun. At sunrise (or 0 degrees of elevation), using crystals of thickness 1.5, I found that about 4600 rays took the SF path and only about 870 took the LS path. Considering also that the LS rays are much more spread apart, it seems that the simulation correctly suggests that the 46-degree halo receives fewer rays per unit visible area than its 22-degree companion.

So far we've assumed random orientations for the crystals because of the presence of a strong wind. But if the wind calms down, then crystals will tend to fall with their hexagonal sides parallel to the ground, like a piece of paper fluttering to the floor. In Figure 1.9a, I've restricted the orientation of the crystals to only 7 degrees plus or minus on the X and Z axes (refer to Figure 1.4), though they were free to rotate about the Y axis. The yellow arcs at the left and right are sun dogs. The 46-degree halo can be seen here to be composed of six different arcs, now distinguished because of the limited crystal orientations. In Figure 1.9b I've extended the X and Z

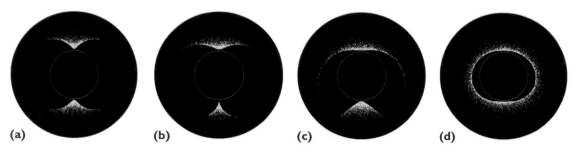

(a) (b) (c) (d)

Figure 1.10
(a) The simulation shows crystals with a length-to-radius ratio of 8 and the sun at 22 degrees. These crystals fall with their long axis parallel to the ground in the absence of wind.
(b) With the sun at 11 degrees, we see the arcs begin to wrap around.
(c) The sun at 30 degrees.
(d) With the sun at 50 degrees, the circumscribed halo comes closer to the 22-degree halo.

rotations to 20 dgrees in either direction, and everything begins to spread out and come closer to complete halos.

So far, we've only looked at the sun on the horizon, but it turns out that the phenomena due to plate crystals don't change much as the sun rises.

THE PLOT THICKENS

Let's now let the crystals return to random orientations, but thicken them so they turn from plates to pencils. The graphs of Figure 1.8 show that for ratios below about 1.5, the LL paths dominate. This makes sense, since they're the largest faces in the crystal. Above that ratio, the SF and SO paths become more common, as the side faces grow larger. The LS paths have a small peak around 1.5, so that's the size that best shows the 46-degree halo and why I chose a ratio of 1.5 for the earlier figures. If we enlarge the crystals to a ratio of 6, as in Figure 1.9c, then the number of rays that contribute to the 46-degree halo drops dramatically. A value of 2 seems to separate the two cases nicely, which is why I used that as a defining point for the two types of shapes.

As before, let's return our attention to a calm day. Unlike the plate crystals, pencils fall with their rectangular sides facing the ground, like logs in a river. The simulation in Figure 1.10a shows crystals with a length-to-radius ratio of 8 (the small circle marks the location of the 22-degree halo). They fall with their long axis parallel to the ground but are free to rotate about the other two axes. Here we see the circumscribed halo effect as in Figure 1.2. But that photograph shows an upper tangent arc that is rather more spread out than Figure 1.10a. That's because the sun in the photo is at an elevation of about 11 degrees, and these effects do change with the sun's elevation. Figure 1.10b shows the result of the same simulation but now with the sun at 11 degrees, and we find good agreement with the photograph. Figures 1.10c and 1.10d show the results with the sun at 30 degrees

10   Chapter One

and 50 degrees; as the sun rises, the circumscribed halo comes ever closer to the 22-degree halo.

IMPLEMENTATION AND NOTES

If you're interested in replicating these figures and experimenting with crystal formations, it isn't difficult; the whole program isn't much more than a simple ray tracer. I'll sketch out my implementation and mention a couple of notes.

I place the camera at the origin, looking down the positive Z axis, and place the sun at infinity on the positive Z axis. The crystal starts centered at the origin, assumes an orientation, and then gets moved into position on the unit hemisphere in front of the camera. In these simulations I use a viewing half-angle of 90 degrees (or a full 180 degrees from one side of the picture to the other)—the most fishy of fish-eye lenses without having eyes on the back of your head! It's a bit extreme, but it allows me to see big effects, like the 46-degree halo and the light that fades out from it. It also makes it easy to plunk down a dot in the right place; if the normalized direction vector of the ray arriving at the eye is (x, y, z), you can just put a point at $(-x, -y)$. As the sun rises, I like to keep the sun in the center of the image; I just rotate everything down to the horizon before plotting.

The main loop in the program picks an orientation for the crystal, rotates it into place, traces a ray, and then plots the ray's outgoing direction. Then I pick a new orientation and repeat. To orient the crystal, I pick some random angles and build a rotation matrix. Because it's pure rotation, I use the same matrix to transform both the points of the crystal and the normals. This is a convenient approach for me because it lets me control the range of angles that can be assumed by the crystal. In the little user interface I built to make the images in this chapter, I can pick independent minimum and maximum values for rotation about each of the X, Y, and Z angles. To orient a crystal, I generate uniformly distributed random numbers in each of these ranges and rotate the crystal sequentially around the X, Y, and Z axes.

Ronen Barzel has observed that different rotation methods will yield different statistical distributions of ice crystals and thus statistically different types of images. He also noted that my sequential approach described above won't generate a really uniform distribution of orientations, but I haven't seen any artifacts. I doubt that a more sophisticated method would yield images that were visually distinguishable from the ones I made, but there probably would be numerical differences.

To start a ray, I pick a "goal" point: this is a point in a disk of radius 1, centered at the origin, lying in the *XY* plane. Then I find the direction back to the sun. Because the sun is so far away, I treat it as a point light source generating parallel illumination rays. Since I assume the sun rises in the *YZ* plane, the vector pointing from the goal to the sun is $(0, \sin(\theta), \cos(\theta))$, where θ is the angle of elevation of the sun. I push the goal point back along this direction by a length of 2 or twice the thickness, whichever is larger—this is just to make sure that I start outside the crystal. This transformed goal point is the origin of the ray, and the ray's direction is the opposite of the direction in which I pushed it.

The first ray-object test is to find out if the ray strikes the crystal, since the crystal will not occupy the entire unit disk. If the ray misses, I just discard that orientation and start the loop again. Otherwise, I follow the ray through the crystal using standard ray-tracing techniques. It's important to keep the selection of the goal point and the rotation of the crystal decoupled; if they correlate, it will introduce artifacts into the results.

The hexagonal prism is a convex solid of convex faces. To intersect a ray with convex faces, I've always liked the enclosure method. For each edge of each polygon, I build a wall—a plane that is perpendicular to the plane of the polygon, passing through the edge, pointing inward. When I find the intersection of the ray with the plane of the polygon, I test that point against each of the plane equations that make up the walls; if it's on the positive side of all the walls, the point is within the polygon. As soon as it's on the negative side of any wall, I can quit the test. This wall-based technique works fine, but if you're looking for something more efficient, take a look at the article by Eric Haines in the Further Reading section.

The only thing left is to pick a wavelength for the simulation, compute the index of refraction of ice at that wavelength, and start orienting crystals.

I built a small pushbutton-style interface that allows me to set global parameters such as the number of rays to trace, the thickness of the crystal, and the angle of the sun. I can select which paths I want to have plotted, the initial orientation of the crystal, and the range of random rotations that can be applied once it's been positioned. These last two steps let me place the crystal properly (e.g., the plate with hexagon side down, or the pencil a rectangular side down) and then constrain how much the wind can cause it to rotate. When a run is complete, I print out some statistics, such as the number of rays that followed each type of path and the number of points plotted. I also keep track of how many rays underwent total internal reflection (TIR) within the crystal and simply extinguish all such rays.

Now We're Getting Warm

Now we're ready to extend the simulation to include energy considerations, smooth images, and color.

ENERGIZED BY OLD FRIENDS

The first thing we'll do to enhance this model is include energy effects, which we will handle very casually. There are lots of places where the light ray can pick up and lose energy, but we'll focus just on the crystal faces. When the ray strikes the first face, it represents a whole beam of light, and thus we need to diminish the energy by the cosine of the angle the ray makes with the face normal. This is just Lambert's law, which forms the heart of almost every hardware polygon-shading algorithm. Similarly, we should apply Fresnel's law, another standard shading model in computer graphics. This accounts for the fact that glancing rays are generally reflected, while rays more perpendicular to the face are better able to penetrate the crystal. Now when we draw a dot in our image, we can draw it with an intensity value indicating the amount of energy it carries.

THE PURSUIT OF SMOOTH COLOR

My process of generating smooth color images involved some trial and error. In a technical paper, people generally present only the answers that worked, not all the dead ends. I thought it might be interesting to present the various approaches I took on my way to finding satisfactory answers.

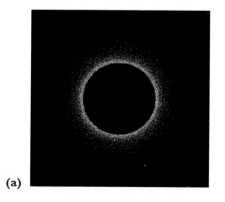
(a)

(b)

Figure 1.11
(a) A dot pattern generated using uniformly distributed random wavelengths in a single simulation.
(b) A close-up of 1.11a.

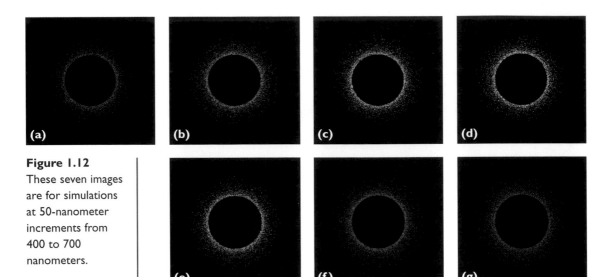

(a) **(b)** **(c)** **(d)**

(e) **(f)** **(g)**

Figure 1.12
These seven images are for simulations at 50-nanometer increments from 400 to 700 nanometers.

Figure 1.13
A close-up of the overlaid upper-left corner of the 400- and 700-nanometer simulations in Figure 1.12. Note that the red dots appear inside the blue ones, and the blue dots predominate at the outside.

40,000 Points of Light

My first extension to the basic algorithm was to include color. My initial approach was to simply pick a different wavelength for each ray of light, follow it through the crystal, and plot it with the right color on the screen. But after throwing lots of rays, I had a very speckled dot pattern of all different colors, as shown in Figure 1.11 for the 22-degree halo. Tracing more

rays just changed the speckle pattern, since new rays overwrote the old ones—the image itself didn't get any smoother. So I decided instead to run several different simulations, each at its own wavelength, and then combine them. I used seven wavelengths from 400 to 700 nanometers, evenly spaced 50 nanometers apart. The results are shown in Figure 1.12. Figure 1.13 shows a close-up view of just the 400- and 700-nanometer simu-

lations, where you can see the inner ring of red generated by the change in the index of refraction with wavelength.

To compute the index of refraction η as a function of wavelength λ, I went to the literature. I found a table for the index of refraction of ice at three different wavelengths for temperatures from 0 to 100 degrees Celsius in 10-degree increments; a plot of this reference data is shown in Figure 1.14a. My favorite formula for approximating η as a function of wavelength λ is Sellmeier's formula, which in two-term form is $\eta(\lambda) = A + B/\lambda^2$ (you can

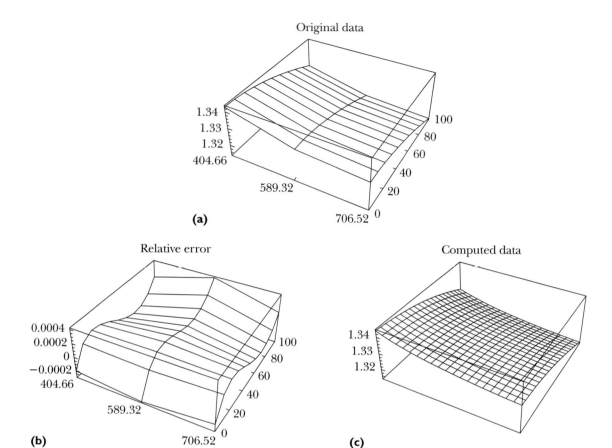

Original data

(a)

Relative error

(b)

Computed data

(c)

add more terms for more accuracy, but I found that the two-term form fit the data with excellent precision). Since the table gave values at different temperatures, I made the coefficients in Sellmeier's formula temperature-dependent:

$$\eta(\lambda, T) = A(T) + B(T)/\lambda^2$$

I used a symbolic algebra program to compute A and B at each of the 11 temperatures, so now I had 11 samples of the functions $A(T)$ and $B(T)$. I found that quadratic polynomials matched both functions very well; these polynomials are

$$A(T) = 1.32491 - 0.0000399278\ T - 0.00000120678\ T^2$$
$$B(T) = 3105.31 + 1.25203\ T - 0.0353608\ T^2$$

Figure 1.14
(a) The reference data for the index of refraction of ice.
(b) The relative error in the approximation used here.
(c) A sampling of the approximation function.

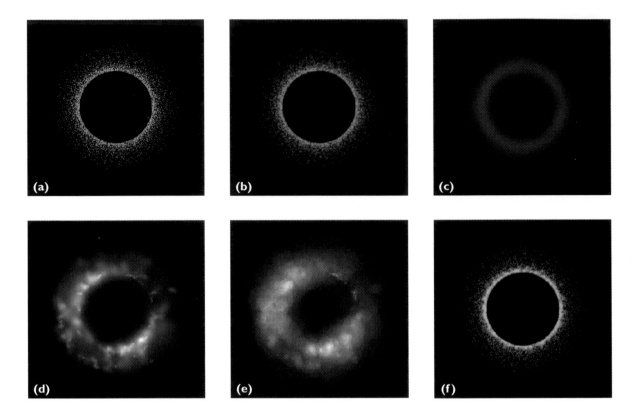

Figure 1.15
First attempts at smoothing.
(a) The original dot pattern at 550 nanometers.
(b) A small blurring of 1.15a still looks speckled.
(c) A large blurring of 1.15a looks too fuzzy.
(d) Using Gaussian blobs produces a splotchy image.
(e) Using disks instead of blobs isn't much better.
(f) Compositing 1.15b with 1.15a, using the intensity of 1.15b as a matte. The inner edge is too blurry, and the outer parts are too speckled.

where T is the temperature in degrees Celsius. So now to find η at any wavelength and temperature, I compute $A(T)$ and $B(T)$, and I plug that into Sellmeier's formula along with the wavelength in nanometers. The maximum absolute and relative errors in this approximation are both less than six parts in 10,000. The relative error is shown in Figure 1.14b, and the values generated by the approximation are plotted in Figure 1.14c. I decided to send my simulations on vacation; all of the figures shown here were made at a balmy 30 degrees Celsius.

My first approach to combining the color runs was to simply add the images together; I hoped that the regions that were dense on all plots would sum to white, and I'd get smooth edges where the different colors faded out. Unfortunately, the result looked just like Figure 1.11a: speckles again. I realized that the density plots had to be smoothed before they could be combined.

My impulsive reaction was to abandon the dot patterns and generate a smooth picture directly by inverting the image-making process. Rather

Chapter One

than orienting the crystal and then tracing rays, I would scan the screen and find the probability of a crystal being in the right orientation to send light through each pixel in the image. This sounded like a simple enough problem: the crystal is rigid, the geometry of refraction is well known, and everything should be straightforward. Indeed, it is straightforward to a point, but things get very messy very fast. Just setting up the equations is complicated, because of all the trig functions involved. But then I realized that in fact there was no single solution: there are lots of different crystal orientations that can send rays back in any given direction. Just as a quick test I selected one pixel on the screen and ran the simulator. Dozens of different sets of angles sent light back in almost the same direction, passing through the same pixel. I decided that I'd stick with the dot patterns and try to smooth them out.

Blurs and Blobs

Looking at the dot pattern of Figure 1.15a, my first thought was to simply blur the density plot. But no value of blur worked well—the small blur of Figure 1.15b didn't get the dots to join up and form a smooth field, and the large blur of Figure 1.15c made the whole picture go fuzzy. My next approach was to draw a Gaussian blob over each spot, like the splatting technique used in volume visualization. I used the distance from each ray to its nearest neighbor to determine the blob's radius and scaled the blob's height by the amount of energy carried by the ray. The radius was set so the blob was at half-height at its nearest neighbor. Finding the nearest neighbor involved saving all the ray locations (at subpixel accuracy) and then searching for neighbors for each ray. To speed the search, I built a data structure of overlapping rectangles in the image, and for each ray only searched the other rays in its rectangle. Because the rectangles overlapped, a ray could belong to more than one such rectangle, so I could avoid the problem where two nearby rays straddle a boundary between rectangles and don't see each other. When the image was built up, I normalized the pixel values to use the whole display range.

Figure 1.15d shows the result of the blobs. The bright spots come from places where lots of rays just happened to land on top of one another (this artifact isn't visible in Figure 1.15a because all of these rays land on the same pixel). This result was disappointing not only because it looked so bad, but because it required a whole lot of additional computation and storage. I thought maybe if I replaced the blobs by flat disks it would look a bit better, but as you can see from Figure 1.15e, this wasn't a success either.

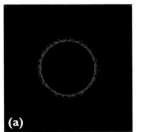 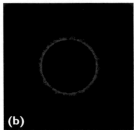 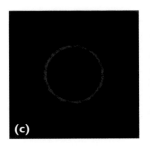 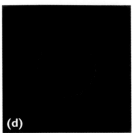

(a) (b) (c) (d)

Figure 1.16
(a) Figure 1.15a filtered from 400 to 300 pixels on a side, then filtered back up to 400.
(b) 1.16a filtered down to 200 pixels on a side, then filtered back up to 400.
(c) 1.16b filtered down to 100 pixels on a side, then filtered back up to 400.
(d) 1.16c filtered down to 50 pixels on a side, then back up to 400.

Fuzzy Thinking

The bridge to a better answer came from looking at the blurry picture and the sharp picture together. I thought that if I could get the blurry picture to show up where the sharp picture was black, I'd get a smooth field. So I turned the blurry picture into its own matte and composited the images together: the result was that where the blurry picture was bright, it dominated the result. As you can see in Figure 1.15f, it smoothed out the inner ring, but the unwelcome bright dots around the outside were still clearly visible. While looking at this picture I realized that if I combined several images that had each been blurred by different amounts, I could probably get what I wanted.

So I created several images, each blurred by a different amount, as shown in Figure 1.16. To make the blurred images, I scaled down the original by increasing amounts and then blew the results back up. My original dot pattern was 400 pixels on a side. I applied a Gaussian filter kernel with a radius of about 1.3 to make a 300-pixel image and then enlarged it back to 400. Then I applied a filter of radius 1.5 to that to make a 200-pixel image, which I then filtered back up to 400. I filtered that image down to 100 pixels and filtered it back up to 400 pixels. Finally, I took that result, reduced it to 50 pixels on a side, and brought it back up to 400. Note that the blurriest image in Figure 1.16d is the result of eight filters applied in sequence (four reducing and four enlarging), not just a single blur to the original. When all the images were back up to 400 pixels on a side I renormalized them to use the full range of image intensities.

At first I simply added the three blurriest pictures together equally, as in Figure 1.17a. That still showed a little too much of the speckling for my taste. So I tried again, this time changing the recipe to use three parts of the 50-pixel image, two parts of the 100-pixel image, and one part of the 200-pixel image. Figure 1.17b shows the result. The inner edge is still relatively sharp, and the outer edges fade out nicely.

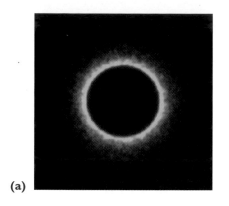

(a)

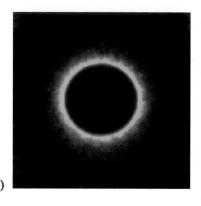

(b)

Figure 1.17
(a) An equally weighted average of Figures 1.16b, 1.16c, and 1.16d. **(b)** A better average using one part of Figure 1.16b, two parts of Figure 1.16c, and three parts of Figure 1.16d.

Nothing New under the Sun

As soon as I made these images, I recognized this process as multiresolution compositing, which is a standard technique in image processing and computer graphics production. I wished I had thought of it before trying all the other approaches, but I did enjoy playing around with this problem looking for a good answer. This approach also has a big efficiency advantage over the Gaussian blob-type solutions, because it's simple image processing and doesn't require lots of additional data structures and processing. Just draw the dot pictures, blur them out, and add them up.

I applied the multiresolution blur and compositing to each of the dot patterns in Figure 1.12, and generated the composite 22-degree halo shown in Figure 1.18a. Comparing it to the photograph shown in Figures 1.2 and 1.3, I think it's a pretty good match. Figure 1.18b shows a close-up of the inner edge; it has a satisfyingly red tint. I ran through the same process for sun dogs, as shown in Figure 1.18c. Note that the sun dogs aren't just slices of the halo; their color fringes have a subtly different shape. The upper and lower tangent arcs for a sun elevation of 30 degrees are shown in Figure 1.18d.

The Movie

I have made a movie of the upper and lower tangent arcs for the rising sun from 0 to 90 degrees. You can find the file for the movie on my Web page at *http://www.research.microsoft.com/glassner/*.

There's a lot more going on up in the sky than I've talked about here. One thing we haven't addressed is what happens to light that reflects off of the crystals, rather than passing through them. These reflections give rise to a

Figure 1.18
(a) The multi-resolution reconstruction of the 22-degree halo.
(b) A close-up of 1.18a, showing the red inner and blue outer bands.
(c) The multi-resolution reconstruction of sun dogs.
(d) The multi-resolution of the upper and lower tangent arcs for a sun elevation of 30 degrees.

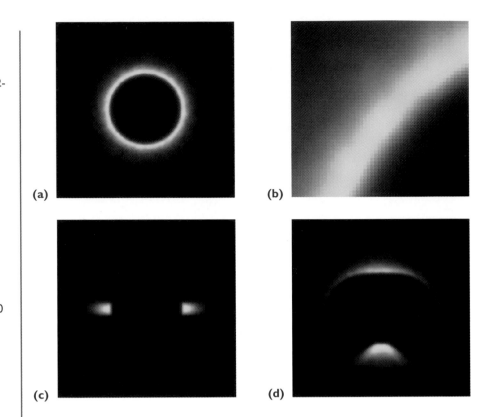

(a)　　(b)

(c)　　(d)

phenomenon called *sun pillars*. I encourage you to write a little simulation program and investigate them yourself.

Most of all, observe the skies around you a little more closely. I find that with increased knowledge comes increased pleasure in the beauty of our world; I hope you find the same.

Further Reading

The basic technique for creating the dot patterns in this chapter was developed by Robert Greenler and his colleagues and is described in his book, *Rainbows, Halos, and Glories* (Cambridge University Press, 1980). If you want to learn more about the colors in the skies, you can look at M. G. J. Minnaert's classic book, *Light and Color in the Outdoors* (Springer-Verlag, 1937, revised 1985 edition). A more recent volume with lots of good information is the book by the Meinels, *Sunsets, Twilights, and Evening Skies* (Aden Meinel and Marjorie Meinel, Cambridge University Press, 1983).

In the implementation section I described the ray-crystal intersection algorithm I used. Eric Haines has presented a simpler and faster algorithm in his article, "Fast Ray-Convex Polyhedron Intersection" in *Graphics Gems II* (Jim Arvo, editor, Academic Press, 1991). According to Eric, the code in the book has a bug, so make sure you use the online version of the implementation (available at *http://www.acm.org/tog/GraphicsGems/*).

My data for the index of refraction of ice came from the *CRC Handbook of Chemistry and Physics* (CRC Press, 1996). You can read up on the index of refraction and different formulas for computing it in my book, *Principles of Digital Image Synthesis* (Morgan Kaufmann Publishers, 1995); I also talk about Lambert's and Fresnel's laws in there.

You can learn more about multiresolution compositing in a graphics setting from the famous "apples and oranges" paper, "A Multiresolution Spline with Application to Image Mosaics" (Peter J. Burt and Edward H. Adelson, *ACM Transactions on Graphics,* 2(4):217–236, October 1983).

Frieze Groups

ANDREW GLASSNER'S NOTEBOOK
May 1996

2

A man goes into a bar and starts drinking hard. The night barman leans over to him and says, "You look sad . . . I can see you're alone." The man shakes his head and sips at his beer, saying, "It's those darn nuclear freeze groups."

Oh, wait, I got that wrong. I'll start again.

A man gets into his car and starts thinking hard. His wife Carmen leans over to him and asks, "You look sad—did you lose the cellular phone?" The man shakes his head and shifts into gear, saying, "It's those darn unclear frieze groups."

There's no reason to get harried over frieze groups. They're only seven in number, not too hard to understand, and pretty useful. The idea is inspired by *friezes*—the decorative horizontal bands that are often used in architecture. Figure 2.1 shows a piece of a storytelling frieze from ancient Egypt. This example shows written language and people at work, but often friezes are simply abstract designs used purely for decoration. In addition to architecture, bands of patterns show up in such diverse crafts as pottery, embroidery, and furniture. When these bands are created by some repeating pattern or motif, and particularly if that pattern has some internal symmetry, there's a good chance the structure of the design can be represented mathematically as a frieze group.

The value of such a description in graphics is twofold. First, you can generate lots of texture by stamping out little textured polygons in the right positions and orientations. Second, you can go the other way and, given a point on a polygon, you can find out what the texture value ought to be. In other words, frieze groups give us an algorithm to turn a little bit of texture into a lot of texture. Because the pattern is algorithmic, we can synthesize it and generate texture (such as when scan-converting) or analyze it to find the texture coordinates we need (such as when ray-tracing).

First, Imagine the Components

The basic idea behind frieze groups is to imagine that you have a design that's printed on a rectangular glass tile. The tile attaches to a metal rod through a fixture at its base, and you want to place copies of the tile along the rod to make a long flat strip. You can't cut or bend the tile, but you can rotate it around the rod, flip it over from left to right, and move it horizontally along the bar, as shown in Figure 2.2. We will restrict our attention to flat bands, so although you can rotate the tiles to change their position and orientation, they must end up in the plane of the page. If you ask yourself how many different kinds of periodic patterns you can generate from the four tiles in Figure 2.2, you're thinking about frieze groups. You may be surprised that there are only seven fundamentally different patterns.

If you remove the rod and generalize the process to the whole 2D plane, then you're creating wallpaper—designs that repeat smoothly across the plane. There are only 17 ways of doing that. Wallpaper patterns are very important in computer graphics, because we often create large textured surfaces by taking a little piece of texture and repeating it over and over.

Figure 2.1
A drawing of a piece of a 4000-year-old kiosk of King Sesoris I. The coloring is not historically motivated.

Figure 2.2
Tiles on a rod. Note that if the tiles are to be in the plane of the page and on the rod, these four orientations are the only possibilities.

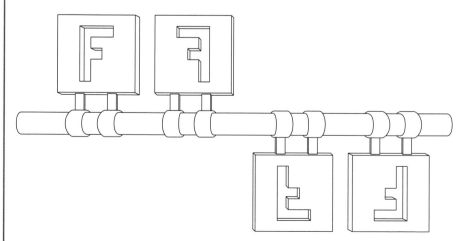

Looking at frieze groups is a good way to get a hold of the basic ideas of this kind of algorithmic texture.

The study of frieze patterns is traditionally associated with group theory, a branch of abstract mathematics. In fact, frieze and wallpaper patterns appear almost universally in books on group theory because they are perfect illustrations of those ideas. The group theory approach to our subject is satisfying in a deep way, because it is very elegant and presents a beautiful chain of thinking that makes the results seem inevitable and certain.

In this discussion I'll take a very informal and visual approach to the subject. I hope you'll believe my arguments, but I'll focus on your intuition. Intuitive mathematics is no substitute for rigor—some seemingly reasonable conjectures can be completely wrong. But developing intuition is a great way to approach a subject for the first time, since you can get the big picture up front and fill in details later if you care to. If you find the subject intriguing, dip into the books in the Further Reading section and investigate the beautiful theory behind these symmetrical patterns.

The Infinite Band

Our goal is to categorize repeating patterns that lie within an infinite 2D band. More precisely, suppose that you have a pair of infinite parallel lines. The region of the plane between them is where we will draw our pattern (I'll talk of the pattern running horizontally, but of course the strip can be oriented in any direction). The centerline of the band is the "rod" upon which we will hang our tiles.

Because we're only going to study repeating patterns, there must be some piece of the pattern that we can isolate and then use as a rubber stamp. In Figure 2.3a, I show a simple band pattern and highlight the *fundamental cell*—that little region that contains the essence of the figure. If we made a rubber stamp of the fundamental cell, we could make the pattern just by stamping out images left and right into infinity. One of the basic ways to repeat a pattern is by *translation*, which here means simply sliding some or all of the pattern along the rod. The result of translating this entire, infinite band by the width of one cell would give us a new band that is indistinguishable from the original.

We say that translation is an *isometry* of such a band. An isometry is a transformation that preserves shape (*isos* = equal, *métron* = measure). For convenience, we will give each isometry its own letter; I will represent

Figure 2.3
Bands generated by
different opera-
tions; the gray zone
is a fundamental
cell.
(a) Translation
along the band.
(b) Translation and
horizontal
reflection; the
reflection axis is
shown by a dashed
line.
(c) Translation
and vertical
reflection; the
reflection axis is
shown by a dashed
line.
(d) 180-degree ro-
tation; the center
of rotation is
shown by a circle.

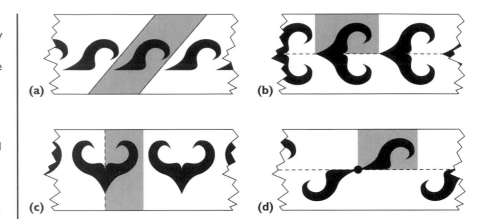

translation simply with the letter T. (Unfortunately, the literature contains lots of conflicting sets of notations for the isometries and the patterns they produce; my choice here is motivated by simplicity.)

My approach in the next few sections will be to first find all the possible isometries that an infinite band might possibly contain, then find all the unique combinations of those isometries.

HALL OF MIRRORS

We've established that translation, T, is an isometry of all infinite, periodic bands. What other isometries might an infinite, periodic band contain?

Suppose that we look at the centerline along the band and reflect every point above the line to its mirror position below, and vice versa for those points below the line, as in Figure 2.3b. The result is indistinguishable from the original. Because the mirror line runs horizontally, such a band has *horizontal reflection symmetry,* which we denote with the letter H.

Now suppose that we place a reflection line perpendicular to the center-line, in the plane of the band, and that we exchange the position of points to the left and right of that line, and the result is just like the original, as in Figure 2.3c. In terms of tiles, it means we feed some onto the bar the same way as before, and some we flip over first. Since the mirror line runs verti-cally, we say it has *vertical reflection symmetry,* which we describe with the let-ter V. The placement of the symmetry line can't be just anywhere—typi-cally it must be right on a border between cells.

Another way to think about these two reflections is as rotations out of the plane of the band. H symmetry spins the band around the center bar like a very wide paddlewheel on an old steamboat. V symmetry spins the band like a giant propeller, the infinite ends slicing through space.

Another type of symmetry that the entire band can share is rotational symmetry within its own plane. Pick a point on the centerline of the band and imagine rotating the band in the plane around that point. If the band is going to have any chance of being unaffected by the operation, it had better spin by some multiple of 180 degrees. A 360-degree rotation brings it right back to where it started. So the interesting rotation is 180 degrees, as shown in Figure 2.3d. If the result of a 180-degree rotation is to leave the band looking the same as when it started, then we say it has *half-turn rotational symmetry,* which we denote R.

These four operations—T, H, V, and R—seem like a pretty complete list. To get an even better idea of how each one works, it helps to think about them in terms of *fixed points*—those points that don't move under the isometry. For translation, everything moves; so there are no fixed points. For both types of reflection, a single line of points remains put—the points along the line of reflection. And for rotation, only a single point stays still—the center of rotation. So our four isometries, taken in turn, give us no fixed points, a line of fixed points (twice), and a single fixed point. Most of the likely sets of possible fixed points seem accounted for.

This does seem like a complete list. But even in a casual study, we want to make sure we cover all the bases. Can there be any other simple isometries of the band that we haven't considered? It's possible that some combinations of these four isometries could make a new isometry that might not be obvious. Let's try combining them and see what happens.

THE MATING GAME

How many useful ways are there to combine our list of four isometries? Let's try applying two isometries, one after the other. We'll read them from right to left, like nested trig operations. So HT means to apply translation and then horizontal reflection. If a result leaves us where we started, then it's just as though we had done nothing at all. We represent that by saying that such a combination is equivalent to the *identity isometry,* written I. The collection of all isometries that preserve the band is called the *symmetry group* of the band; we say the band is *invariant* under these operations.

First we'll try each operation twice, as shown in Figure 2.4. Applying T two times in a row simply shifts the band over by the width of two cells instead of one. Since the band is infinite, this is identical to shifting it only once or

Figure 2.4
Pairs of repeated
transformations.
(a) Translation (T)
repeated twice.
The original tile is
black, the result of
the first operation
is green, and the
second result is
red.
(b) Vertical
reflection (V) re-
peated twice.
(c) Horizontal
reflection (H) re-
peated twice.

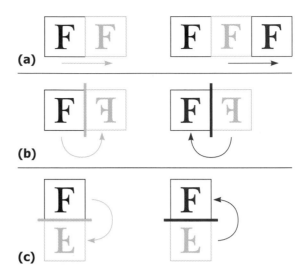

even not at all. In other words, two translations are indistinguishable from any number of translations, including zero. So in our informal shorthand, we can say that two translations, one after the other, are equivalent to one translation. Representing multiple operations with an exponent, this gives us the odd-looking identity $T^2 = T$. The conclusion is that multiple translations don't give us any new isometries.

Applying H twice leaves us right where we started: the second flip undoes the first. So there aren't any new isometries to be found there. Similarly, doubling up V or R also leaves us where we started, so there's nothing new hiding in those combinations either. In our notation, we can summarize these results as $T^2 = T$ and $H^2 = V^2 = R^2 = I$.

Note that this notation doesn't capture everything about these particular isometries. For example, when we write $T^2 = T$, we only mean that the equivalent of two translations is one translation. We're not saying how long each translation is. This is just to avoid cluttering everything up with additional notation that isn't really useful right now.

How about the other combinations? There are six other pairs, each in two forms, as illustrated in Figure 2.5. Most of the combinations reduce to one of the simpler isometries. For example, consider HR. First we rotate the cell, then we flip it over the centerline. The result is indistinguishable from applying V directly, so HR = V.

There are only two types of odd ducks in the flock. The first is TV, in Figure 2.5b. When we flip the cell across the vertical line, the direction of translation flips with it, so then the translation stamps the tile (in a new

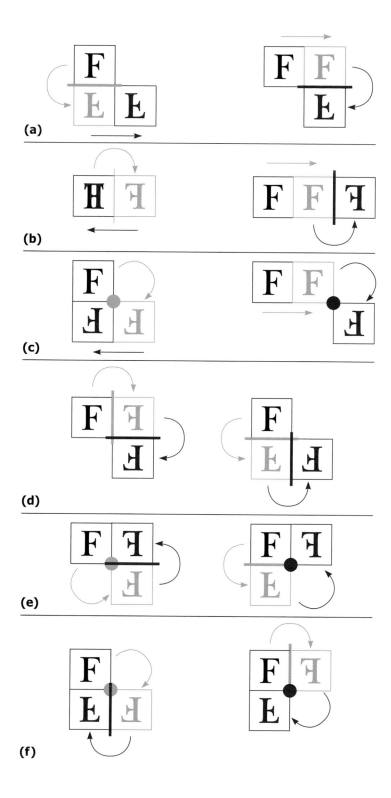

Figure 2.5
Pairs of different transformations. The original tile is black, the result of the first operation is green, and the second result is red. A rotation is represented by a circle at the pivot point, and a reflection by a thick line at the mirror.
(a) TH = G and HT = G.
(b) TV = X (illegal) and VT = V.
(c) TR = R and RT = R.
(d) HV = R and VH = R.
(e) HR = V and RH = V.
(f) VR = H and RV=H.

orientation) on top of its original image. This is a corruption of the fundamental cell that makes up the pattern, and it is certainly not a new kind of symmetry! If the fundamental cell has an internal V-style symmetry, then the result is the identity operation; otherwise it's easiest just to classify this operation as invalid.

The other odd combination is H and T, shown in Figure 2.5a. Consider HT. First we translate the cell, and then we reflect it about the centerline of the band. We get the same result with TH. This result isn't like any of the other isometries, and it is the one isometry we missed in the previous section. This combined move-and-flip isometry is called *glide reflection* and is symbolized by G. Applying G twice means we undo the flip, so two G's in sequence give just a double-length translation: $G^2 = T$. Note that G has no fixed points.

If you can think about combining G with the other four isometries, you'll find that nothing new comes of it. One way to see this is to think about writing G as either TH or HT. Following this combination with any other isometry X, you can write $X(TH) = (XT)H$ and then simplify using the rules we've already seen. If that leads to trouble, use HT instead. I know this section hasn't been a proof, but I hope it's suggestive. You can find solid proofs aplenty in the references noted in Further Reading.

Leading the Band

Now we know about all five isometries. Suppose you wanted to make a periodic band pattern containing one or more of these isometries. How many different such patterns could you make? You might think the number would be huge, but it boils down to only seven. Let's see why.

I wanted to use infinite bands to illustrate this section, but then I realized it would require infinite amounts of trees to print them. So instead, we'll just focus on a little piece of the band and imagine it repeating infinitely to the left and right. I like to use the letter F in the cell, because it is easy to recognize in any orientation and has no symmetries of its own.

Because we're making a periodic pattern, by definition we know we always need the translation operator T, even if we have nothing else. In fact, translation alone creates the first frieze pattern, which we call F1, as shown in Figure 2.6a. Now let's add each of our other isometries to T.

Remember what we're after now is to analyze the possible symmetries in a band. So we're not applying isometries to a fundamental cell, but rather analyzing the whole band to see what isometries it has. We'll write the

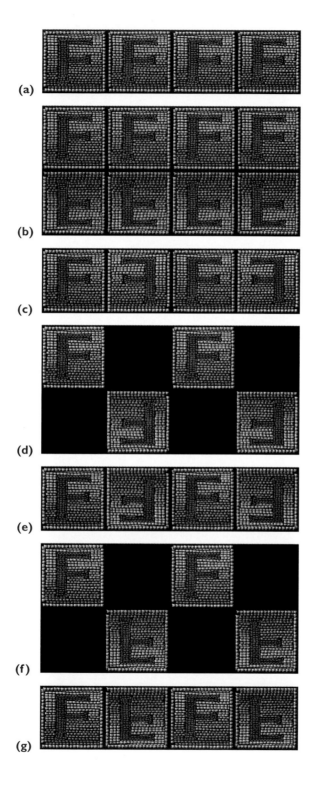

Figure 2.6
(a) [T].
(b) [TH].
(c) [TV].
(d, e) Two bands of the form [TR]. Note that in 2.6d the center of rotation is at the bottom-right corner of the original tile, while for 2.6e the center of rotation is in the middle of the right side.
(f, g) Two bands of the form [TG].

Figure 2.7
(a) An even num-
ber of reflections
in parallel lines is
equivalent to trans-
lation.
(b) An even num-
ber of reflections
in lines that all
meet at one point
is equivalent to
rotation.

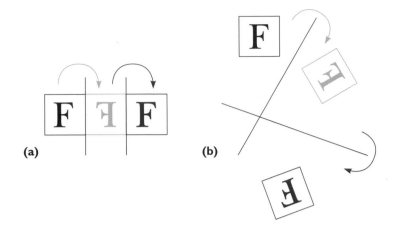

(a)   **(b)**

symmetry group for the band in square brackets, e.g., [TH], to make it clear that for now the order doesn't matter. So F1 is simply [T].

Combining T with each of the other isometries gives us patterns that support [TH], [TV], [TR], and [TG], as shown in the rest of Figure 2.6. That's patterns F2, F3, F4, and F5. Note that Figures 2.6d and 2.6e are the same pattern, except that in the latter figure I moved the center of rotation to the middle of the right side of the fundamental cell. Similarly, Figures 2.6f and 2.6g are also the same pattern.

The next step is to start combining more than two isometries. We know we always need translation in order to make a repeating pattern. So we only need to look at combinations of the other four.

These combinations get very simple if you look at them the right way. The trick is to think about successive reflections. Consider Figure 2.7a, where I show two reflections in parallel lines. The result is just translation, and this is always true for parallel reflections. In Figure 2.7b, I show successive reflections in two nonparallel lines. The result is the same as rotation about the point of intersection. You can prove this is always true. So any two reflections sort of cancel each other out—they turn into either translation or rotation, which are handled by their own isometries. So as we build our combinations of isometries, we can only use one of H, V, or G, or we lose them both.

Since we need T, that leaves us with only three ways to combine three isometries: T and R, plus one of the reflections. Figure 2.8a shows [TRH] and [TRV]. These two symmetry groups describe the same pattern, which

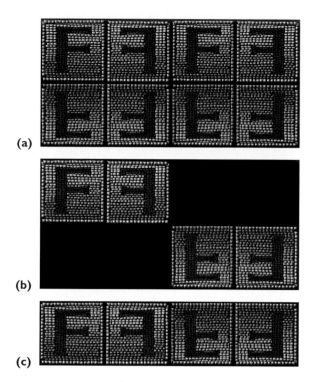

(a)

(b)

(c)

Figure 2.8
(a) [TRH] and [TRV].
(b, c) Two bands of the form [TRG].

is F6. And [TRG] is pattern F7, shown in two forms in Figures 2.8b and 2.8c.

We've exhausted the possibilities! Adding in any more isometries will cause them to simply reduce to something we've already covered. To recap, we found that an infinite, repeating strip could only have five possible symmetries. Then we found all the ways to combine those symmetries, and we discovered that there were only seven different patterns. Perhaps more surprising is that these seven include the five symmetries created by the basic types themselves; there are only two new combinations of two or more symmetries.

Figure 2.9 offers a set of band patterns, one of each type. The coloration and surface texture is not part of the symmetry pattern; if you want to practice recognizing bands using these examples, focus your attention on the basic shapes of the patterns, not the little details.

Interlocking Tiles

A common use of 2D wallpaper patterns is to create interlocking tiles. The humbler, 1D frieze patterns discussed here can be made to interlock as

Figure 2.9
The seven frieze groups.

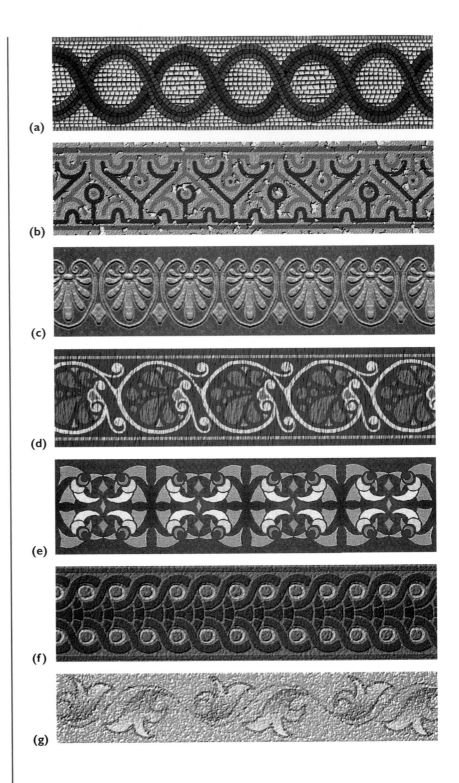

(a)

(b)

(c)

(d)

(e)

(f)

(g)

well. The idea is to design tiles that will fit together into the given patterns without creating any overlaps or leaving any gaps.

You can design rules for building interlocking tiles for each of the seven patterns. Basically you just have to make sure that the edges that touch will fit together and that they don't self-intersect. It's fun to come up with the little geometric instructions for making these interlocking tiles. If you get stuck, take a look at Doris Schattschneider's paper in the Further Reading section—she shows how to build most of the tiles for interlocking frieze groups.

Coding It Up

Symmetry programs are great fun to write. The resulting textures can be used to create wood grain on moldings and borders on furniture, hallway carpets, and so on, giving the textures a little more pizzazz than just rubber-stamping the fundamental cell over and over. To create a frieze group image, just pick one of the seven patterns, create the fundamental cell, and replicate it as needed. To create interlocking tiles, you can write a program that allows a designer to draw curves freehand somewhere on the edge of the tile and automatically generates the appropriate, necessary curves on other edges.

Free-running programs can create eye candy of all sorts, from screen savers to animated backgrounds. Consider creating a long band that winds back and forth across the screen, with a changing pattern replicated across it, and maybe passing through a random series of band types.

There are some fun programming projects associated with frieze groups. You can write each of the isometries as a matrix operation, so any combination of isometries can be captured by a single composite matrix. You might try writing out the matrices for each of the five isometries T, H, V, R, and G. Then write a program that takes a texture tile as input and generates appropriately transformed versions of that tile to make a band. Another useful routine takes an original tile, a band type, and a point anywhere on the band as input; the routine analyzes the position of the point to return the appropriate point in the original tile that corresponds to the selected point. For example, if the original tile ran from $(0, 0)$ in the lower left to $(1, 1)$ in the upper right, the band pattern is [TH], and the input point is $(3.2, 0.6)$, the routine would return $(0.8, 0.6)$—the location in the original tile that ends up at the input point after being transformed there.

If you want to get into color, look in the Further Reading section for some information on color symmetry.

When you allow repeated reflection lines throughout the plane (rather than the special horizontal and vertical orientations we used here), you can fill the plane with images. Those beautiful patterns can be seen by looking into a kaleidoscope. The kaleidoscope's class of symmetrical designs can be understood from the point of view of point groups.

Further Reading

A book that develops group theory with lots of pictorial illustrations from many different cultures is *Symmetries of Culture* by Dorothy K. Washburn and Donald W. Crowe (University of Washington Press, 1988). Another big book that offers tons of examples of different symmetry patterns is *Handbook of Regular Patterns* by Peter S. Stevens (MIT Press, 1981). A wonderful warehouse of copyright-free examples of many types of patterns can be found in *Decorative Symbols and Motifs for Artists and Craftspeople* by Flinders Petrie (Dover Publications, 1986).

If you want to get into the math, a good visual starting place is *Groups and Their Graphs* by Isreal Grossman and Wilhelm Magnus (Random House, 1964). Another visually oriented book, but much heavier on the mathematics, is *Incidence and Symmetry in Design and Architecture* by Jenny A. Baglivo and Jack E. Graver (Cambridge University Press, 1983). The study of isometries and their interactions is called *transformational geometry;* any good introduction to group theory will give you the tools to till this field.

A great introductory paper on color symmetry for frieze groups is "In Black and White: How to Create Perfectly Colored Symmetric Patterns" by Doris Schattschneider (*Computers & Mathematics with Applications,* 12B(3,4):673–695, 1986).

Origami
Polyhedra

ANDREW GLASSNER'S NOTEBOOK
July & September 1996

3

There's something very beautiful and elegant about the simple 3D shapes known as *Platonic solids*. When you hold one in your hand, your fingertips and muscles join in with your mind to create a rich 3D understanding of the graceful underlying structure. The famous polyhedral solids named for Plato have wonderful properties that can tantalize and entertain the intellect. Looking at pictures of these solids, and thinking about them, is very rewarding. But when you hold them in your hands, you pick up another level of understanding. Our bodies know things that our minds can't even name, and it's great to learn from both perspectives.

One of the appealing things about computer graphics is that it lets us make pictures of things that can't be seen, or be built, or even exist. And when this is our only way to get near to these things, it's great. But when we can actually build the objects under scrutiny, sometimes it's worth the effort because it leads to deeper understanding of the underlying structure. I think geometry is really important to graphics, and a good geometric intuition is an important tool for most graphics people. A good way to develop that intuition is to build models and play with them. This chapter will discuss how to make polyhedral models that are interesting to build and study. They're also attractive to look at.

A Model to Have and to Hold

The traditional way to make a model of a polyhedron is to begin with what's called a *net*. Suppose we start with the cube of Figure 3.1a and unfold it, as in Figure 3.1b. Completely unfolding the cube and laying it out flat gives us Figure 3.1c, where I've also added some small tabs on the sides of some of the faces. If you cut out Figure 3.1c, fold it along the edges, and glue the tabs to insides of the appropriate faces, you can build a cube; a flat diagram like Figure 3.1c is a net diagram for the cube. You can build any polyhedron with this approach, though you might have to glue together several different nets.

Building polyhedra from nets is the topic of Chapter 7 in this book. It's a fine technique, but recently an entirely new way of building polyhedral models has appeared. It's an adaptation of the art of *origami,* based on paper folding. Origami polyhedra are assembled without any cutting or gluing—you just fold paper and assemble the pieces by tucking flaps into pockets. This chapter is about building polyhedra with origami.

You've probably seen origami creations at some point, and you may even have built a few—most kids have built a hat or "fortune-teller" or other toy at some point by folding up paper. Origami is an ancient Japanese art (*ori* = folded, *kami* = paper) that always involves starting with a simple shape of paper and folding it into an attractive, surprising, or simply interesting shape. Different places and times have had different definitions of just what can be considered origami. Generally the differences revolve around what else you can do in addition to folding the paper. Some people like to cut away pieces with scissors; others only cut slits, so they don't remove any paper; some use glue or tape; and so on.

In this chapter, I'll stick with a pretty simple and popular description of origami. You start with a single sheet of paper, and you're only allowed to fold it. There are no tools allowed except for your own fingers—no pencils, measuring sticks, compasses, and so on.

Figure 3.1
(a) A folded-up cube.
(b) Unfolding the cube.
(c) The net diagram, complete with tabs, for constructing the cube.

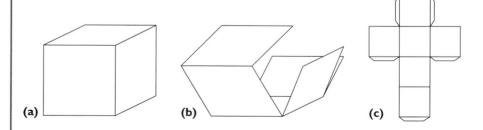

I'll allow two variations, though. The first is to start with something other than a square: in origami books, for example, you can find lots of designs that are based on dollar bills. Second, we'll create most of our models by assembling several different pieces together. The assembly must not require tape or glue, though for some of the flimsier models you may want to apply a few dabs of glue here and there so that the model doesn't completely unravel if you should drop it. (I speak from experience!)

Origami paper is available in most craft and art stores. It's usually glazed and colored on one side and unfinished and white on the other. Animals tend to be very popular subjects for origami, and many of the packages of paper come with a set of folding instructions for some simple models. Figure 3.2 shows a kangaroo I folded from a gray square of paper.

Unit Origami

Frankly, I've always found traditional origami to be rather difficult. The notation is very simple (and we'll see some of it below), but often while I'm following some instructions from a book I get lost in one of the steps and I just can't figure out where I went wrong. Sometimes I plow on, and sometimes I give up. But every now and then I'll dig out one of my books and try again—and once in a while I do manage to make a creature of some sort.

Recently my success-to-failure ratio went way up, because I found two new books. The first book talks about how to make traditional models, such as animals. Working from Lang's *The Complete Book of Origami* I've actually been able to complete each model I've attempted, which is a bit of a feat for me. I folded the kangaroo in Figure 3.2 from the instructions in this book.

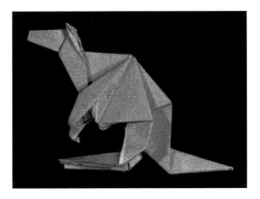

Figure 3.2
An origami kangaroo.

The other big news was my discovery of Tomoko Fusè's book *Unit Origami*. The basic idea behind unit origami is that you build many instances of a single piece, or unit, and assemble them to build a more complicated model. Unit origami is mostly directed toward building geometric polyhedra such as the Platonic solids, rather than organic creatures such as squids or dinosaurs. The main trick behind unit origami is to build a unit that combines *pockets, flaps,* and *locktabs.* A pocket is like a kangaroo's pouch: there's an open burrow into which you can place a flap from another unit. A flap is a little bit of paper that sticks out from the unit, generally shaped the same as the pocket it's intended to mate with. When the flap slides into the pocket, the two pieces are joined together. Sometimes there's a little extra bit that hangs off of a flap, which I call a locktab—this usually wraps around a fold in the model to keep the flap firmly in its pocket.

There are generally three types of units that you fold in unit origami, which I call *face, edge,* and *vertex* units. As the name implies, a face unit is a piece that you fold up to represent a single face. For a cube, you'd make six square faces, each one from its own piece of paper. Each square would probably have some tabs and pockets, and you'd assemble the cube by connecting the faces. An edge unit spans an edge and includes at least some of the face on each side; for the cube, we'd have 12 edge units, each one probably with a pair of triangles on each side of the edge. Finally, vertex units contain a corner of the model and generally some edge and some face parts; for the cube, we'd have eight vertex units.

Some models can be built in all three ways. Generally the trade-offs are stability, complexity, and time. For our hypothetical cube, we would need six, eight, or 12 units for face-, edge-, and vertex-based assemblies. Generally it will take longer to build 12 units than six, though of course the relative complexities of the units make a difference. Sometimes the time savings from a smaller number of units is lost in the assembly stage, because the pieces have to fit together more precisely. Generally the models built with smaller numbers of units are less strong than their more complex counterparts. So a model with only a few pieces can be pretty quick to fold, but it might be harder to assemble and a little flimsier than a more numerous version. In this chapter I'll show you several different modules that allow you to build models based on equilateral triangles, and if you build the models you'll see some of these trade-offs firsthand.

To get the ball rolling, I'll first cover the little bit of traditional notation that we'll need.

The Rules of the Game

Figure 3.3 summarizes the notation that I'll use in this chapter. This notation was developed by Akira Yoshizawa and is now very standardized; almost all books on origami use these symbols. And this is about half of the total symbols that are used—it's really a very simple and spare system.

Everything is described from your point of view, as the person holding the paper. A *valley fold* is represented by a dashed line, and it's a fold that forms a valley from your point of view. That is, the two sides of the fold rise up toward you, so if you dropped a kernel of corn into the fold, it would roll down to the crease. A *mountain fold* is the crest of a mountain, and it is represented by alternating dashes and dots. If you dropped a kernel of corn onto a mountain fold, it would roll off to one side or the other and down.

Figure 3.3a shows a piece of paper that has a valley fold and a mountain fold indicated. Solid lines in the drawings refer to either the edges of the paper or creases that you've already made. Often arrows are used to show you where to make the fold; if an arrow has two arcs, as in Figure 3.3b, it means you should make the fold and then unfold the paper, rather than leaving it folded. The symbol to flip the paper over is an arrow with a built-in loop, as in Figure 3.3c. The colored side of the paper is indicated by gray shading.

Generally you should work on a hard, flat surface. When you make a fold, get it roughly into position with your fingers. Once everything is in place, smush it down; this way you can still maneuver a little bit to get the pieces aligned. When the paper seems set up correctly, go over the fold again with your fingernail, making a sharp crease. You'll find the sharper your creases, the better your models will look and the easier they'll go together.

It's very important, particularly in unit origami, that your folds be accurate. A little error in alignment early on will magnify on each subsequent fold, until the resulting model is really quite off. It's worth a little care to

Figure 3.3
(a) Solid lines are paper edges or old creases. A dashed line is a valley fold, and a dash-and-dot line is a mountain fold.
(b) An arrow with two arcs means fold (and make the crease), then unfold.
(c) An arrow with a loop means to turn the model over.

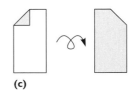

(a)   **(b)**   **(c)**

make sure that all of your folds are precise and sharp. To rephrase a carpenter's maxim: measure twice, fold once.

There are two kinds of folds in unit origami, which I call *reference folds* and *construction folds*. A reference fold is made only to provide some sort of calibrating mark for further folds. For example, we'll see below that we can make an equilateral triangle by folding up the corners of a square sheet until they meet the centerline; this centerline is simply a crease running up the middle of the page, created by folding it in two. There's often no further use for this crease once it's been used to form the triangle. On the other hand, a construction fold directly contributes to the shape of the final piece. Reference folds need to be precise, but you don't have to make them as sharp or enduring as construction folds, which should fundamentally reshape the paper.

Many folds make a model. Generally I learn a new unit by building it a few times slowly. Each unit has its own tricks to getting it built fast and accurately.

One technique that works for me on long folds is to place my fingernail at one end, particularly if it's near the edge of the paper; then I can use that as an anchor to pivot the folded-over piece around. Another trick is to notice when you're going to fold something over twice (i.e., in half, then in half again). If you make the first fold a tiny bit shorter than it ideally should be, you will have compensated for the thickness of the paper when you make the second fold and everything will still align correctly. You may think it's pretty unlikely that the thickness of the paper would be much of a consideration, but when a fold is four or eight layers thick, then the offset can make a visible difference. Plus, there's a certain pleasing aesthetic to making a nice unit, and a sharp point or a clean edge is both gratifying while you're building and attractive to look at when you're done.

Sometimes these models are very fragile and prone to falling apart while you're assembling them. I use artist's removable tape (made of the same adhesive found on the back of those yellow sticky notes) to hold the pieces together while I'm building; it comes off without a trace once the model is assembled and strong enough to hold itself together. As I mentioned earlier, some of the weaker models may be strengthened with a bit of glue in strategic places to keep them together so that you (and others) can handle them without fearing that holding and turning the model will cause it to disintegrate.

Finally, once I understand how to build the unit, I'll wait until there's something I want to hear on the radio, or I'll select a CD I'd like to listen to. Then I'll put on the radio or the CD player and fold while mostly paying attention to the other stuff. Folding lots of copies of the same unit can be a meditative experience, but if you're not in that frame of mind it can get pretty boring. At those times, folding can be a nice experience if you're just keeping your hands busy while concentrating on something else.

The Platonic Solids

The Platonic solids are the starting point for almost all discussions of 3D geometric solids. Entire books have been written about these five shapes—I couldn't even begin to skim the surface here. Jim Blinn gave instructions on how to find the coordinates of these solids in his book (see the Further Reading section). More information on them can be found in almost any book on 3D geometry.

We'll begin by building the Platonic solids. They're familiar, attractive, and they seem to have endless layers of ever-more subtle but rewarding structure, both within and between each solid. I will illustrate the construction of each solid with a different origami unit, so we'll see five different units as we build the five different solids.

THE TETRAHEDRON

The simplest Platonic solid is the *tetrahedron*, shown in Figure 3.4. The tetrahedron has four faces, each an equilateral triangle. Every of the four vertices joins three triangles, which meet along six edges.

We will build this model from rectangular pieces with sides in the ratio 2:1. This might immediately seem like an almost impossible task. How could we possibly start with a rectangular piece

Figure 3.4
A tetrahedron built from edge equilateral triangle units.

of paper and make an equilateral triangle, without using a compass, ruler, protractor, pencil, or anything else? Aren't there all sorts of irrational numbers running around inside an equilateral triangle? True enough, but this is a special case. Remember the 30–60–90 triangle, shown in Figure 3.5.

Figure 3.5
The geometry of
the 30-60-90
triangle.

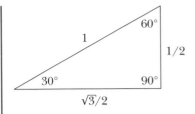

If the hypotenuse has length 1, then the length of the edge opposite the 30-degree angle is 1/2. This is the central observation to folding a tetrahedron.

Let's first see this trick in isolation. Figure 3.6a shows a square piece of paper, one unit on a side. We'll begin by making a valley fold up the middle as in Figure 3.6b—just fold the left half over the right, crease, and open it up again. Now we have two vertical rectangles, each of height 1 and width 1/2. Now fold the bottom-left corner up until it reaches the centerline, as in Figure 3.6c. The result is Figure 3.6d. This is a good place to use the fingernail pivot trick: plant your fingernail right on the bottom-right corner and work the folded-over bottom-left corner around until it lands on top of the centerline. These two points will determine where the corner ends up. Just let it land where it falls naturally when you crease the fold, making sure the other two vertices stay in place as you make that crease.

The geometry of the situation is shown in Figure 3.6e. Consider triangle $\triangle EFH$. The original square's edge was of length 1, and that edge is the hypotenuse EH of this triangle. Since the hypotenuse is 1 and the far side is 1/2, then the angle $\angle EHF$ at the bottom must be 30 degrees (remember Figure 3.5), and since angle $\angle CHG$ is 90 degrees, angle $\angle EHG$ is 60 degrees. Now consider the folded triangle $\triangle EHD$. The gap it left behind, triangle $\triangle DHG$, is exactly the same shape. So the 60-degree angle $\angle EHG$ is bisected, meaning angle $\angle EHD$ is 30 degrees as well. We have trisected a right angle! Now we can make units with angles that are any multiple of 30 degrees.

Let's now return to the tetrahedron. We begin with units that are rectangles, twice as wide as they are tall, as in Figure 3.7. If you want to be a purist and only use square pieces of paper, just fold the paper in half once before starting. I cut along that fold to make two rectangles before proceeding,

Figure 3.6
Creating a 30-
degree angle.
(a) Start with a
square.
(b) Fold in half to
make a crease up
the center.
(c) Pivoting around
the lower-right
corner, fold the
lower-left corner
up until it falls on
the midline.
(d) The result.
(e) The geometry
of the result.

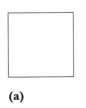

(a)

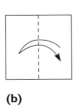

(b)

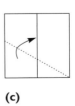

(c)

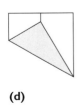

(d)

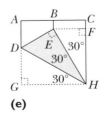

(e)

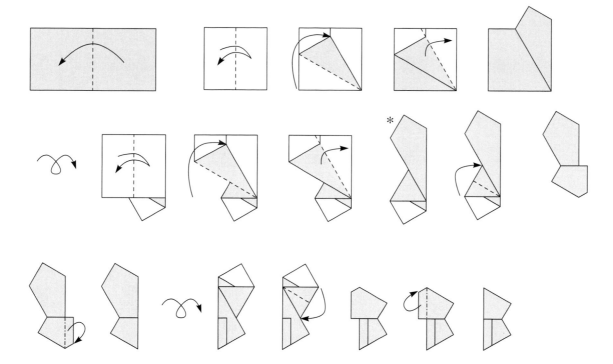

because it saves on paper and keeps the pieces from getting too thick and unwieldy.

Begin by folding the rectangle in half to create a pair of squares. Then fold up the bottom piece, as in Figure 3.6, and fold it up again. Try to get the right side of the paper to align with the right side of the square. Then you flip the paper over and repeat the process. Once the top and bottom have the same shape, fold up the bottom part. Use the tip of the triangle as one endpoint of the fold, and try to bisect that angle by bringing up the lower-left point of the triangle to the top point, as shown by the arrow. Then fold the remaining flap over to the back; this will be a locktab. Now flip the unit over and repeat the process.

When you're done, unfold these folds until you reach the starred picture in Figure 3.7. Then open the piece by unfolding once along the edge at the right of that picture. The piece, seen from the top and bottom, should look like Figure 3.8a. Assembling the pieces is shown in Figure 3.8b—slip the tab of one piece into the flap of the other, and let the locktab slide down into the bottom of the pocket.

This is the *edge equilateral triangle unit*. The open flap along the diagonal of the piece turns into an edge of the model. Because the tetrahedron has six

Figure 3.7
Folding the edge equilateral triangle unit. When you've completed the folding, unfold back to the step marked with a star.

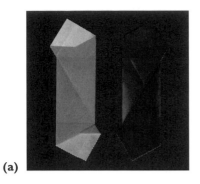
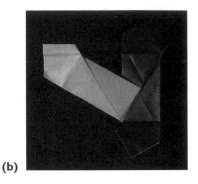

(a) **(b)**

Figure 3.8
(a) The edge equilateral triangle unit.
(b) Assembling two units.

edges, you'll need to build and assemble six of these pieces to build the model. It can be a little tricky to see how the pieces fit at first, so give yourself a quiet space and some time to play with it. It may feel like a puzzle—in fact, the tetrahedron is one of the hardest models to build! This isn't because it's complicated, but rather the folding that you have to do to get the pieces to lock together seems really implausible until after you've done it—at least, that's how it seemed to me. The implausible part is to realize that the prongs at the ends of the units need to wrap around to the other pieces already in place—after all, only three triangles can meet at each vertex. It takes a little patience and diligence, but if you fiddle with it a bit you'll eventually get the pieces together as in Figure 3.4, and then you'll wonder why you thought it was

Figure 3.9
A cube built from harlequin strut units.

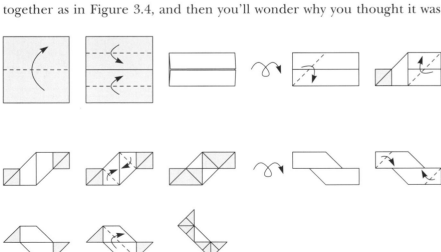

Figure 3.10
Folding the harlequin strut unit.

Chapter Three

hard! When you're done, every face, vertex, and edge will look like every other (except for colors, if you use differently colored papers). In Figure 3.4, I used two pieces each of red, green, and blue papers.

If you look closely, you'll see that in the center of each face is a small irregular hexagon formed by the middles of the edges and the folds on the paper that make up the faces.

THE CUBE

Probably the next simplest Platonic solid is the *cube*. The cube has six faces, 12 edges, and eight vertices. We saw the net for the cube in Figure 3.1; here we'll build one out of origami units.

In the last section we built a tetrahedron from edge-based pieces: we created six pieces, which corresponded to the six edges of the solid. We'll do the same thing for the cube, creating 12 struts that correspond to the cube's edges. Figure 3.9 shows the model, based on what I call the *harlequin strut unit*. Folding instructions for the strut are shown in Figure 3.10. Start with a square piece of paper, colored side up. The resulting piece is shown from two points of view in Figure 3.11a. To photograph them, I've flattened out the pieces, but to assemble them you'll need to fold them into right-angled bars.

The result of the folding process is a little right-angled strut with flaps at right angles at the top and bottom and two pockets along the strut. To put them together, you slide the flaps into the pockets, with the new pieces at right angles, as in Figure 3.11b. Because three units meet at each vertex, you'll need to slide another unit with the other two, as in Figure 3.11c. The entire cube is assembled by putting together 12 units. This model is particularly floppy as it's going together, so you might want to use artist's adhesive tape to temporarily hold the pieces in place during assembly. Once

Figure 3.11
(a) The harlequin strut unit.
(b) Assembling two harlequin strut units.
(c) Including the third unit makes a single vertex of the cube.

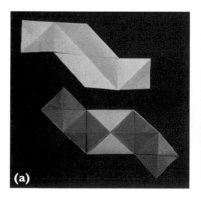
(a)

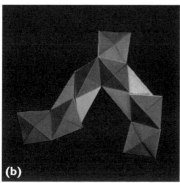
(b)

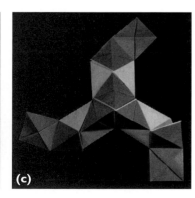
(c)

built, though, you can take off the tape and the model will hold together quite well.

The harlequin strut unit has the interesting property that it can be tightened up to create a triangular shape as well. The strut becomes tighter and flatter in this configuration, but there's no distortion. The piece remains planar, though—you can't use these struts to build a tetrahedron.

THE OCTAHEDRON

The next Platonic solid we'll consider is the *octahedron*. It has eight faces, each of which is an equilateral triangle. Each of the 12 edges joins two faces, and each of the six vertices joins four triangles. We can build the octahedron from the same edge equilateral triangle units that we used for the tetrahedron above; Figure 3.12 shows the result. Because there are 12 edges, this model requires 12 of these units.

Figure 3.12
An octahedron built from edge equilateral triangle units.

An alternative construction uses only four units, each of which covers two faces. I call these *double-face equilateral triangle units.* As the name implies, each of these units correlates to two faces of the finished solid; Figure 3.13 shows the octahedron assembled with these. Folding instructions for this unit are shown in Figure 3.14; the result is four equilateral triangles in a strip, with locktabs at the top and bottom. Figure 3.15a shows the pieces from the top and bottom.

Figure 3.13
An octahedron built from double-face equilateral triangle units.

To assemble the pieces, line them up as in Figure 3.15b, and slip one flap into one pocket. Then get the other flap into the other pocket, as in Figure 3.15c. These two pieces now create a square-based pyramid, which forms the top half of the octahedron. You can assemble two pieces in the same way to make the bottom half, and then connect the top and bottoms together by tucking the flaps into the pockets.

The little locktabs at the end of each large flap serve to lock the model together; they extend over the octahedron's edge and into the adjacent face. I typically get these into place by sliding the flap into the pocket from the

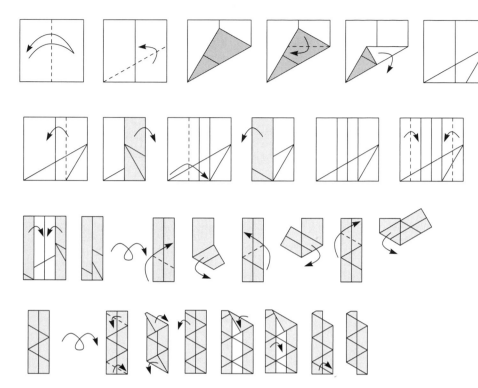

Figure 3.14
Folding the double-face equilateral triangle unit.

edge of the unit. Toward the end of construction it gets hard to angle the little flaps around the edge, so I fold them back against the big flap. Then I just slide the flap into the pocket. The model is stable enough with a few of the little locktabs in place that it will still hold together. It is flimsier than the version in Figure 3.12, but it only takes half the paper and half the effort to build.

There's something very cool about this construction: in the opening section, we trisect the edge of the original square! The geometry behind this

Figure 3.15
(a) The double-face equilateral triangle unit.
(b) Assembling two double-face equilateral triangle units.
(c) Completing the assembly.

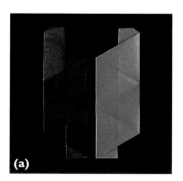

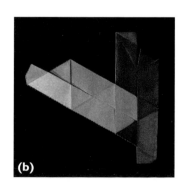

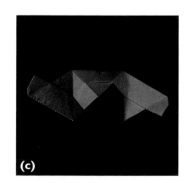

is shown in Figure 3.16. As we've seen before, triangles $\triangle FGE$ and $\triangle FCE$ are identical 30-60-90 triangles. Since the original edge FG has length 1, both CE and EG have length $1/\sqrt{3}$, and the shared hypotenuse EF has length $2/\sqrt{3}$. When we fold down the point at C to bisect angle $\angle CEF$, we create two new triangles. Triangle $\triangle CED$ is another 30-60-90 triangle. Working from the known edge CE (now opposite the 60-degree angle $\angle CDE$), the new hypotenuse DE has length $2/3$ and thus the new short side CD has length $1/3$. Because CF

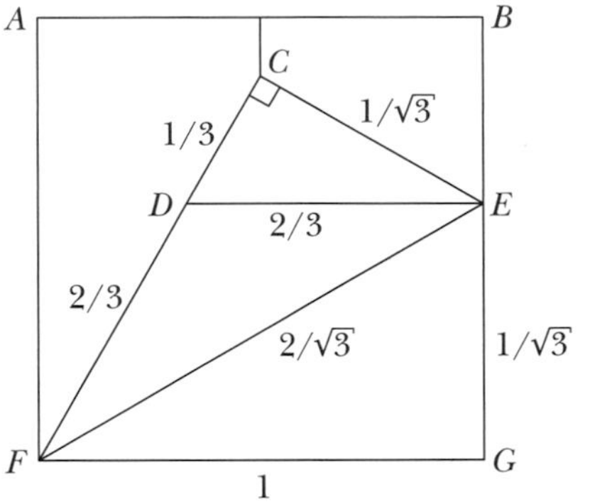

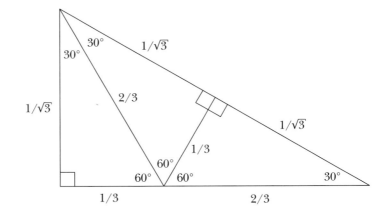

Figure 3.16
The geometry of the double-face equilateral triangle unit.

Figure 3.17
The 30-60-90 triangle is a reptile: it can be composed of three smaller copies of itself.

has length 1, the remaining piece DF must have length $2/3$, just like DE. CF is one of the original edges of the square; when we unfold the square, the crease at D marks one-third the square's edge.

Figure 3.17 shows the geometry of this situation in a more familiar orientation. This is basically a dissection of the 30-60-90 triangle into three smaller, equivalent triangles. The hypotenuse is bisected, and the long edge is marked off at one-third from the right angle. A figure like this 30-60-90 triangle that can be dissected into smaller copies of itself is called a *reptile*.

THE DODECAHEDRON

Our next Platonic solid is the *dodecahedron:* this is a solid of 12 pentagonal faces, three of which meet at each of the 20 vertices; there are 30 edges. To build the dodecahedron, we'll again adopt a framework design. Figure 3.18 shows the model we will build, using a vertex-based unit.

The dodecahedron is built from a piece I call the *triangular vertex unit*. To build the triangular vertex unit, we start with a piece of paper that is an equilateral triangle. To form an equilateral triangle from a square piece of origami paper, use the opening steps of the tetrahedron construction in Figure 3.7 to create a 60-degree angle at each end of an edge of the square; the triangle will be formed by the points of the original square at both ends of this edge and the point where the two creases intersect along the midline.

Figure 3.18
A dodecahedron built from triangular vertex units.

If you're a purist, you'll probably want to fold these two pieces in and under to make the triangle, and then continue with the folding of the unit. I admit that I take scissors to these folds and cut along them to make a triangle-shaped piece of paper. The advantage of cutting out the triangle is that the resulting unit comes out completely symmetrical and isn't a bit thicker in some places than others. I recommend that you do the same, but if you find the idea of actually *cutting* a piece of origami paper to be shocking, you can build the model just fine if you fold the pieces under.

Figure 3.19 shows how to fold the triangular vertex unit. Start with the colored side up, and fold the triangle in half each of the three ways. This gives you the center point. Then fold the vertices to the center, and flip the unit

Figure 3.19
Folding the triangular vertex unit.

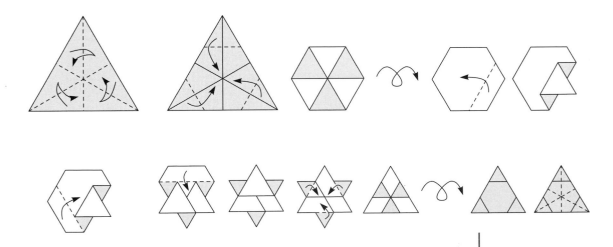

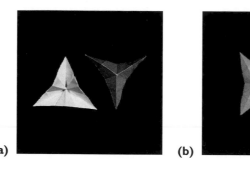

Figure 3.20
(a) The triangular vertex unit.
(b) Assembling triangular vertex units.

(a)　　　　　**(b)**

over. With one of the flipped-over pieces at the top, fold the top, bottom-right, and then bottom-left pieces to the center, creating a new triangle. Fold in the little triangles of the star that stick out, and turn the piece over. Now to give the piece some strength, you're going to fold it up like a starfish, with mountain folds along the arms and valley folds between them. Fold down on both sides of the three arms and fold up in the creases between them to make a little triangular connector with small arms sticking out. Figure 3.20a shows the pieces from the top and bottom.

To combine two triangular vertex units, slide the arm coming out of one into the pocket of another, as in Figure 3.20b. It doesn't seem to really matter which piece goes into which, since the pieces look the same and end up the same thickness whichever way they're assembled.

Since the dodecahedron has 20 vertices, you'll need 20 of these modules to make the model.

THE ICOSAHEDRON

Our final Platonic solid is the *icosahedron:* it has 20 faces and 12 vertices, held together by 30 edges. Each face of the icosahedron is an equilateral triangle, so we could use either of the two triangle forms we've seen so far. Using the edge equilateral triangle unit we'd need 30 pieces, which is simply a whole lot of folding. The double-face

Figure 3.21
An icosahedron built from four-triangle face units.

equilateral triangle unit is much more attractive, requiring only 10 pieces to cover the 20 faces.

Just for variety, I'll present here an alternate double-face unit, which I call the *four-triangle face unit.* This unit has a property that crystallographers describe as *enantiomorphic:* there's both a left-handed and a

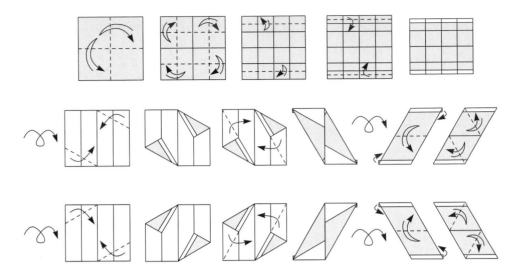

right-handed version (anything with this property, such as a glove, is called an *enantiomorph*). This piece also uses both the front and back of the paper. This tends to make it a little weaker than most of the other units, so the model tends to be a little floppier during assembly and a little more fragile once built.

An icosahedron built from the four-triangle face unit is shown in Figure 3.21. Folding instructions for this unit are shown in Figure 3.22; the resulting piece is seen from above and below in Figure 3.23a. The second line of Figure 3.22 shows how to make the right-handed version, while the third line shows how to make the left-handed version. They go together as in Figure 3.23b.

Recall that the previous stack of four triangles, in the double-face equilateral triangle unit, had a little bit of paper left over that was absorbed into the locktab at one end of the stack. There doesn't seem to be any paper

Figure 3.22
Folding the four-triangle face unit. After following the top row, fold the second row for a right-handed piece or the third row for a left-handed piece.

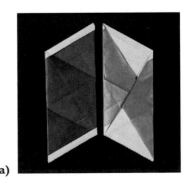

(a)

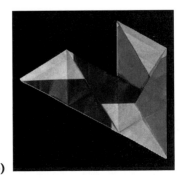

(b)

Figure 3.23
(a) The four-triangle face unit.
(b) Assembling two units.

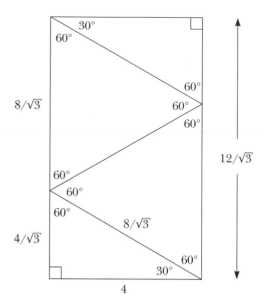

Figure 3.24
The geometry behind the four-triangle face unit.

left over in this unit, which struck me initially as pretty special. Of course, we make this happen by doing all of that folding of ever-smaller strips at the top and bottom at the beginning, but still we only do that a couple of times and we don't use any tools. It turns out that this works because of a nice numerical approximation.

Consider Figure 3.24. I built a 30-60-90 triangle in the corner and then a couple of equilateral triangles above it. Suppose that the bottom edge is 4 units across. Then the edge of the triangle is $8/\sqrt{3}$, and the short leg on the left side is $4/\sqrt{3}$. So the upper part of the left edge also has length $8/\sqrt{3}$, for a total of $12/\sqrt{3}$ for the left side of the figure. This has a value of about 6.928, which for paper folding we can think of as being pretty close to 7. So this figure is 4 units wide by about 7 units tall, and the two triangles fit just about perfectly, with a half-triangle remaining at the top and bottom.

This is then why we make those opening folds in Figure 3.22; they turn the original square into a rectangle that's 8 units wide by 7 units high (it's 8 units wide because we're going to build four triangles, not two). If we think of the side of the square as 1 unit, then essentially we approximated the irrational value $3/\sqrt{3}$ as $2(1-(1/8))$. The resulting error of about 2 parts in 100 is pretty close for paper folding.

To assemble the modules, insert one of the triangular flaps into one of the triangular pockets of the other model, as shown in Figure 3.23b. Then continue adding pieces, always bringing together five triangles at a vertex,

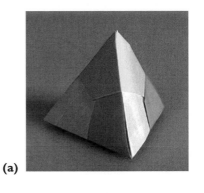

(a)

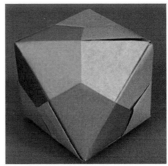

(b)

Figure 3.25
Other models built
from four-triangle
face units.
(a) A tetrahedron.
(b) An octahedron.

Figure 3.26
A teapotahedron.

until the model is closed. You'll need 5 right-handed and 5 left-handed units for the icosahedron.

You don't need both forms of this module for all models. The tetrahedron and octahedron can both be built from just left-handed or right-handed units—2 and 4 of them, respectively. Figure 3.25a shows a tetrahedron from these pieces, and Figure 3.25b shows an octahedron. They're considerably more fragile than the versions we built earlier.

THE TEAPOTAHEDRON

In 1987, the graphics world was stunned when Jim Arvo and David Kirk announced in the Siggraph '97 paper proceedings that they had discovered a new primitive solid, which they dubbed the *teapotahedron*. No discussion of the Platonic solids since then could be complete without inclusion of this new fundamental shape. Figure 3.26 shows my origami approximation to the teapotahedron. This version is deficient in several ways; most noticeably, it's flat. It would be wonderful to have a nice 3D origami teapotahedron.

Archimedean Solids

The Platonic solids were a great place to start when studying unit origami: they're the classic 3D polyhedra, and there are only five of them. Now we'll move on to a closely related family of polyhedra, called the *Archimedean solids*. There are a bunch of these, but we'll only look at the ones that are mixtures of pairs of Platonic solids, or stepping-stones along the way of transforming between different Platonic solids. Before we get to that, we need to first look at what *duals* are all about.

THE CUBE/OCTAHEDRON DUAL

Suppose we take the cube of Figure 3.27a and mark the centers of the six faces with dots. Each dot has four other dots that are closest to it. If we draw a line between every dot and its nearest neighbors, we get Figure 3.27b. Removing the cube, we see in Figure 3.27c that we've created an octahedron. The six vertices of the octahedron correspond exactly to the six faces of the cube. Use your imagination to think about what would happen if we repeat the process on the octahedron. If you put a dot at the center of each of the eight triangular faces of the octahedron, then each dot has three nearest neighbors. Connecting those dots, you create the outline of a cube: the eight faces of the octahedron correspond exactly to the eight vertices of the cube. The cube and the octahedron are called *dual polyhedra* or, simply *duals*.

Figure 3.27
(a) A cube.
(b) Mark the center of each face and connect each dot to its four nearest neighbors.
(c) This forms an octahedron.

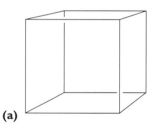
(a)

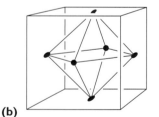
(b)

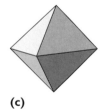
(c)

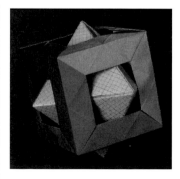

Figure 3.28
Nested cube and octahedron.

We can show this relationship with our origami models. I was sneaky in my choice of units for the Platonic solids because I showed how to build a framework cube and a solid octahedron. That was so that I could make the nested pair shown in Figure 3.28. You may have to play a little to get the sizes right, but the results are worth it. I built

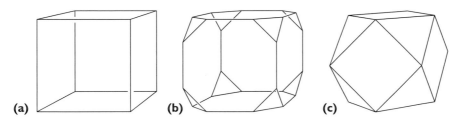

(a)   (b)   (c)

Figure 3.29
(a) A cube.
(b) The corners sliced a quarter of the way off.
(c) The corners sliced down to where the triangles meet, forming a cuboctahedron.

both models and then simply opened up the cube to place the octahedron inside.

We can look at the dual construction in a slightly different way. Suppose we begin with the cube of Figure 3.29a, and we start to slice off the corners. Figure 3.29b shows a step along the way: the square faces become octagons, and each vertex turns into a triangle. As we deepen our slices, the triangles in the corners grow larger and larger, until they touch, as in Figure 3.29c. Now the faces are squares again, but they're rotated 45 degrees with respect to their previous orientation. If we continue shaving down the corners, we'll be left with an octahedron.

The shape in Figure 3.29b is, in some sense, halfway between a cube and an octahedron. It's an Archimedean solid known as a *cuboctahedron*. This is a celebrated shape. Buckminster Fuller had a particular fondness for this structure, which he called the *vector equilibrium*, and believed it was a basic building block of the universe.

We can build a cuboctahedron with origami, as shown in Figure 3.30. The basic building block is a vertex unit with four radiating arms; it's a lot like the triangular piece we used last time to build the dodecahedron. Folding instructions for the *square vertex unit* are given in Figure 3.31. The piece is illustrated in Figure 3.32a, and you can see how to put them together in Figure 3.32b.

THE TETRAHEDRON/ TETRAHEDRON DUAL

Now that we've seen the basic idea behind duals, think about what the dual of the tetrahedron might be. You can use the point/face connection approach of Figure 3.27 or the shaving-down approach of Figure 3.29, but you'll reach the same answer either way:

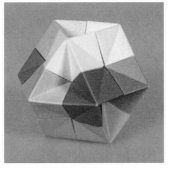

Figure 3.30
An origami cuboctahedron.

Figure 3.31
Folding the square
vertex unit.

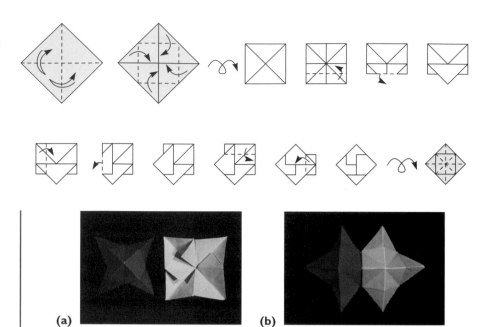

Figure 3.32
(a) The square
vertex unit.
(b) Assembling
two units.

(a)   (b)

the dual of the tetrahedron is another tetrahedron! We say that the tetrahedron is *self-dual.*

Figure 3.33
A pair of nested
tetrahedra.

Figure 3.33 shows a pair of tetrahedra, nested inside one another. Notice that just like the other pairs of duals, if you file down the corners of the larger, framework tetrahedron, you'll get the one inside. The framework tetrahedron was made with a slightly altered version of the *little turtle unit,* described in the next section.

If you use the corner-shaving process and stop halfway, you'll reach another Archimedean solid known as the *truncated tetrahedron,* shown in Figure 3.34. You can build this model from six hexagonal pieces of paper: three will end up forming the big hexagonal faces and three will form the triangles. To get a hexagonal piece of paper from a square, take a look at Figure 3.35a. The basic idea is to fold a 30-60-90 triangle at each

Figure 3.34
An origami truncated tetrahedron,
half of the way
from one tetrahedron to another.

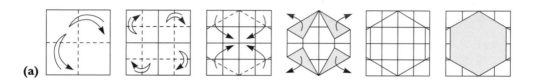

(a)

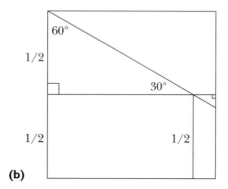

(b)

Figure 3.35
(a) Creating a hexagonal piece of paper from a square one.
(b) The geometry behind 3.35a.

corner and then get rid of the triangles and the flaps on the sides. The geometry behind this is shown in Figure 3.35b; basically you're making sure that each side of the hexagon has unit length and meets the other sides at a 60-degree angle. The two pieces involved are shown in Figure 3.36.

Figure 3.37 shows how to build the hexagonal piece. There are a couple of places where you need to be careful; this is a good one to expect to practice on for a bit. Folding over those flaps while getting the inside part to fold under is a snap once you see what to do, but you might find yourself fighting with the paper for a bit before you get the hang of it. (That's what happened to me, anyway.) The step in parentheses is meant to show you that you have six flaps going around at that step—you don't need to actually open up the flower. The last few steps involve tucking in three of the flaps. The result is a hexagon with pockets on three sides.

Figure 3.38 shows how to build the triangular piece. This is a little triangle with three flaps, which go into the pockets of the hexagons. The model will hold together this way, but loosely. You might want to reinforce it with some glue, or tape hidden in the inside.

(a)

(b)

Figure 3.36
The pieces that make the truncated tetrahedron.
(a) From the top.
(b) From the bottom.

Figure 3.37
Folding the hexagonal face of the truncated tetrahedron.

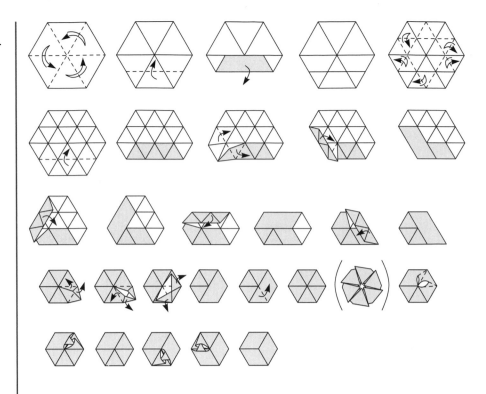

THE DODECAHEDRON/ICOSAHEDRON DUAL

The remaining two Platonic solids are the dodecahedron and icosahedron, and as you probably expect by now, they are also duals of each other. Figure 3.39 shows the dodecahedron and icosahedron of the previous sections together; as with the other duals, you can see the points of the icosahedron poking out of the center of the faces of the dodecahedron.

Figure 3.38
Folding the triangular face of the truncated tetrahedron.

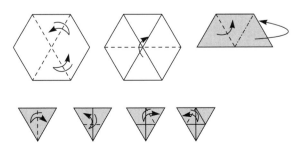

If you whittle down the points of one of these solids and stop when they start to touch, you reach the Archimedean solid called the *icosadodecahedron*. This is a big object—it combines the 12 pentagons of the dodecahedron and the 20 triangles of the icosahedron, for a total of 32 faces in all. It has 30 vertices and 60 edges.

Figure 3.39
Nested dodecahedron (the outer shell) and icosahedron (the inner solid).

I tried a lot of approaches to building this model, but it's tricky to get something this complex to stay together; almost everything was too flimsy. The problem is that any two faces that touch are almost coplanar; if a flap sticks into a pocket, there's nothing to keep it from just slipping out again. Finally I modified an edge-based unit called the *little turtle*, and the model hung together, more or less. My icosadodecahedron based on the modified little turtle unit is shown in Figure 3.40. The morning I took this 12-inch diameter model from home to the photographer's studio, I accidentally dropped it, from the incredible height of about 4 inches. One whole side of the model dented inward and, as I tried to tease it back into a spherical shape, the whole thing started to unravel. Stable, yes, but don't sneeze near it. This is a very good candidate for a bit of glue here and there.

Figure 3.40
An origami icosadodecahedron, halfway between a dodecahedron and an icosahedron.

The folding diagram for the little turtle is given in Figure 3.41. For the variant that I used here, I opened up the triangle at the top and bottom of the unit, as shown in parentheses at the very end. Figure 3.42a shows the opened-up little turtle, and Figure 3.42b shows how to put them together.

Be patient as you assemble this model, because as I've mentioned it's delicate. It's also big—once you're done folding the necessary 60 pieces, you'll be able to do more in your sleep. I found that artist's removable tape was

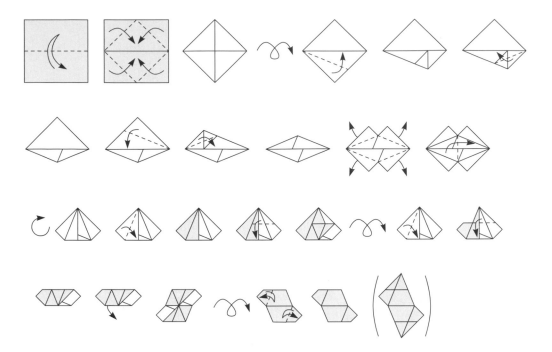

Figure 3.41
Folding the little turtle. The final figure in parentheses is the opened-up version for the icosadodecahedron.

invaluable in putting it together and, as I mentioned, I recommend adding some tape or glue when you're finished, to help keep it together.

Variations on a Theme

There are many directions in which we can generalize the techniques we've seen in this chapter. We can move on to entirely new models and new classes of models, or we can create some variations on the models we've already built. I'm going to take the latter approach here, because most of my

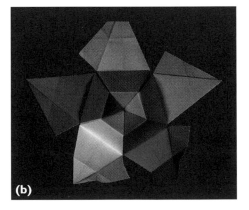

Figure 3.42
(a) The little turtle.
(b) Assembling turtles together.

own understanding of how unit origami works came from playing with variations such as these.

First, Figure 3.43 shows an opened-up version of the cuboctahedron. It takes a little more folding, but I like those windows that show through. Figure 3.44 shows you how to fold the piece; it looks a lot like the square vertex unit when you're done, except that the pockets don't reach all the way to the center. Figure 3.45a shows the pieces from above and below, and Figure 3.45b shows how to assemble them.

Figure 3.43
Another origami cuboctahedron.

You can use the little turtle to build most of the other models that have square or triangular facets. I used a variant of the little turtle to make the shell of the tetrahedron in Figure 3.33. Figure 3.46 shows the result; Figures 3.47a and 3.47b show the pieces and how to assemble them.

The great dodecahedron is a beautiful model. Each face of the dodecahedron is effectively replaced by a little inset pentagonal star, as shown in Figure 3.48. It's easy to make. You start with a pentagonal piece of paper and fold it up just like the triangular and square vertex units, as shown in

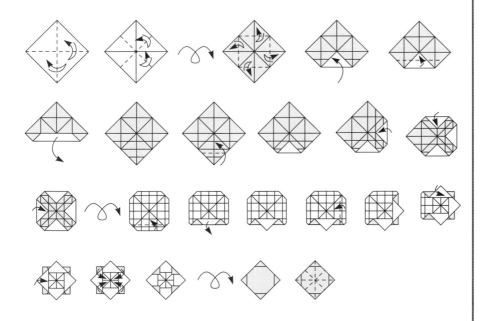

Figure 3.44
Folding the variant for Figure 3.43.

Figure 3.45
(a) The variant square vertex unit.
(b) Assembling two units.

Figure 3.49. The pieces are shown in Figure 3.50. You assemble them just like the cuboctahedron and dodecahedron, sliding the points into the corresponding flaps.

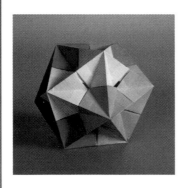

Another way to experiment is to take a model and play around with the folding pattern. The example I'll use is a form of stellated icosahedron, shown in Figure 3.51a. The folding pattern for this model is shown at the top of Figure 3.52; the open arrows indicate where you tuck a piece under another flap. The pieces are shown in Figure 3.53a. Assemble as in Figure 3.53b—the

Figure 3.46
An octahedron built from shiny little turtles.

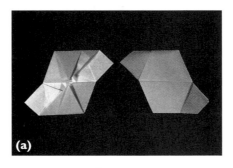

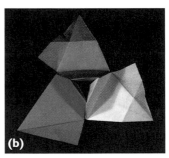

Figure 3.47
(a) The little turtles.
(b) Assembling unit turtles.

idea is that you fold the end of one piece into a pocket in the middle of another. Do this three times and you have a little triangular pyramid. The rest of Figure 3.52 shows variants on the folding pattern; there are just four simple variations, but they really make things look interesting. I mixed them up pretty much at random on Figure 3.51b.

Figure 3.48
The great dodecahedron.

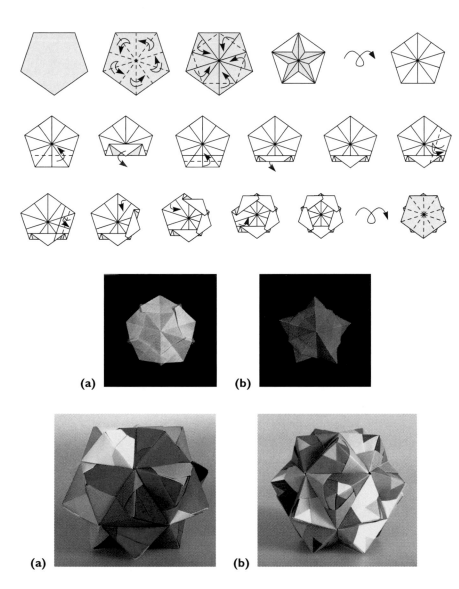

Figure 3.49
Folding the pentagonal vertex unit.

(a) (b)

Figure 3.50
The pentagonal vertex unit.

(a) (b)

Figure 3.51
(a) A stellated icosahedron.
(b) The stellated icosahedron with variant pieces.

Try cooking up your own variations on these themes; you'll find that after a while you can begin to imagine what the results will look like even as you dream up new ways of folding the paper.

Coding the Fold

There are a bunch of interesting programming projects hiding within the subject of origami and within unit origami in particular. Certainly one of the most straightforward is to write a program that will read some form of origami notation and create a 3D geometry file of the result that you can

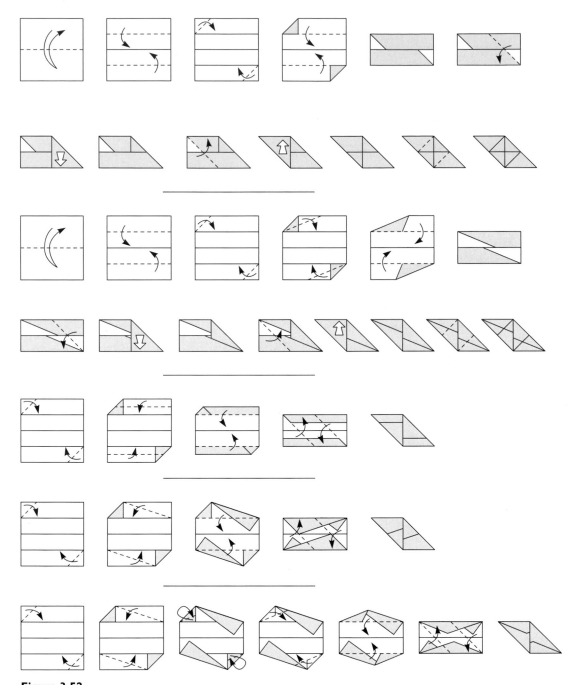

Figure 3.52
Folding the stellated icosahedron. Each of the last three
rows represents a different variation. The open arrows
indicate that a flap is tucked under another.

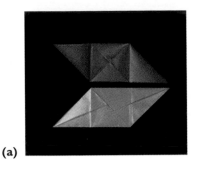

(a)

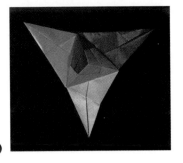

(b)

Figure 3.53
(a) The triangular stellation pieces.
(b) Assembling the triangular stellation pieces.

render. Or you can use the same information to create folding diagrams. These are both very hard problems if you go into them deeply. The folding problem requires keeping track of the thickness of the paper at each fold and how it slides around (for example, if you have two layers of paper involved in a fold, the outermost layer requires more paper than the inner layer). The diagramming problem is pretty tricky, because getting the right point of view, and picking the right steps to illustrate, is a very personal choice.

I made the diagrams in this chapter by hand with a computer-aided drafting program. With my trusty calculator, I computed all the angles and lengths to make sure that everything lined up just where it ought to be; I got very good at remembering the values for $\sqrt{3}$ and $1/\sqrt{3}$, as well as a few other key ratios. After I finished these diagrams, I learned about Maarten van Gelder's program ORIDRAW, which reads a text file with folding instructions and produces PostScript output (see the Further Reading section).

As I mentioned at the start, I really think the best way to apply the ideas of origami is to actually fold the models, using your hands as well as your eyes. Then you can feel the paper as you assemble the model, and you can hold the result, turning it in your hands and feeling its shape. This simple act will tell you things about the structure of the model that you could never learn just by looking at it. Then the next time you find yourself dealing with a shape you can only approach by looking (for example, a rendered image), some of these experiences can come to your aid to help you develop an intuitive understanding of the structure.

Moving On

I've only touched on the tip of the unit origami iceberg—this is a field that's only a few years old, and it's growing quickly. If you find the subject interesting, there's lots of room out there for original experimentation and invention.

I encourage you to build some of the models I've discussed and play with them for a bit. They make for nice decorations, and many people like to hold them in their hands. I've given away most of the models in the photographs here as gifts; I've been surprised at how much people like these little constructions! Try cooking up some variations of your own, using paper with decorations, or mixing up some modules to make really weird shapes. I used a variation on the tetrahedral units to make a moving card the last time I moved. I sent friends three colored squares with writing and a page of folding instructions; the results are shown in Figure 3.54.

Figure 3.54
A moving card built from unit origami.

Much more information on origami units and models can be found from the books in the Further Reading section. Fusè is largely credited with having invented unit origami, and his book is wonderful. The book by Gurkewitz and Arnstein, though a bit harder to follow, also contains some terrific origami units. Happy folding!

Further Reading

For a basic introduction to origami, I heartily suggest *The Complete Book of Origami* by Robert J. Lang (Dover Publications, 1989). If you've conquered that book, some good places to move on to include *Folding the Universe* by Peter Engel (Vintage Books, 1989), *Origami* by Robert Harbin (Harper & Row, 1979), *Animal Origami for the Enthusiast* by John Montroll (Dover Publications, 1985), and *Origami for the Connoisseur* by Kasahara and Takahama (Japan Publications, Inc., 1998). For more fun with paper, take a look at *Paper Dinosaurs* by David Hawcock (Sterling Publishing, 1988) and *Paper Capers* by Jack Botermans (Henry Holt, 1986).

Two of Robert Lang's technical articles on origami are particularly interesting. "Mathematical Algorithms for Origami Design" appeared in *Symmetry: Culture and Science,* 5(2):115–152, 1994. "Origami: Complexity Increasing" appeared in the CalTech quarterly magazine *Engineering & Science,* LII(2):16–23, Winter 1989.

The basics of unit origami were first put forth in *Unit Origami* by Tomoko Fusè (Japan Publications, Inc., 1990). The book *3-D Geometric Origami* by Rona Gurkewitz and Bennett Arnstein (Dover, 1996) is a little light on discussion but presents a wide selection of units. An application of unit origami to box-making is given in *Origami Boxes* by Tomoko Fusè (Japan Publications, Inc., 1989).

Finding coordinates for the Platonic solids can be tricky but also fun. Jim Blinn gives some recipes in Chapter 4 of his book, *Jim Blinn's Corner: A Trip Down the Graphics Pipeline* (Morgan Kaufmann Publishers, 1996).

Maarten van Gelder's program ORIDRAW is freely available from *http://www.rug.nl/rugcis/rc/ftp/origami/programs/oridraw/.menu.html;* a whole bunch of other origami-related programs can be found there. To get involved in the very active online world of origami, a good place to start is Joseph Wu's origami page, located at *http://www.cs.ubc.ca/spider/jwu/origami.html.*

Going the Distance

ANDREW GLASSNER'S NOTEBOOK
January/February 1997

Quick, what's the fastest way to get from one point to another?

A straight line, right?

Well, it depends on what you mean by "straight."

One of the fun aspects of non-Euclidean geometries is discovering how familiar shapes are changed under different rules. The new rules mean we have to think about distances differently from how we consider them in the flat world that Euclid described. For example, suppose you want to travel from Paris to New York. In practical terms, you can't take the straight-line path—that choice would require you to drill a tunnel through the Earth. Instead, you might take a boat or a plane, both of which travel in curved paths over the Earth's surface. Compared with the tunnel, the plane takes a longer path and you'll need more fuel, but at least your wings won't get ripped off.

Let's take a look at a couple of simple 2D geometries that obey rules different from those in the world of the flat plane.

The Euclidean World

We'll start with the familiar world of 2D Euclidean geometry. The distance d_E between two points A and B is given by the familiar formula

$$d_E(A, B) = \sqrt{(A_x - B_x)^2 + (A_y - B_y)^2}$$

Let's put this formula into action. Suppose we have a circle of radius r, centered at point M. Points P on the circle are those where the value of the function C are 0:

$$C(P, M, r) = d_E(P, M)^2 - r^2$$

Figure 4.1 shows a region of the plane with this function plotted. In all of the figures in this chapter, the range of values in the plotted domain has been scaled to place black at the minimum value and white at the maximum. The yellow curve indicates where the function has a value of 0. Of course, it's a circle.

More interesting than the circle is the blob. There are lots of blob functions; I like the one developed by Wyvill, McPheeters, and Wyvill. It's a circularly symmetric shape parameterized by the distance r from the center and the size R of the blob. The blob equation B is given by

$$B(A, B, r) = 1 - \begin{cases} \dfrac{\alpha(22 - \alpha(17 - 4\alpha))}{9} & 0 \leq \alpha \leq 1 \\ 0 & \text{otherwise} \end{cases}$$

where

$$\alpha = \left(\frac{d_E(A, B)}{r} \right)^2$$

This is plotted in Figure 4.2.

Figure 4.1
(a) A height-field plot of the circle function, centered at (0.1, 0.2) with radius 0.5.
(b) Heights are mapped to shades of gray. The yellow curve is that set of points with the value 0.0.

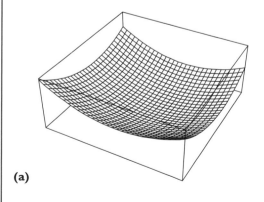

(a)

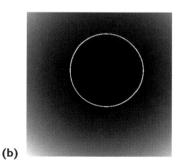

(b)

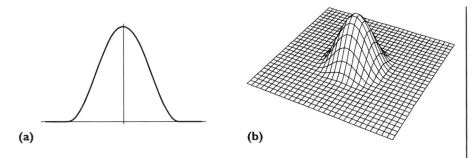

(a)　　　　　　　　　　　　　**(b)**

Figure 4.2
(a) The blob function $B(r, 0.5)$.
(b) A 3D plot of $B(r, 0.5)$ using the Euclidean distance metric d_E to find the value r between a point on the plane and the blob's center at the origin.

Figure 4.3 shows three blobs in the plane. Where blobs overlap, their values are simply summed up. The yellow line here indicates the curve where the value is 0.5.

Another interesting function of distance comes about from your recent wedding.(Congratulations!) Now the question is where to live so that you and your spouse are both the same distance away from your respective workplaces. If your job is at point A and your spouse works at point B, then your house at P can be anyplace where $d_E(P, A) = d_E(P, B)$. If we plot

$$H(P, A, B) = d_E(P, A) - d_E(P, B)$$

then we're once again looking for points P where the value of H is 0. This is shown in Figure 4.4 by the thick yellow line.

Our three formulas each depend on d_E to give us the distance between two points. Thanks, Euclid.

Taxicab Geometry

You can't get there from here.

Well, you can, but you have to take a cab.

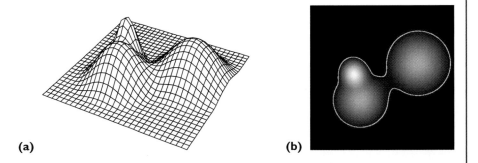

(a)　　　　　　　　　　　　　**(b)**

Figure 4.3
(a) Three blob functions. The centers are at $(0.5, 0.2)$, $(-0.3, -0.3)$, and $(0.4, 0.1)$, with radii 0.7, 0.6, and 0.3, respectively.
(b) The grayscale version of the three blobs. The yellow line is an isocontour at a height of 0.5.

Figure 4.4
(a) The equal-distance function. One workplace is at $(0.6, 0.2)$ and the other is at $(-0.3, -0.4)$.
(b) The grayscale version. The yellow line is the set of points equally distant from the two workplaces.

(b)

(a)

Figure 4.5
Two points A and B, and a taxicab's route between them. The taxi needs to cover a distance of 7 blocks, though the Euclidean distance is only 5.

Suppose that you live in a city that's laid out on a grid, like midtown Manhattan. For simplicity, we'll assume it's a perfect square grid. If you want to take a cab from point A to point B, how far do you have to travel? Figure 4.5 shows the situation.

A little thought reveals that the *taxicab distance* $d_T(A, B)$ is given by

$$d_T(A, B) = \left| A_x - B_x \right| + \left| A_y - B_y \right|$$

Simply put, you need to go horizontally and then vertically. Strictly speaking, this is the shortest taxicab distance. As anyone visiting an unfamiliar city knows, a cab can take a very circuitous path from one place to another, and you can pay for many more miles than were actually required. But conceptually, the distance d_T is all that you need to cover.

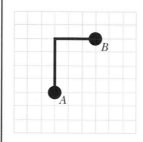

Let's revisit our three functions from the previous section, using d_T rather than d_E. Figure 4.6 shows the same functions with this new measure. The circle has become a diamond, as in Figure 4.6a. This makes sense if you think about it in terms of the form of d_T. Suppose we are sitting on a point P where $d_T(P, C, r) = 0$ and the center of the "circle" is to our northwest; that is, $C_x < P_x$ and $P_y < C_y$. Then as we move left, we have to move an equal amount down to keep the function at 0. This equal trade-off keeps us moving in a straight line.

Similarly, we'd expect the blob function to also turn into diamonds, and Figure 4.6b shows that they do. Figure 4.6c is a little more interesting. Some of the points that are equidistant from the two workplaces still lie

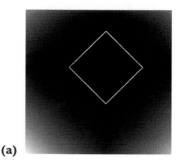
(a)

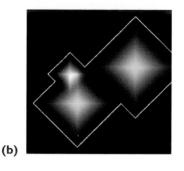
(b)

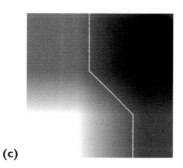
(c)

along a line between the two, but then the line turns vertical. As we move along those vertical segments, we move the same taxicab distance from both workplaces.

Figure 4.6
The three test functions using the taxicab metric. **(a)** The circle. **(b)** The three blobs. **(c)** The two-workplace distance.

Polar Bear Geometry

Last night I shot a polar bear in my pajamas. How a bear got into my pajamas, I'll never know (thanks, Groucho). These guys live up north, where instead of a square grid we can plot the landscape in a latitude-longitude format, as in Figure 4.7.

Up there at the North Pole, there are lots of ways to compute distance. Commonly, we first convert a point P from Cartesian (x, y) format to polar (r, θ) format, representing the radius from the pole and angle made with respect to a particular line. This rectangular-to-polar conversion is simply

$$A_r = \sqrt{A_x^2 + A_y^2}$$
$$A_\theta = \tan^{-1}(A_y/A_x)$$

You can prove to yourself that using these values you can compute a distance d_N that is the same as d_E:

$$d_N(A, B) = A_r^2 + B_r^2 - 2\,A_r\,B_r\,\cos(A_\theta - B_\theta)$$

That's nice, but because $d_N = d_E$, if we plot our three functions again, they'll look just the same as for the Euclidean measure. So let's cook up something that's a little different, but still interesting. Just like the taxicab distance, we can simply add up the difference in the

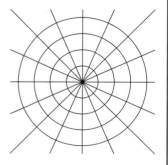

Figure 4.7
A polar grid for measuring distances at the North Pole.

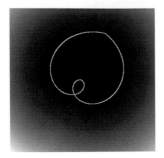 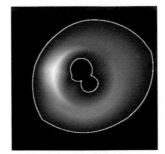 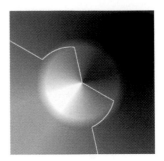

Figure 4.8
The three test functions using the modified polar metric d_P

radii and the difference in the angles. To make the images look interesting with the same equations that we used above, I arbitrarily decided to scale the angle measure down by dividing by 2π. One gotcha with the angles is that we want the difference between 5 degrees and 355 degrees to be 10 degrees, not 350. The cosine operator did that for us in the definition of d_N; we can do that procedurally for our *polar bear distance* d_P:

$$d_P(A, B) = \left| A_r - B_r \right| \frac{\min\left(\left| A_\theta - B_\theta \right|, 2\pi - \left| A_\theta - B_\theta \right| \right)}{2\pi}$$

This is how far you'd have to travel under a spoke-and-ring type of monorail system. Figure 4.8 shows our three functions under the polar bear measure of distance.

Other Metrics

It's easy to change the definition of the distance function to try out other metrics. Here are a few fun metrics that I cooked up. The first one that I played with involved mapping the horizontal interval $(-1, 1)$ to the interval $(0, 2\pi)$ and then taking the sine of that value. The metric is the arclength of the fragment of sine curve between the X components of the two points, scaled by their vertical distance. In symbols, using $s(f, x_0, x_1)$ to represent the arclength of function f between arguments x_0 and x_1, the arclength metric d_A is

$$d_A(f, A, B) = s(f, A_r, B_r) \left| A_y - B_y \right|$$

Our three functions plotted with this metric using $f(x) = \sin(x)$ are shown in Figure 4.9.

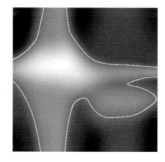

The star metric d_S has a sort of polar-ish feel:

$$d_S(A, B) = d_E(A, B) \cos\left(2\pi \tan^{-1}\left(\frac{A_y - B_y}{A_y - B_y}\right)\right)$$

The results are shown in Figure 4.10.

Finally, the ring metric d_R takes the Euclidean distance and maps it into the sine curve:

$$d_s(A, B) = \sin(2\pi\, d_E(A, B))$$

The ring metric images are shown in Figure 4.11.

Plotting Implicit Functions

The yellow curves in this chapter were created using a program that plots contours of implicit functions. Basically you give the program a function $f(x, y)$ and a level value a, and it finds that set of points (or *locus*) where $f(x, y) = a$.

There are plenty of commercial programs out there that will do this job for you. But not everyone has such a program at their disposal; I didn't have

Figure 4.9
The three test functions using the arclength metric d_A with the sine function.

Figure 4.10
The three test functions using the star metric d_S.

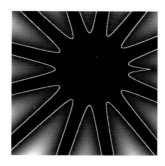
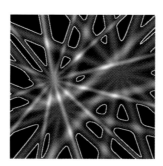
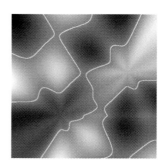

 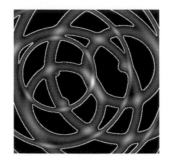 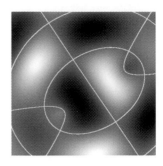

Figure 4.11
The three test
functions using the
ring metric d_R.

one on my home computer when I felt like playing around with these curves. Happily, it's both easy and fun to roll your own. In this section I'll give you the general approach that I followed, which does the job pretty well. It only took me a couple of hours to write the first version in BASIC; it took about the same amount of time to write a much spiffier second version in C, with which I made all the figures in this chapter.

I found that it was useful to have four runtime controls: the size of the graph (in this chapter all of the plots are 400-by-400 points), the choice of the function to plot (e.g., circles or blobs), the choice of metric (e.g., Euclidean or polar bear), and the threshold (usually 0). The accuracy of the algorithm is controlled by four other values, described below.

The first step is to draw the grayscale picture. To do this, I evaluated all the points in the image and kept a record of the minimum and maximum values of the function. Then I evaluated all the points again, this time scaling them to the range 0–1, which I mapped into grayscale values 0–255. If you have lots of memory and a slow processor, you could save the points in an array and then scale them in place instead of recomputing them all. Then I just drew the scaled points into the screen and forgot about them.

I used a very simple strategy to draw the level curves. I began by searching the function to find a point that was on the curve. I looked around that point and followed the curve as far as I could in both directions. Then I searched for another point. This way if there are several disconnected curves or segments, I could pick up each one in turn, at the risk of going over some of them more than once.

The first step in finding a curve to follow is to find a point on the curve. If we're plotting a function $z = f(x, y)$, then we're looking for points P where $f(P) = 0$. If we find two nearby points A and B such that $f(A) < 0$ and $f(B) > 0$, then we can search the line AB for points where the function goes through 0. I find these points by scanning a coarse grid on the domain. The density of this grid needs to match the high-frequency content of the function being plotted; smooth functions can be sampled loosely, while wiggly ones need a denser mesh. In this chapter, I sampled Figures 4.1, 4.3, 4.4, and 4.6 with a mesh 10 samples on a side; the other figures used a 30-by-30 grid. Figure 4.12a shows the coarse grid.

Next, I used this grid to search for points with different signs. For each point on the grid (with the exception of the top row and rightmost column), I compared the sign of the point with the sign of the point to its right and the one above. If the signs were the same I moved on. If they differed, then I found a point on the curve between them, followed and drew the curve, and then returned to test the next pair of points. Figure 4.12b shows the grid marked with lines that join points of different sign.

I trapped the curve with binary subdivision, recursively halving the input interval to always contain a point P where $f(P) = 0$. The recursion stopped when the interval was too short or the midpoint was nearly 0. I used a minimum length of $1/ks$, where I'd pick k and s was the largest side of the display grid (in these pictures, $s = 400$). I also chose a tolerance ε (so I'd stop when $|f(P)| < \varepsilon$). For plenty of functions you can fly by the seat of your pants, set these around $k = 4$ and $\varepsilon = 1 \times 10^{-6}$, and all is well. You can be less conservative and draw your pictures more quickly if you know something about the function being plotted. Most of the functions in these figures are pretty smooth and these values worked fine. These two values k and ε are the first two of four numbers that control the algorithm's precision.

Returning to the job of drawing the curve, the binary searcher returns a starting point S that is on, or near, the curve. Hey, one point! Now, if we only had a second point, we could draw a line (Euclid really did have this all figured out).

Figure 4.12
(a) The coarse resampling grid for the circle function measured with the Euclidean metric. Red circles are positive values, and green are negative.
(b) Lines join resampling points of different sign, and the small circle indicates the starting point for the curve along that line.
(c) The grid, starting lines, and the followed curve.

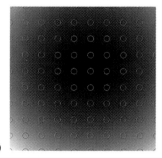

(a)

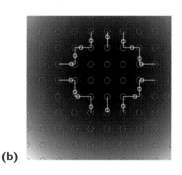

(b)

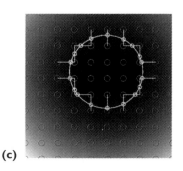

(c)

I assumed that if we stand on the point S and look around, we would see two branches of the curve leaving the point, in opposite directions. Of course, they could turn around really fast, but when we face one branch the other is at our back. This assumption can fail—for example, if S is a cusp. I'll get back to this later. But usually it is true. To keep the bookkeeping simple, I handle the two branches independently.

To find a branch, I search a circle around S, looking for points on the curve. This circle is specified by the other two numbers that set the accuracy of the algorithm: the radius r of the circle and the number of samples n taken around it. The radius of the circle controls the length of the little line segments that make up the curve. Adding more steps around the circle lets us follow wigglier curves.

So I sample the function at n points on the circle and look for adjacent points of different sign. Figure 4.13 shows a curve passing through S. The two-branch assumption above says that we'll find two pairs of adjacent points with different signs. Each of these pairs surrounds a point on one of the branches.

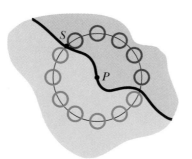

I take the two pairs in turn, following (and drawing) the curve passing through one and the repeating the process for the other. If the curve is a circle (as in Figure 4.1), then this means I'll end up following the curve twice, once clockwise and once counterclockwise. It wastes some time, but there's no other harm done.

Given a point S and one pair of points on the circle, I again hand the pair of points to the binary subdivision routine. It gives me back a new point P on the line between the points and on the curve. That's the second point! I immediately draw the line SP with a thick yellow line.

Now it's time to follow the curve. I can repeat exactly the same circle-searching procedure around the point P, finding two pairs of points that contain the curve. One of those pairs contains the branch we just came in on, where the other pair holds the new branch. We can try to determine either the old branch or the new one. We can find the old branch by finding the one that contains S, then the other branch is the new one. That works fine, but we can make the algorithm a bit more robust without any more cost by doing this a bit differently.

Suppose that the curve crosses over itself at P, like at the left of Figure 4.8. Then there will be four branches coming out of P. If we find the one containing S, we still don't know which of the remaining three to take. But suppose we use the pair that is farthest from S. Then we'll always head out in the direction opposite to the way we entered, and as long as the two intersecting lines aren't nearly parallel, we'll follow each one just fine. So to find a new point, I search around P for pairs that contain the curve, and then pick the pair farthest from S. To test for a pair's distance from S, I found the distance from S to the pair's midpoint. To determine this distance I always used the conventional Euclidean metric, though I didn't bother with the square root (this is a standard trick, which works because I was only looking for the biggest distance and the square-root function doesn't change that).

So I'd draw another thick yellow line from P to the new point. The new point becomes P, the old point becomes S, and I repeat the procedure, pushing forward one circle-radius at a time. When I'm done following the first branch, I follow the other branch, and then return to the coarse grid to find another starting point.

There are four criteria that I use to determine when I'm done following a branch. First, if the branch went offscreen, I stopped. I figured that even if the curve came back onscreen, I'd catch that new piece from another starting point. Second, if the branch closed itself, I stopped. To determine that, I saved the very first point S. As I followed the curve, I checked the distance of each new point against this original point. If I got within a pixel, I joined the gap and stopped following the curve. This test only cut in after I'd already drawn 10 pixels, so I didn't accidentally stop as soon as I'd started. Third, I had an arbitrary upper limit on the number of steps I would take on a branch; I used 5000. This made sure the program didn't get stuck in an infinite loop. This could arise, for example, between two narrow cusps—the tracker could just ping-pong between the two cusps forever unless otherwise stopped. Finally, I stopped if for any reason I couldn't find a new point to move to.

That's it. The algorithm's a bit wasteful (since most branches are drawn a few times), but it's robust enough for playing around with the sorts of functions in this chapter. This simple algorithm runs pretty quickly: all of the grayscale figures in this chapter were first created by my original draft of the program in interpreted BASIC in less than 15 seconds each on a 90-MHz Pentium machine. I then redrew them with my improved C version of the program. The compiled C code ran much faster.

This algorithm is hardly bulletproof. I mentioned earlier that cusps could be a problem. These are places where the curve makes a sudden about-face and has a discontinuous first derivative. In fact, any tight U-turn is a problem for this algorithm, whether it's pointed or just a sharp turn. Suppose that we're at a point P that is on (or near) a cusp. As we search the circle around P, we find that there aren't any pairs of points with differing sign—Figure 4.14 shows the problem. In my implementation, I quit, using criterion 4 from above. There simply wasn't anywhere to go. You can actually handle this problem with another subdivision step. Find the pair of points

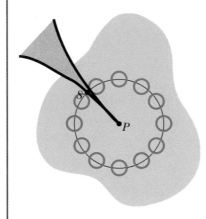

that included S and subdivide that interval. You'll need to follow all the branches of the tree, but sooner or later you should find a point that has a different sign from the others, and this will give you a pair of intervals. Pick the one that doesn't contain S, and that will contain the new branch.

There are lots of other improvements that could be made to make this a more general algorithm. One of the pleasures of hacking up your own routine is that you can design it to work perfectly well

Figure 4.14
A cusp at P results in both arcs leaving the circle through the same pair of points.

for your particular needs—a special-purpose tool for a special-purpose job. Making that tool more general, more efficient, and so on is also fun. Here are a few starting places for making this program better.

First, the coarse sampling grid can miss small features. This is a standard sampling problem, but because you draw the grayscale version first you can use information from that to help guide a smarter search strategy. Second, big flat basins are something of a problem; if a whole big region has the value 0, the tracking routine can wander around erratically. Third, you could run some numerical analysis routines on the function being plotted to gather initial estimates and values for the four accuracy controls described above.

Different measures of distance can lead toward all kinds of non-Euclidean geometries. I find that the connection between the math of the space and the aesthetics of the imagery is captivating. Playing around with different metrics and functions is a lot of fun, and after a while I find my intuition gets pretty good at predicting what's going to happen.

Further Reading

An elementary introduction to taxicab metrics can be found in *Taxicab Geometry* by Eugene F. Krause (Dover Publications, 1987). If you're looking for interesting functions to play with, a great starting place is *A Catalog of Special Plane Curves* by J. Dennis Lawrence (Dover, 1972). The blob function comes from "Data Structures for Soft Objects" by Wyvill, McPheeters, and Wyvill, in *The Visual Computer,* 2(4), April 1986. You can find some discussion of contour-tracking in *Numerical Continuation Methods, an Introduction* by E. Allgower and K. Georg (Springer-Verlag, 1990) and some practical discussion in "Automatic Contour Map" by G. Cottafava and G. Le Moli (*Communications of the ACM,* 12(7), 1969). One way of avoiding the problems of the coarse sampling grid is by using interval analysis, as discussed in "Interval Analysis for Computer Graphics" by John Snyder (*Computer Graphics,* 26(2), July 1992).

If you're interested in this kind of algorithm, here are some more references that you might want to look at in order to develop a more efficient and accurate program:

- Chandler, R. E. "A Tracking Algorithm for Implicitly Defined Curves." *IEEE Computer Graphics and Applications,* 8(2):83–89, March 1988.

- Cohen, E. "A Method for Plotting Curves Defined by Implicit Equations." *Computer Graphics,* 10(2):263–265, summer 1976.

- Nakartsuyama, M., Kanno, K., Nagahashi, H., and Nishizuka, N. "Curve Generation of Implicit Functions by Incremental Computers." *Computers and Graphics,* 7(2):161–168, 1983.

- Sutcliffe, D. C. "An Algorithm for Drawing the Curve $f(x, y) = 0$." *The Computer Journal,* 19(3):246–249, August 1976.

- Taubin, G. "Distance Approximation for Rasterizing Implicit Curves." *ACM Transactions on Graphics,* 13(1):3–42, January 1994.

Situation Normal

ANDREW GLASSNER'S NOTEBOOK
March/April 1997

5

In the pantheon of science, having your name attached to something is a pretty high honor. Graphics isn't terribly big on this practice of eponymy—most of our techniques bear descriptive names, such as the Z-buffer algorithm, ray tracing, and the RGB color space. But there are exceptions. Two of the most famous are derived from shading algorithms by Henri Gouraud and Bui-Tuong Phong. Their techniques have been implemented in thousands of pieces of hardware and software throughout the world.

Both of these methods use various hacks to smooth out the shading of a polygonal surface. So rather than looking like an assembly of flat slabs, a smooth-shaded model seems to be, well, smoother. The sharp creases between polygons are gone, replaced by a continuous change in tone or color.

But if the original polygons aren't being rendered directly, then the shading doesn't correspond to the original model. What model does it correspond to? In other words, what is the smooth surface which, when rendered accurately (that is, without interpolation tricks), has the same appearance as a Phong-shaded polygonal model? That's the surface that Phong shading is pretending is actually under there.

Often we know what we want that surface to be, because we started there. For example, if we begin with a cylinder, chop it up into polygons, and render the polygons with Gouraud or Phong shading, we would like the final rendered picture to have the same intensities that we'd get from an accurate point-by-point rendering of the original cylinder. Even when we don't start with a smooth mathematical object, we often imagine that the polygons form a framework over which an elastic sheet is stretched; this sheet is conceptually the smooth surface we want to represent. How close do these shading methods come to these goals?

Before we plunge in, I'd like to make the standard distinction between the two very separate ideas that are often lumped together as "Phong shading." The first is the process of computing a point's surface normal by linear interpolation of the components of two normals at either end of a line containing that point; this is Phong *normal interpolation*. This normal may then be used as part of a shading equation that takes into account specular highlights in an empirical manner; this is Phong *illumination*. Throughout this chapter, I will deal only with perfectly diffuse surfaces lit by a single light source, so Phong illumination isn't part of the discussion. And we will assume that the light source is conveniently located at infinity (so the direction in which we look at that light doesn't change from point to point over the surface).

So here, "Gouraud shading" means the process of interpolating a color component to find intermediate color values across a polygon. And "Phong shading" means interpolating surface normals to find intermediate normals that are then evaluated with respect to the light source to find a color for that point.

Under the Surface

Let's look first at Gouraud shading. In this discussion, we're going to do everything in 2D, to keep it simple. Suppose that we're rendering the top half of a cylinder. Figure 5.1a shows the basic idea: the purple curve is the cylinder, and the four yellow lines are four polygonal facets that approximate the cylinder. There is one light source, directly to the northwest. Figure 5.1b shows the intensity profile created by Gouraud-shading the yellow facets. Our goal is to find out what surface is represented by this intensity profile.

Because everything is so simple, we can use a very primitive shape-from-shading algorithm. The first step is to recall the basic equation of Gouraud

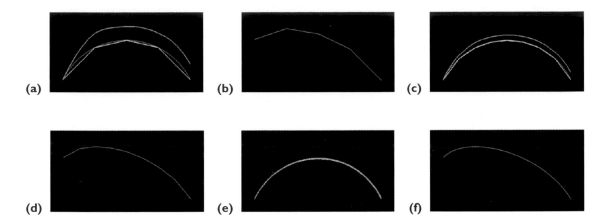

(a)　　(b)　　(c)

(d)　　(e)　　(f)

shading that relates surface normals and illumination geometry. For a perfectly diffuse, grayscale world,

$$I = k_d(\mathbf{N} \cdot \mathbf{L}) = k_d \cos \theta$$

where I is the resulting intensity, k_d is a scalar that controls diffuse reflectivity, $\mathbf{N}$ is the (unit-length) surface normal, and $\mathbf{L}$ is the (unit-length) vector to the light source. Figure 5.2a shows the geometry of the situation.

In Gouraud shading, we evaluate this equation only at the vertices of the facets, then interpolate the value of I across the facet. To find $\mathbf{N}$ at a vertex, we often average the values of the facets that share that vertex. For this chapter, I had access to the underlying curved shapes, so I used the actual surface normal computed from the surface at that vertex. If the normals at the endpoints are $\mathbf{A}$ and $\mathbf{C}$, then we compute I_A and I_C and linearly interpolate them to find the Gouraud intensity I_G (for utter simplicity, let's assume that $k_d = 1$):

$$I_G = \alpha I_A + (1 - \alpha) I_C = \alpha(\mathbf{A} \cdot \mathbf{L}) + (1 - \alpha)(\mathbf{C} \cdot \mathbf{L})$$

In shape-from-shading, we need to invert this equation: we're given I (the shade), and we want to find $\mathbf{N}$ (which reveals the shape). Then we easily find that $\theta = \cos^{-1}(I)$. Given the light source direction $\mathbf{L}$, there are only two vectors in the plane that make an angle θ with $\mathbf{L}$, as shown in Figure 5.2b. The quick-and-dirty approach (it works well here) says to pick the choice that is closest to the neighboring surface normals. To start this

Figure 5.1
Gouraud shading applied to a cylinder. In part a, the purple curve is the original cylinder, approximated by yellow facets. The single light source is directly to the northwest. The green curve is the shape derived from the shading.
(a) A four-facet approximation.
(b) The intensity profile for 5.1a.
(c) An eight-facet approximation.
(d) The intensity profile for 5.1c.
(e) A 50-facet approximation.
(f) The intensity profile for 5.1e.

Figure 5.2
The geometry
behind diffuse
shading.
(a) The normal
and light make an
angle θ.
(b) Only two can-
didate normal vec-
tors make an angle
θ with the light.

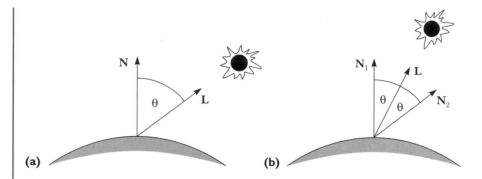

(a) **(b)**

process, you guess (or cheat) to get one normal somewhere on the surface, then work outward from there.

In Figure 5.1a, I knew that the normal at the far left was pointing almost due west, so that was my starting normal. Then I marched across the intensity graph in Figure 5.1b, looking up I, computing θ, and choosing the closest **N**. To plot the surface, I drew a little green line that had a horizontal span of one pixel that started where the last bit of surface ended and was perpendicular to **N**. Then I just marched on to the next pixel, got the next I and θ, and continued the process.

Notice that it is, in fact, a smooth curve. That's why Gouraud shading looks smooth: it's faking this smooth surface. But there's something wrong, because this green curve seems to rise too high over the underlying faceted approximation. Remember that this curve is the shape of the underlying surface. Well, is it really such a problem? Notice that the rightmost three-quarters of the curve tracks the facets (and the cylinder) pretty well, but it's just too high. Since the light's at infinity, and we're not using the Gouraud values to compute depth information, this isn't really a problem at all. But it is worth thinking about why it goes wrong.

The reason the Gouraud surface rises up is because the interpolated shade values in the leftmost segment don't do a good job of tracking the actual shade values of a smooth cylinder. Each of those little errors accumulates along the facet. The problem here is not that there aren't enough facets, but that the illumination over the facets doesn't match the illumination that would derive from the actual cylinder.

Figures 5.1c and 5.1d show the same process repeated for eight facets. The situation is generally quite improved. This is because with more facets, there are more places where the Gouraud shading is locked down to the actual computed illumination values. Figures 5.1e and 5.1f pump up the subdivision to 50 facets, and now the surface that is implied by Gouraud shading matches the underlying cylinder very well.

Let's try the same process with a sine curve. Figures 5.3a and 5.3b show the four-facet approximation (the middle two facets are colinear and look like one long straight line, but they actually have a shared vertex where they cross the purple sine curve). The intensity profile has five facets, not four, because I've clipped it at 0. (Otherwise I'd have to suck the photons out of your eyes when you look at the rendered image and, while not particularly painful, this can be dangerous.) It's reassuring to see that crinkly little sine-wave-ish green curve in the figure, but it's not really correct for the surface. Of course, we're asking way too much of Gouraud shading to try to handle this much variation in surface with only four facets, but it's interesting to see that it still gets things vaguely right.

Figures 5.3c through 5.3f show the eight- and 50-facet versions, respectively. As you would expect, things get much better with improved subdivision.

Figure 5.3
Gouraud shading applied to a sine curve. The images are arranged as in Figure 5.1.

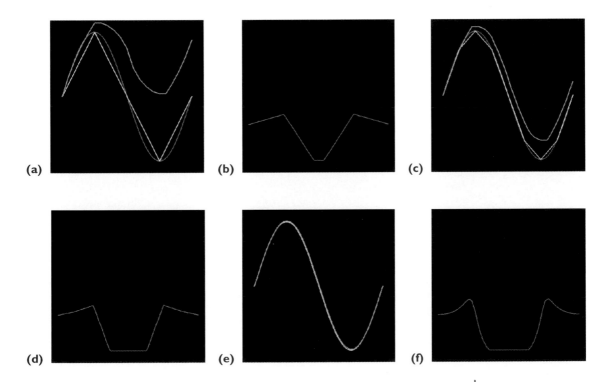

(a) (b) (c)

(d) (e) (f)

Approximately Normal

Let's now turn our attention to Phong normal interpolation. We will use exactly the same shading equation presented above, but we'll change how we find the normal. Just as in Gouraud shading, Phong shading finds the normals at the vertices of the polygon. But remember that Phong shading we interpolate the normals across the polygon's face, then recompute the illumination value at each point.

Just how to interpolate the normals has been a subject of much debate, and we'll return to it below. For now, though, we'll use the method originally proposed by Phong and the one that is most widely implemented. If **A** and **C** are the normals at the two ends of a line, then the normal **B** at a point between them that cuts the line in the ratio α can be found from

$$\mathbf{B} = \frac{\alpha \mathbf{A} + (1-\alpha)\mathbf{C}}{\left| \alpha \mathbf{A} + (1-\alpha)\mathbf{C} \right|}$$

In words, we just linearly interpolate each of the components, then normalize the result. Then we plug it into the shading formula to find the Phong intensity I_P:

$$I_P = \mathbf{B} \cdot \mathbf{L}$$

Figure 5.4
Phong shading applied to a cylinder. Compare with Figure 5.1.

Figures 5.4a and 5.4b show the same four-faceted cylinder that we used in Figure 5.1, only now we've used Phong shading. It's easy to see how much closer the derived curve follows the underlying surface. It also links up

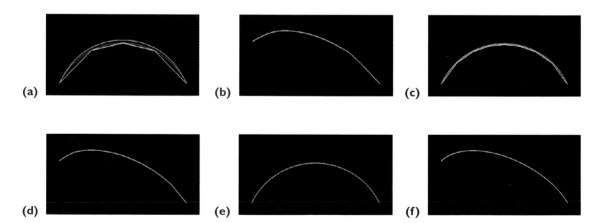

(a)　　　　　　　　　(b)　　　　　　　　　(c)

(d)　　　　　　　　　(e)　　　　　　　　　(f)

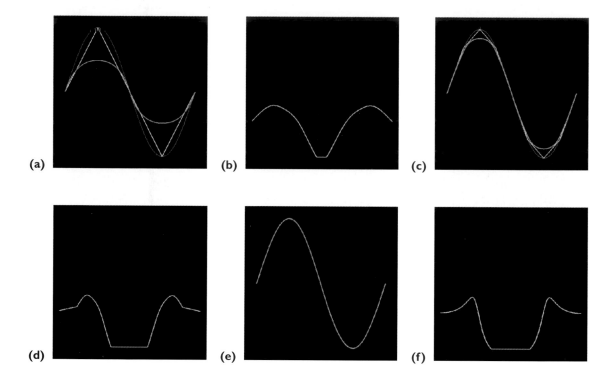

(a)   (b)   (c)

(d)   (e)   (f)

with the far point of the cylinder. Figures 5.4c through 5.4f show the 8- and 50-faceted cylinders; the match in Figure 5.4e looks about perfect.

Figure 5.5 shows the same sine wave as before. The green curve almost looks like a B-spline built on the control polygon of the yellow facets (but it doesn't stay within the convex hull they define). Notice how much more symmetrical the figure is compared with the Gouraud-shaded version.

Figure 5.5
Phong shading applied to a sine curve. Compare with Figure 5.3.

Bright Answers

Let's compare the Gouraud and Phong illuminations. Tom Duff expanded out the dot product in his 1979 paper to find

$$I_P = \frac{\alpha \mathbf{A} + (1-\alpha)\mathbf{C}}{\left|\alpha \mathbf{A} + (1-\alpha)\mathbf{C}\right|} \cdot \mathbf{L} = \frac{\alpha(\mathbf{A} \cdot \mathbf{L}) + (1-\alpha)(\mathbf{C} \cdot \mathbf{L})}{\left|\alpha \mathbf{A} + (1-\alpha)\mathbf{C}\right|} = \frac{I_G}{\left|\alpha \mathbf{A} + (1-\alpha)\mathbf{C}\right|}$$

I found this to be a really surprising result! In words, Phong shading produces the same values as Gouraud shading, except that they are scaled by a normalization factor that is always in the range 0 to 1. So in equivalent situations, Phong shading will *always* produce a brighter image than Gouraud

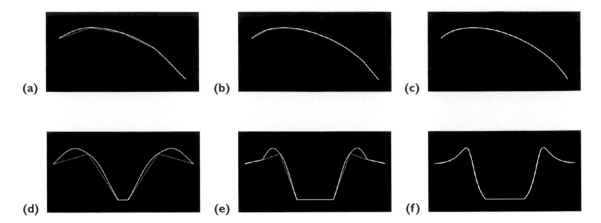

(a)   **(b)**   **(c)**

(d)   **(e)**   **(f)**

Figure 5.6
Phong shading (cyan) is always brighter than Gouraud shading (purple).
(a) The intensity profiles for the four-facet cylinder.
(b) The eight-facet cylinder.
(c) The 50-facet cylinder.
(d) The intensity profiles for the four-facet sine wave.
(e) The eight-facet sine wave.
(f) The 50-facet sine wave.

shading. Remember that this has nothing to do with highlights—we're simply looking at the purely diffuse component here.

Tom observed that sometimes people talk about speeding up Phong shading by skipping the renormalization step—that is, you interpolate the normal components, but you don't bother scaling the result so that it has unit length. In other words, that assumes that the denominator in the above equation is 1. So computing Phong shading by interpolating the normals, but not scaling those normals to unit length before computing the shading, results in exactly the same values as Gouraud shading.

Sure, it may be slower, but it's more expensive.

Figure 5.6 shows the intensity profiles for Gouraud and Phong shading overlaid for the cylinder and the sine wave. You can see that the Phong values are never less than the Gouraud values.

What is the nature of this normalization factor? Figure 5.7 shows the geometry of the situation; we're basically sweeping through a triangle to find the interpolated normal, then extending it to reach the unit circle. The trick here is that we're not stepping by equal angles. Because we're interpolating components by equal amounts, we're stepping by equal lengths along the chord. Figure 5.8 shows a plot of the length of the interpolated normal as a function of α for various values of θ.

Who's to Say What's Normal?

This whole process of interpolating normal components has seemed pretty suspect to a lot of people, myself included. After all, why should that be the best way to interpolate normals?

The answer, of course, is that it's not the best way. But there is no better way. In other words, it's an arbitrary hack based on the assumption that the default shape resulting from this interpolation is a reasonable building block to match the underlying shapes we're modeling with polygons. Other interpolation methods will produce other types of curves. As with any approximation, sometimes one type of guess will be better than another; there's no "right" way to interpolate normals unless you know what kind of surface you're trying to match.

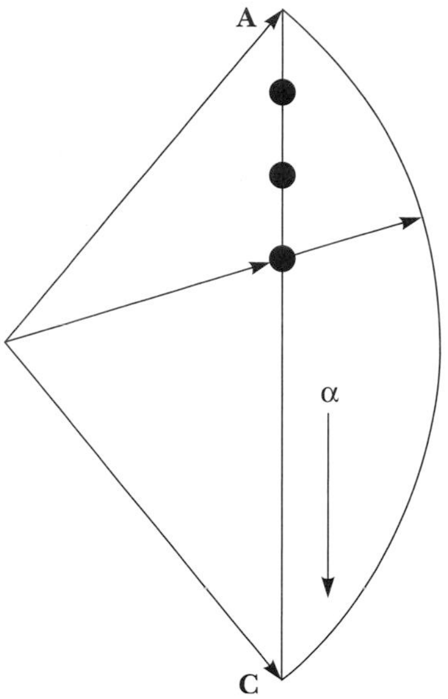

But it is interesting to look at alternatives. One of the most popular approaches is to think of interpolating the normal in equal angular steps, rather than equal steps along the chord between them. So what we want is a formula to find the interpolated normal vector between two end vectors as a function of α, which is the percentage of the angle between the extremes. This is the *equal-angle interpolation formula*.

My favorite geometric derivation of this formula was developed by Frits Post. Take a look at Figure 5.9. The point C is at the center of a circle of unit radius, and we've marked off the two extreme vectors **P** and **R,** which both have unit length. We're going to write the interpolated vector **Q** as a

Figure 5.7
When interpolating normals using component interpolation, we are effectively moving along a straight line between the two endpoints. We step in equal increments along this line, not in equal angular steps between the extremes. The interpolated normal must then be scaled to unit length.

Figure 5.8
The length s of the interpolated normal as a function of the angle θ between the extremes and the interpolant α between them. Note that when the angle is small, the interpolated lengths are very close to 1. When $\theta = \pi/2$, the normal at $\alpha = 0.5$ has length 0 and is undetermined. We divide by the value in this plot to scale the interpolated normal to unit length.

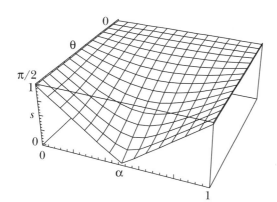

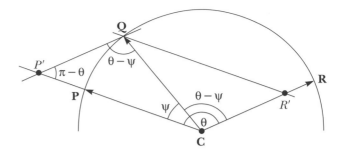

Figure 5.9
The geometry behind equal-angle interpolation.

linear sum of **P** and **R,** or $\mathbf{Q} = \beta_1\mathbf{P} + \beta_2\mathbf{R}.$ What are these two scaling factors?

We'll start by labeling a bunch of angles and lengths; then finding the unknowns will be pretty simple. For convenience, I'll write the point at the tip of any vector as that vector's name without boldface; that is, point P is at the tip of vector **P.** Angles will be identified by the three points that compose them (e.g., $\angle QP'C$), though when it's unambiguous I'll just use a single point (e.g., $\angle P'$).

In the figure, I've marked points P' and R', which are the tips of the scaled vectors $\beta_1\mathbf{P}$ and $\beta_2\mathbf{R}.$ Then we have a parallelogram formed by $CP'QR'.$ Note that the line QP is in general not going to be tangent to the circle. $\angle PCR$ is θ, our original angle between the vectors **P** and **R.** And $\angle PCQ$ is the interpolated angle, $\psi = \alpha\theta.$ So $\angle QCR$ is $\theta - \psi.$ Because CR' is parallel to $P'Q$, $\angle CQP'$ is the same as $\angle QCR'$, or $\theta - \psi.$ That just leaves $\angle P'$, which must be $\pi - \theta.$ By construction, $|CP'| = \beta_1$ and $|CR'| = \beta_2.$

Now we can use the law of sines to write down the relationships between angles and lengths in triangle $\Delta P'QC$ and solve:

$$\frac{\sin P'}{|QC|} = \frac{\sin Q}{|P'C|} = \frac{\sin C}{|P'Q|}$$

Recalling that $\sin(\pi - \theta) = \sin(\theta)$, we can replace these distances with the lengths we've assigned them:

$$\frac{\sin\theta}{1} = \frac{\sin Q}{\beta_1} = \frac{\sin C}{\beta_2}$$

Chapter Five

Solving for β_1 and β_2 yields

$$\beta_1 = \frac{\sin(\theta - \psi)}{\sin\theta}, \quad \beta_2 = \frac{\sin(\psi)}{\sin\theta}$$

So our interpolation formula for $\mathbf{Q}(\alpha)$ leads us to

$$\mathbf{Q}(\alpha) = \frac{\sin(\theta - \psi)}{\sin\theta}\mathbf{P} + \frac{\sin(\psi)}{\sin\theta}\mathbf{R}$$

where $\psi = \alpha\theta$. You can prove to yourself that this doesn't require a normalization step; in other words, the vector $\mathbf{Q}$ computed by this formula always has unit length.

Equal-angle interpolation will yield results different from component interpolation, but how different? Figure 5.10 shows a comparison of the two techniques on a two-element version of the sine curve. This is about as extreme a test as you can hope for, because the normals are almost antiparallel at the two ends. The two techniques yield pretty much the same intensity profile. Under less severe conditions the two methods are usually very close—much closer than Gouraud and Phong shading.

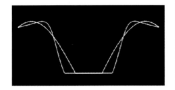

Figure 5.10
A comparison of intensity profiles for equal-angle interpolation (in yellow) and Phong shading (in cyan) for an extreme case.

Further Reading

There have been lots of interesting papers on Phong shading over the years; here are just a few. A nice discussion of Phong shading can be found in Tom Duff's paper, "Smoothly Shaded Renderings of Polyhedral Objects on Raster Displays," in *Proceedings of SIGGRAPH '79,* pages 270–275. A way to speed up the computation is offered by Gary Bishop and David Weimer in "Fast Phong Shading," in *Proceedings of SIGGRAPH '86,* pages 103–106. There's a famous paper by Bui-Tuong Phong and Frank Crow on smoothing out Phong-shaded images, which is sadly all but unavailable; the official citation lists "Improved Rendition of Polygonal Models of Curved Surfaces" in the *Proceedings of the 2nd USA-Japan Computer Conference,* 1975. Nelson Max has investigated smoothing out models in a variety of ways, so that silhouettes and intersections are rounded as well, in "Smooth Appearance for Polygonal Surfaces," published in the June 1989 issue of *The Visual Computer,* pages 160–173.

Signs of Significance

ANDREW GLASSNER'S NOTEBOOK
May/June 1997

6

You're in a train station you've never been to before, and you're late. You know that you want the 22:15 train to Magritte, but as you look around, your tired arms holding heavy suitcases, you realize you're lost. There seem to be thousands of corridors with thousands of branches. So you look for the signs. And you see your destination in bright yellow letters on a big sign halfway down one of the tunnels. You take a breath, lift your bags, and walk to the train with confidence.

Signs are great. They are the visible labels of our geography. If you're a relativist, you never really know where you are in the absolute, but you always know where you are with respect to some landmarks. And often signs serve as those landmarks, either simply as part of the remembered geography or as active fountains of information.

Because they're so important, they need to be very clear. Consider the special case of signs that change, like the destination signs in a train station. The information must be succinct. And the presentation must be very direct, only contributing to the information and not conflicting with it. How do you avoid conflicting with something unpredictable?

Be simple and be bland. Simplicity means that you don't risk the style of the presentation conflicting with the underlying message. Blandness means you avoid contamination or distortion of the message. So a simple, bland sign should be perfectly legible and perfectly boring. If you're careful and clever, you can work in some design as well, so that the sign has some visual appeal and connection to its environment.

In my experience three types of varying signs are the most popular: mechanical, electromechancial, and electronic. Examples of mechanical signs include a whiteboard and a movie marquee. Electromechanical signs are often found on the fronts of buses and in rotating billboards. Some are very clever indeed; I particularly like the grids of little disks, black on one side and yellow on the other, that flip under control of a magnetic field.

In this chapter I'll focus on a third type of sign, the purely electronic displays that are typically implemented with LEDs (light-emitting diodes), LCDs (liquid crystal displays), or light-emitting panels. I think the evolution of the electronic digital display provides a fascinating example of graphic design cooperating with technology. Digital displays also demonstrate the practical importance of economy: not only must they be easy to read, displays must be economical to make and buy—or no one will do either.

Early Digital Displays

Computer-controlled illuminated electronic displays probably began with the Nixie tube, which came to prominence in the '50s and '60s. The Nixie tube was a clear glass envelope with a plastic base that looked like a regular vacuum tube, but things were different inside. A loop of wire was formed into the digit 0 and vertically centered in the tube. Behind it, another bit of wire was shaped into the digit 1 and behind it a 2 and so on. Electrically, each of these wires was treated as a cathode, and there was a single anode at the top. The tube itself was filled with neon gas. To display a particular number, you pulsed the appropriate pin at the base with around 200 volts (which you could then reduce to sustain the display). The neon gas around the selected wire would glow an orange-amber color, creating a clear and legible number. Because the digits were formed individually with wires, they looked quite nice, with curves and joins just the way you'd draw them. The glowing neon was bright enough that even the numbers at the back were easily legible through all the wires in front of them. Nixies were used for everything from large-scale electronic computers to desk calculators.

By all accounts Nixie numbers were attractive and very legible, but the tubes were expensive and ran at high voltages. A replacement tube consisted of a black sheet mounted vertically inside the envelope. Sitting above

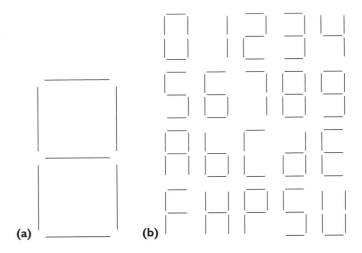

Figure 6.1
(a) A simple seven-segment display made of wires.
(b) The digits and a few recognizable letters.

(a) **(b)**

the sheet were seven incandescent wires, arranged in a rectangle with a horizontal bisector, as in Figure 6.1a. This was the first *seven-segment display*. By running electrical current through the different segments, you could cause them to light up, like the wires in your toaster. This incandescent design required plenty of juice, and eventually the filaments burned out.

The beauty of the seven-segment displays was economy: they were cheaper than Nixies. But they were much less attractive, because the nicely curved numbers in the Nixie tube became boxy. We partly lost something pretty—our familiar numbers—and got back something functional but bleak. On the good side, all 10 digits were clear and easily distinguishable. The design represents a fascinating compliance with the constraint of absolute economy—I don't think you can pull this problem off with fewer than seven segments. And it fits our simplicity and blandness criteria to a tee. Except for the annihilation of beauty, it's a terrific solution. Figure 6.1b shows the digits formed by this simple format.

A nice bonus was that the seven-segment display was also capable of showing a variety of letters. To my mind, the letters that worked best were the uppercase A, C, E, F, H, I, J, L, O, P, S, U and lowercase a, b, c, d, e, g, h, l, o, q, r, u. Not a bad list—it has all the vowels and a few consonants. Note also that it includes the first six letters of the alphabet, which was perfect for hexadecimal systems (where A–F stand for the numbers 10–15). In the figures I've shown A–F, as well as H, P, S, and U. You can also make some letters upside down (to receive a calculator's greeting, punch in 07734 and turn the display upside down).

The seven-segment display easily made the leap to solid state. When LEDs began to appear on the scene, the most commonly available form was as single blobs of light—a little red or green gumdrop with a couple of leads coming out of the base. After a short time seven independent LEDs were housed in a single rectangular block, and they were built to illuminate little polygons. The designers took the opportunity to bevel the edges, as shown in Figure 6.2.

I remember discovering the beauty of this display. One of my first home-brew electronics projects in the early '70s was an electronic deck of cards. I had used my paper-route money to buy an early RAM chip, the 7489, which had 64 bits of memory, arranged as 16 words of four bits each. While wondering what to do with it, I realized that this organization corresponded naturally with a deck of cards, which has 13 cards in each of four suits. So I built an electronic card deck. The user interface consisted of two fingertip-sized red pushbuttons (they were cheap) and two seven-segment displays (they were expensive). When you pushed the "deal" button, a very high frequency counter ran through the addresses of the bits on the chip; when you let go, it stopped on the current bit. The idea was that the counter ran so fast that you couldn't control it, and the memory bit it stopped on was thus a random choice. If that bit was 0 (indicating that the card had not yet been dealt), I set it to 1 and displayed the appropriate card on the two seven-segment LEDs. If the bit was already 1, I stepped through the memory sequentially from that point, looking for the first 0 bit I could find (ignoring the last three words). If I came full circle, I shuffled the deck by resetting everything to 0, then dealt the next card. There was also a "shuffle"

Figure 6.2
(a) The seven-segment display with bevels.
(b) The digits and a few letters.

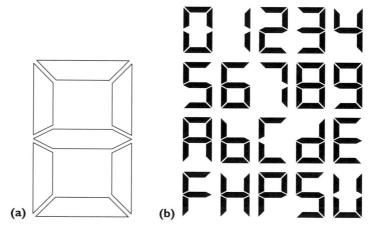

(a)   (b)

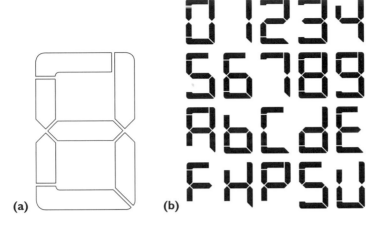

Figure 6.3
(a) The seven-segment display picks up some curves.
(b) Notice that the numbers improve but the letters suffer.

(a) (b)

button available for manual resets. I think I used about a half-dozen TTL chips and a 555 counter for this.

Through the magic of the seven-segment display, all four suits were available: S for spades, C for clubs, H for hearts, and d for diamonds. The cards themselves could be shown by A for ace, 2–9 for number cards, J for jack, q for queen, and (here was a stretch) r for regal, for the king. It worked pretty well, except that the cheap versions of these memory chips were kind of flaky and kept burning out; they'd get stuck on a single address and never move. The three of hearts forever!

Many of the seven-segment LCDs used in today's digital watches use curved corners, breaking up the symmetry as in Figure 6.3. Notice that although some of the numbers look better, the letters suffer. It's an interesting tweak, because the watch designers improved the design for what mattered (numbers), and let the other symbols suffer.

A different enhancement was to increase the number of segments to 14 by cutting the middle segment in half, and adding a plus and an X to the display, as in Figure 6.4. I have only seen this display using little line segments, as in the figure—I haven't seen it with thickened segments, like Figure 6.2. This was a great step forward, because it made available the entire alphabet, but it was hardly the tops in aesthetics; the B in particular relies pretty heavily on people guessing the letter from context. For some reason, I've seen this one a lot in elevators.

Figure 6.4
(a) The 14-
segment display.
(b) The alphabet
and digits. Note the
really lame B.

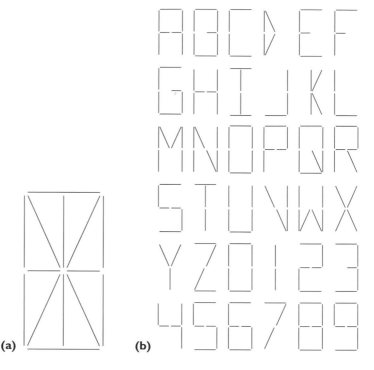

(a)   (b)

Moving to Mosaics

Eventually people were able to stuff a whole bunch of little dot LEDs onto a chip. Most popular was the 5-by-7 grid, which allowed you to represent all the digits and the alphabet with pretty good clarity, as in Figure 6.5. The results looked something like a Lite-Brite toy, but it was perfectly legible. Larger, premium grids were also manufactured, usually 9-by-11 or 13-by-15.

I also remember meeting the grid.

When I was in high school, our school computer was a PDP-8/E, manufactured by Digital Equipment Corporation. It had an enormous 8-kilobyte core memory. Unfortunately, the BASIC interpreter required about 4K, so that left just a few thousand bytes in which to store the text of your program; every character counted. Often several of us would tackle a project simultaneously but independently, trying to figure out the most elegant and compact solution and learning tricks from each other along the way. I remember two of my tricks: starting my line numbers at 1 rather than 10 (thus saving one character per line), and saving words in string variables: for example, A$=" PHASER " requires 13 characters to make the assignment, but only four to use (e.g., PRINT "YOUR"A$"EXPLODED"), so if

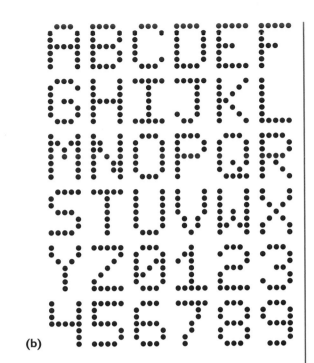

Figure 6.5
(a) The 5-by-7 grid.
(b) The alphabet
and digits.

you print the word " PHASER " more than twice you save characters and can write more code. (We probably shared a lot of attitude with the guys who chiseled stone tablets.)

We talked to the computer using two old Teletypes and saved our programs on paper tape. One of my favorite programs printed out banners on tape—you entered a message, and it punched holes in the tape to make the appropriate letters. It was basically a grid eight holes tall and as long as you liked. The nice thing about the paper tape is that it had a little ribbon of holes off center, which engaged the teeth of a wheel in the reader to pull the tape through. This dotted line left five circular punches on one side and three on the other. This suggested three attractive designs: setting lowercase letters on the bottom five holes and letting uppercase fill all eight; using the upper three holes for ascenders (e.g., the high part of d); and putting the five holes on top and leaving the lower three for descenders (e.g., the tail on g). All three designs had their charm, and I designed alphabets for each one. I used to love to watch my banners chug out of the paper tape punch at 10 rows per second.

A couple of years ago when I was in Vienna, I noticed a very interesting mosaic display in the underground subway system, where it was used to announce train destinations. Figure 6.6 shows the display, along with the alphabet. Each of the segments could be individually illuminated, and they glowed with a steady, flat yellow light. This display contains 66 elements and is almost symmetric. Note the addition of 45-degree edges, which provide little bevels to round out the sharp corners.

This display has a lot to recommend it: the letters are mostly pretty nice from a reasonable distance, where the little divots and bumps aren't so noticeable. And they're very legible even from far away. The line weight is good, and there's no possible confusion among any of the letters or numbers. Some letters are great—the S and R are particularly good-looking. However, the W and M aren't much to cheer about, and the V is a disaster. But still the signs led me to my destination with utter clarity.

In the summer of 1998 I attended the annual Siggraph conference in Orlando, Florida. The hotel I was staying in used a mosaic display in their elevators to indicate the floor. Since a couple of the floors had nonnumeric labels (such as L for lobby), they needed something better than just the seven-segment displays we saw earlier. By riding the elevator a lot, I managed to get drawings of the numbers 1 through 5, and a couple of letters, in an 83-element pattern shown in Figure 6.7a. Returning home, I set

Figure 6.6
(a) The 66-element Vienna Underground mosaic.
(b) The alphabet and digits. The V is quite unfortunate.

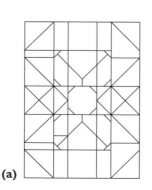

(a)

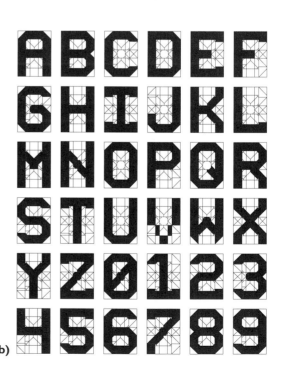

(b)

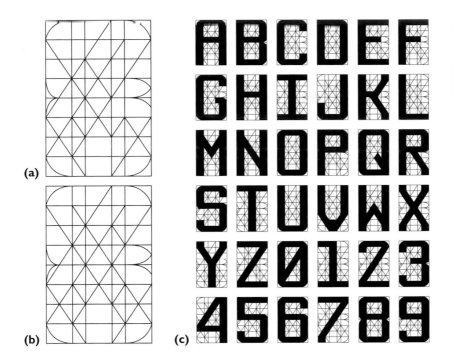

Figure 6.7
(a) The original 83-element Orlando mosaic.
(b) The 87-segment modified Orlando mosaic.
(c) The alphabet and digits.

about developing the rest of the alphabet and digits from this mosaic. It was terrible—there was no way to make the K look anything but embarrassing, for just one example. So I added a few segments to get the modified 87-segment display shown in Figure 6.7b; it's amazing how much you can improve things just by adding a few extra segments. The alphabet I derived for this mosaic is shown in Figure 6.7c.

Making My Mosaic

Just for fun, I tried cooking up my own display. I wanted to make letters with rounded forms and use fewer than even the 66 segments in the Vienna display. My results of this amateur font design are shown in Figure 6.8. On the up side, I managed to do it with only 55 segments. On the down side, my letters are much stronger than the Vienna letters; they look like a bold-style typeface. This may not be a bad thing, but I would have preferred a more delicate touch. Even so, most of my characters look pretty good to me.

This turned out to be a very interesting exercise. I started by making a list of the most important letters and letting them guide the design. Because my native tongue is English, I started with the English letter-frequency

Figure 6.8
(a) My 55-element mosaic.
(b) My alphabet and digits.

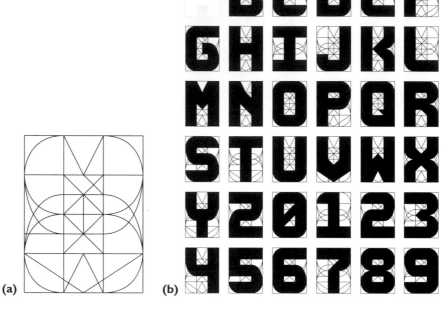

(a)   (b)

table: E is the most common letter in the alphabet, then the table continues with TAOINSHRDLU. These had to look really good, even if at the expense of infrequent letters.

I tried to compromise the letterforms carefully. For example, the two curved arms of the K aren't well distinguished on the right-hand side of the letter, which could be a problem, but the sharp point where they join the left-hand vertical saves things and makes it a recognizable K. It's fun to try to find various characteristics of letters that you can sacrifice or reinforce in order to keep them legible. As another example, I could have saved six segments if I'd left off the two diagonal lines at the bottom—they are only used for the V. It was tempting, but then I'd have ended up with the same embarrassing V as in the Vienna design. Why should V always be the one to suffer? (Historically, V has seniority; the letterforms U and W were both derived from the V in the Middle Ages.) I felt that the sharp point at the bottom was the essence of V in this design. So, I jumped from 49 to 55 segments—three on each side. Symmetry is both an ally and a nemesis in this problem.

Net Results

ANDREW GLASSNER'S NOTEBOOK
July/August 1997

7

Poker players fold. Film directors cut. Recording engineers tape. In this chapter we'll do all three.

In Chapter 3 I discussed how to fold interesting polyhedra using origami techniques. The idea there was to build 3D shapes from square or rectangular pieces of paper by doing nothing but folding them. This time I'll throw out that restriction and use scissors and glue as liberally as folds. Actually, we'll only use scissors to cut out the initial shape; from there on, it's just folding and gluing.

My motivation here is the same as before. A valuable asset for anyone working in 3D graphics is a good 3D visual imagination. One of the best ways to develop that imagination is to build models and hold them, turn them, and study them. If you build them yourself, there's significant value in the physical process of assembly—you get to really feel how the pieces go together, which helps deepen an understanding of the pieces and their relationships. I find that building models helps me keep my 3D visual eye tuned up and active.

We'll begin, as in Chapter 3, with the Platonic solids. I'll show an unfolded shape, such as a tetrahedron made of four equilateral triangles, and include small assembly flaps. The conventional rotation for these drawings differs from the origami rotation. Each solid line, including the ones between the triangles and the flaps, indicates a mountain fold—this means that you should fold the pieces of paper on both sides of the line away from you, so that the fold itself rises up toward you. Dashed lines indicate valley folds, which recede from you.

Construction Tips

To build these models, I recommend card stock. This isn't as heavy as thick cardboard, but it's stiff enough to resist buckling. Something a little thicker than a standard business card should do the trick. You can buy this sort of paper at any art or hobby store.

You'll want your models to be larger than the diagrams. I recommend that most edges be around 2–3 inches long for nice models. It's usually advantageous to work as large as possible—larger pieces cover up minor errors in measuring, folding, and cutting, and they are usually more satisfying to hold and work with. I generally use one of three different enlargement methods, depending on the diagram's complexity. The first is to draw the pattern directly onto the card stock, measuring it out from the geometry of the original diagram. When I don't want to measure right on the surface, I use two other approaches. Both begin by creating a full-size drawing of the diagram on a big piece of paper (or a few pieces of paper taped together), either by measuring it out or by using an enlarging photocopier on a pre-existing diagram. One way to transfer this full-size drawing to the card is to first scribble on the back of the paper with a soft-lead pencil. Then tape down the paper over the card stock and draw over the diagram with a sharp pencil. This transfers the lead from the back of the paper onto the board, leaving a light line for cutting and scoring. For some diagrams, I tape the paper down and use a pin to make a few pinpricks through the paper onto the board underneath, usually at intersection points and external corners. Then I make creases and cuts with the help of a straightedge lined up to the pinholes.

To prepare for folds, I recommend scoring the card by running a blunt butter knife over the fold lines. You can also bear down with a ballpoint pen—you can use one without ink if you don't want to leave a mark.

To get the models folded up may take some trial and error, particularly for the ones at the end of the chapter. I recommend artist's layout tape for holding the pieces together while you play with them. This tape uses the same tacky but removable adhesive that's on the back of those yellow sticky notes.

You can use any regular glue to assemble the flaps. But be careful if you're decorating your model using paper glued over the thicker card: you'll want to remove the paper from the flaps and their destinations so that you're gluing the thick card directly to itself. If you don't want to use glue, you can use regular sticky tape. You can place the tape inside the model if you don't want it to show, but that becomes tricky to apply. Alternatively, you can place the tape on the outside. I find this is the best way to play with the models, because it lets you take them apart easily to study the relationship between the 2D diagram and the 3D model. When you want to make them permanent, glue's the way to go.

Nets and Efficiency

The unfolded tetrahedron in Figure 7.1a is the simplest of the Platonic solids. The standard hierarchy then continues with the cube, octahedron,

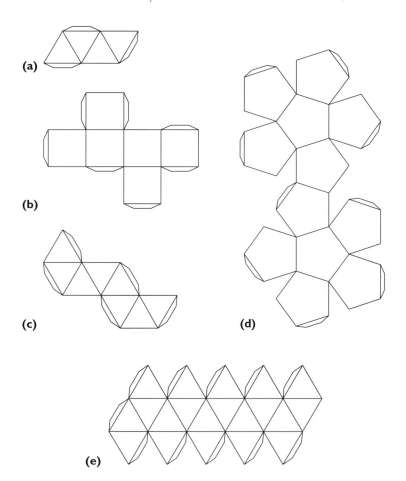

Figure 7.1
Nets for Platonic solids.
(a) Tetrahedron.
(b) Cube.
(c) Octahedron.
(d) Dodecahedron.
(e) Icosahedron.

Figure 7.2
(a) A net for the cube.
(b) Showing 50% efficiency.
(c) Tiling the net.

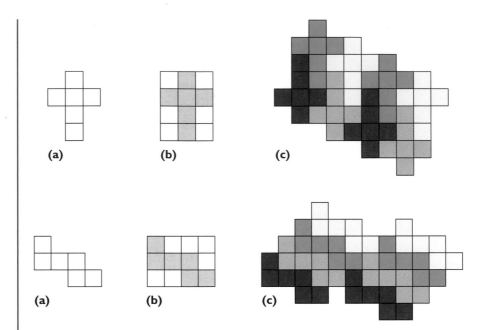

(a)　　　**(b)**　　　**(c)**

Figure 7.3
(a) A second net for the cube.
(b) Showing 50% efficiency.
(c) Tiling the net.

(a)　　　**(b)**　　　**(c)**

dodecahedron, and icosahedron. Unfolded diagrams, or *nets*, for these other solids are shown in the rest of Figure 7.1.

If you're just making a few little models for fun, then it's fine to just draw the net somewhere on a piece of board and cut it out. But suppose that you need to make thousands or millions of models, one per rectangular piece of board. Can different nets give you more or less efficient use of the board?

Figure 7.2a shows the most traditional net for the cube (I'm going to exclude flaps for now; including them would change the numbers a bit, but not the thrust of the discussion). Assuming that the edge length of each square is 1, the net has an area of 6 and sits in a rectangle of area 12, as in Figure 7.2b. So the efficiency is 50%. If efficiency were really an issue, you'd want to make use of that empty area within the rectangle. Happily, just as 3D cubes fill space, these 2D nets tile the plane, as in Figure 7.2c. So

Figure 7.4
(a) A third net for the cube.
(b) Showing 60% efficiency.
(c) Tiling the net.

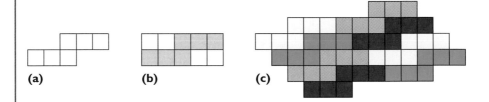

(a)　　　**(b)**　　　**(c)**

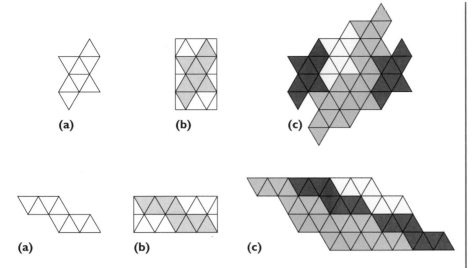

Figure 7.5
(a) A net for the octahedron.
(b) Showing 50% efficiency.
(c) Tiling the net.

Figure 7.6
(a) A second net for the octahedron.
(b) Showing 50% efficiency.
(c) Tiling the net.

the efficiency goes up to 100% in the middle of the paper where they tile, and you only lose the little bits of trim at the boundaries of the sheet.

Figure 7.3 shows another net for the cube. Although the pieces have been moved around quite a bit, this net also has an efficiency of 50% and tiles the plane. Figure 7.4 shows yet another tiling net for the cube, but this one has an efficiency of 60%. I don't know of a net for the cube with better than 60% efficiency.

Figure 7.5 presents the net for an octahedron. It also tiles, and this time has an efficiency of 50%. A little transposition gets a different efficiency of 50% in Figure 7.6. Figure 7.7 shows the best efficiency: 66%. Although each of these nets has eight equilateral triangles, they also have the necessary connectivity. When fooling around with nets, it's important to make sure that you don't accidentally move the pieces around so that you can't make the desired shape. Finally, I can't resist providing in Figure 7.8 the

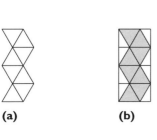

Figure 7.7
(a) A third net for the octahedron.
(b) Showing 66% efficiency.
(c) Tiling the net.

net for the Archimedean solid called the cuboctahedron, which was Buckminster Fuller's favorite shape.

Flowering Polygons

So far we've folded up flat diagrams into static 3D shapes. There are all kinds of dynamic 3D models that you build from very simple nets. One of

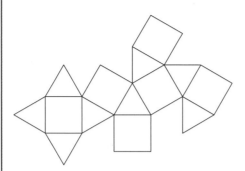

my favorites is simply called the *polyhedral flower*. Figure 7.9 shows the flower, with the petals inside just rising up and starting to spread.

Figure 7.10 shows the net for the flower; you'll need two of these. Figure 7.10 also shows a suggested coloring; if you use this scheme, use the same coloring for each of the two pieces. Cut them out carefully, and score the mountain and valley folds very precisely; accuracy will pay off in a more stable and beautiful model. Figure 7.11 shows how a piece should look when it's ready for as-

sembly. When the two nets have been scored, glue the flaps at the bottom of each piece to the top of the other, so that you create a cylinder with the colored side facing outward.

Now comes the tricky part—but it's also the fun part. It took me a bit of fumbling before I figured out how to get this thing together, but when assembled it's quite lovely. I'll describe how I finally managed it, but there's nothing quite like holding the model in your hands and seeing it. Expect to have to experiment a bit.

The most important thing is to have good folds. Holding the cylinder so that its axis runs vertically, pull together the triangle pairs on the top until they begin to come together, causing the diamond shapes on the outside to fold inward. Figure 7.12 shows how this should look. You can use artist's

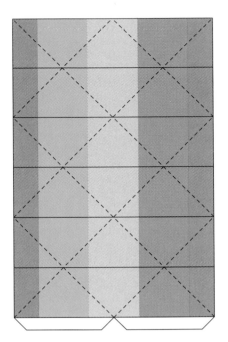

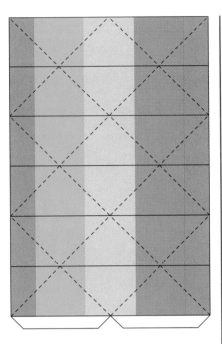

Figure 7.10
The net for a polyhedral flower. The two pieces are glued to one another to make a long cylinder, colored side outward.

temporary tape to hold the folds together. Now do exactly the same thing on the other side. There's no phase shift here— that is, the model is exactly symmetrical (except for color) on both sides of an imaginary plane that cuts perpendicular to the axis of the cylinder. When you're done, you'll have something like a polygonal donut.

Figure 7.11
A piece of the flower ready to be assembled.

Now comes the easy part. Take off the tape and let the top part flop open a little, while keeping the bottom points together. Pull out on the red points at the top, while pushing in on the yellow points at the bottom. This will cause the whole ring to rotate around itself. The top part will open up into a hole, and the points from below will pop up and begin to spread apart. If you

Figure 7.12
Folding the flower.

continue to rotate the ring, it will settle into a stable position with the center part forming a fountain of color in the midst of an enclosing cup, as in Figure 7.9. You can continue to turn the ring around and around, causing the flower to fold into itself and then bloom again.

Kaleidocycles

One of the most interesting dynamic polyhedral models is the *kaleidocycle*. This is a ring of nonregular tetrahedra that rotates like the flower but doesn't open up. Figure 7.13 shows a kaleidocycle, but to really appre-

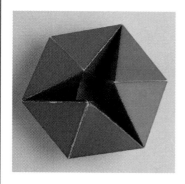

ciate it you need to build one and turn it in your hands. The amazing thing is that the pieces just turn and turn indefinitely, even though the tetrahedra are only hinged along two edges.

The net for a hexagonal kaleidocycle is shown in Figure 7.14. Note that the triangles are not equilateral, but isosceles. The long altitude of the triangle is the same length as the short side it is erected from. You can work out the dimensions from basic trig: if

the short leg has length 1, the long legs are each of length $\sqrt{1.25}$. The acute angle is $\cos^{-1}(0.6) \approx 53.13$ degrees, and the other two angles equally divide what remains of the 180 degrees allotted to every triangle—they are each about 63.43 degrees. You'll only need one copy of the net to build the model.

Figure 7.15 shows the folding process. It's a lot easier to construct than the flower. Begin by forming a ring, so that the top colored triangles overlap

Figure 7.13
A partly open kaleidocycle.

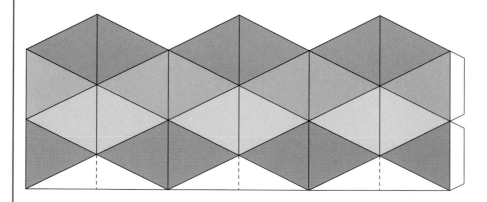

Figure 7.14
The net for a kaleidocycle.

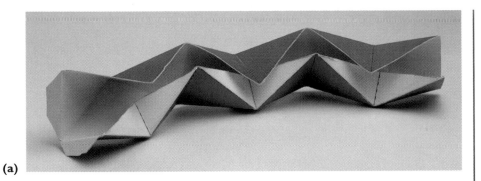

(a)

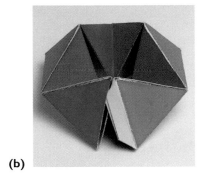

(b)

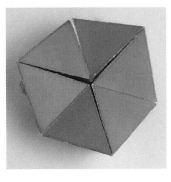

(c)

Figure 7.15
Constructing the kaleidocycle.
(a) Form a tube, and glue the uncolored pieces under the colored ones.
(b) Tuck the end flaps into the open slot.
(c) The assembled kaleidocycle.

with the uncolored ones at the bottom; put glue on the bottom flaps and adhere them to the bottom of the upper triangles. Then put glue on the flaps at the end and tuck them into the hole at the other end, forming a ring.

Now as you turn the ring, it will stay together as a single stable structure, showing you four distinct images as you turn the pieces. It's fascinating to watch the shapes move around one another, seemingly unfolding forever.

If you're interested in decorating your kaleidocycle, Figure 7.16 shows a schematic of how the pieces connect when they form images. The four colors make up the four images, and the letters indicate which arrows join together. If you get continuity across the arrows, then you'll be able to form images from each set of six triangles.

For an even greater challenge, you can try to get continuity around the ring as well as within each image; this is indicated by the white arrows in Figure 7.16. The full-blown version of this is shown in Figure 7.17, which provides the symmetry constraints to pull off this more complicated continuity. You'll recognize the F motif as my favorite way to indicate an oriented tile; all tiles with the same color here should have the same internal

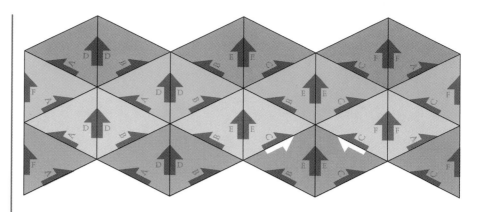

patterns. Notice that although there are 60 tiles, there are only 24 different designs. There are 12 pairs, which are the ones that run vertically in the figure; these are the triangles that are adjacent in the unfolding pattern because they are adjacent in the net. There are also 12 quadruplets, each arranged in what looks to me like butterfly wings. Technically, these little symmetry markings are sufficient but not necessary. That is, they will do the job, but they're overkill. You really only need continuity of design across the edge; as long as they mesh where they touch, the contents of every tile can be different.

If you use Figure 7.17 as the guide to decoration for a kaleidocycle, don't get confused. When I folded this to make sure I drew the figure correctly, I started folding along all the solid lines, which is unnecessary and makes for a very floppy model. These lines are just the boundaries around each tile, not the folding pattern; that's in Figure 7.14.

Happy cutting, folding, and taping!

Figure 7.17
The F motif indicates the orientation of the tile. Tiles with the same color contain the same decoration. There are 12 pairs and 12 quadruplets in the 60 tiles.

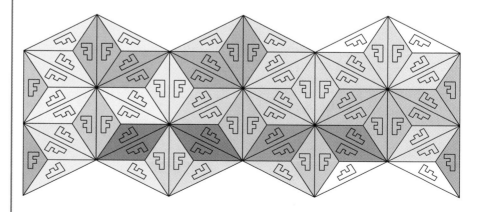

Further Reading

A great book for making all kinds of fixed models is *Polyhedron Models* by Magnus Wenninger (Cambridge University Press, 1974). I also recommend his other books very highly.

I first saw the polygonal flower in a little book called *Mathematical Curiosities 1* by Gerald Jenkins and Anne Wild (Tarquin Publications, 1985). It contains nine interesting little math curiosities, each of which is illustrated with a small model. The book contains full-color pages that you can cut out and score to build the models. Figure 7.10 uses their four-striped decorating scheme.

A beautiful decoration of kaleidocycles is presented in the book *M. C. Escher Kaleidocycles* by Doris Schattschneider and Wallace Walker (TACO, 1987). Besides giving a nice description of the symmetries in Escher's tiled drawings, they show how to adapt his drawings to different kaleidocycles. The book contains high-quality, prescored die-cut nets for building your own models.

The Perils of Problematic Parameterization

ANDREW GLASSNER'S NOTEBOOK

September/October 1997

8

Whenever you want to model a perfectly flat surface, polygons are a great geometric primitive. Of course, truly flat surfaces are rare: book covers, desktops, and even the walls of rooms usually have some wobbles and surface variation. With color and displacement textures, polygons can follow some of these irregularities.

Smoothly curved surfaces are another thing altogether. Ideally, we'd like to model and render these shapes with primitives that are also smoothly curved. Sometimes we can achieve this goal. Often, though, practical considerations lead us to approximate these curved surfaces with polygons. Sometimes the polygons are only introduced at the very end of the rendering phase, where they are smaller than a pixel. Other times we start out modeling with polygons and stick with them all the way through.

No matter how or when polygons are used to approximate a curved surface, we need to be very sure that they match that surface closely. I can think of two ways to check this match: visually and mathematically. A visual check requires looking at the rendered imagery with a critical eye: if the surfaces are free of polygonal artifacts, then the match is acceptable. This is obviously pretty tough to quantize and implement in software. The mathematical approach suggests that we find some descriptive measurement that we can apply to both the original model and the polygonal approximation.

In this chapter I'll compare the quality of a polygonal approximation to the original curved object by comparing their surface areas. If the areas are way off, then that implies something is wrong with the approximation. But if the areas are the same, we can't say much. As an example, we could start with a curved model of a lion and create a polygonal approximation of a bat. If they both have the same surface area, this measure won't tell us that there's any difference at all! On the other hand, if the areas are way off, then we might be prompted to take a closer look.

There's a folk theorem in graphics that says if we want to improve the quality of a polygonal approximation, then we should use triangles, reduce their size, and use more of them, making sure of course that their vertices always lie on the surface. The resulting model can't help but get better and better, right? Nope. Read on.

Approximating Lines with Curves

There's a nice 2D example that illustrates the sort of problem we're going to encounter in this chapter. Just for fun, I'll flip the problem over on its head and try to approximate a straight line with little curves. I'll try to increase the quality by using more curves of ever-smaller size.

In Figure 8.1a I've drawn a circle with radius r, so its diameter is simply $2r$. In Figure 8.1b I've placed two circles side-by-side along a diameter, each circle with radius $r/2$. If we take just the top half of the left circle and bottom half of the right circle, we get the top curve in Figure 8.1c. This is our first (albeit lousy) approximation to the diameter of the circle. Since each semicircle has arclength $\pi r/2$, the length of the two semicircles together is $2\pi r/2 = \pi r$. Now we'll repeat the process, in the second curve from the top

Figure 8.1
(a) A circle of radius r.
(b) In the larger circle, two smaller circles of radius $r/2$.
(c) Replacing each semicircle with two of half-diameter.

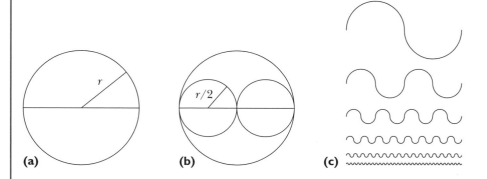

(a)　　　　(b)　　　　(c)

in Figure 8.1c. We halve the radius again from $r/2$ to $r/4$ and double the number of semicircles from 2 to 4, giving us a total length of $4\pi r/4 = \pi r$.

Figure 8.1c shows several more steps in this process. It looks like this wiggly curve is approximating the diameter as we wished, and we might expect its length to approach $2r$ as the wiggles get smaller and smaller. Although the squiggles indeed get ever smaller in amplitude and ever closer together, the length of the curve does not tend to $2r$. This is because we'll always have s semicircles, each with length $\pi r/s$, so the total arclength of the curve is $s\pi r/s = \pi r$, no matter how many squiggles we use!

There's nothing tricky going on here. The reason the length of the curve doesn't go to the diameter of $2r$ but to something rather larger is because the squiggles never completely go away. As the height of each bump is reduced, there are just enough more of them to compensate. You might enjoy creating 3D versions of this phenomenon.

We'll now move on to the so-called *Schwarz paradox.* It shares some of the ideas we've just seen, but with a twist. The basic idea will be to approximate a cylinder with polygons. That probably doesn't seem so hard. But wait, for the chilling truth may shock you.

Mild-Mannered Approximations

We'll begin with a garden-variety circular right cylinder, as shown in Figure 8.2a. Everyone knows that if we ignore the end caps, a cylinder with radius r and height h has a surface area $A = 2\pi rh$.

Our first polygonal model will be like a farm silo: we'll just erect m rectangular boards so that the corners lie on the surface, as in Figure 8.2b, leaving us with the m-sided prism in Figure 8.2c. It's not too hard to find its surface area. The area of each board is wh, where h is the height of the cylinder and w is the width of the board.

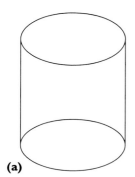  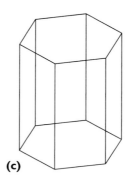

(a)   (b)   (c)

Figure 8.2
(a) A right circular cylinder.
(b) A six-sided approximation of 8.2a.
(c) The resulting prism.

Figure 8.3
(a) The geometry
of one face of the
prism.
(b) Finding the
width of the face.

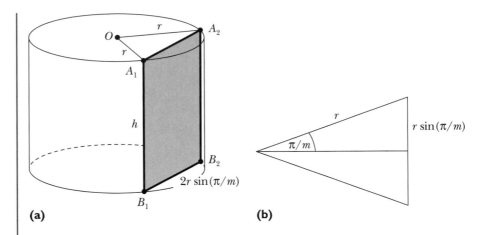

Figure 8.3a shows the geometry for finding these lengths. The height h of each board is simply the height h of the cylinder. The width can be found from the distance from A_1 to A_2. These are both the same distance r from the origin O at the center of the cylinder. Figure 8.3b shows this triangle. The angle at the origin is $2\pi/m$, so half that is π/m. From that, simple trig tells us that the far face of the upper triangle is $r\sin(\pi/m)$. Since that's half the width of the board, we have found that $w = 2r\sin(\pi/m)$.

There are m of these rectangular polygons altogether, so the surface area A_r due to m rectangles is

$$A_r = mwh = m2r\sin(\pi/m)h$$

A plot of the surface area for different values of m is shown in Figure 8.4, where I've set $r = h = 1$. Notice that the surface area seems to approach 2π, which is of course what we want.

Just to make sure that this intuition is right, let's find the limit of the surface area as the number of polygons goes to infinity:

$$A_r = \lim_{m \to \infty} m2r\sin(\pi/m)h$$

Now what happens as we increase m toward infinity? Let's factor out the term $2rh$ for a moment, since it doesn't depend on m, leaving us with $m\sin(\pi/m)$. If we multiply this by π/π, we get

$$m\sin(\pi/m) = \pi\frac{\sin(\pi/m)}{\pi/m}$$

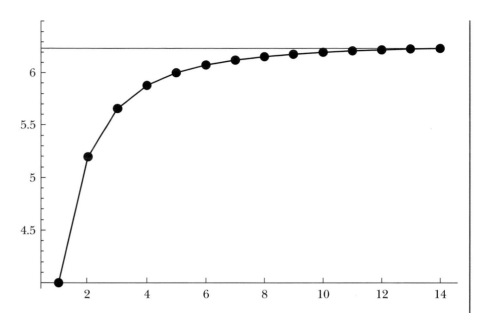

Figure 8.4
A plot of the approximated surface area versus the real surface area, for $r = h = 1$. The horizontal line marks 2π.

Now let's make the replacement $x = \pi/m$. As $m \to \infty$, $x \to 0$. Recall that the sinc function goes to 1 at the origin; that is,

$$\lim_{x \to 0} \frac{\sin x}{x} = 1$$

We can use this limit to find that

$$\lim_{m \to \infty} \pi \frac{\sin(\pi/m)}{\pi/m} = \pi$$

I will use this identity several times throughout this chapter, sometimes juggling things into place to apply it. Putting this all together, we have

$$A_r = \lim_{m \to \infty} m\, 2r \sin(\pi/m)\, h$$

$$= 2rh \lim_{m \to \infty} \pi \frac{\sin(\pi/m)}{\pi/m}$$

$$= 2rh\pi$$

This is reassuring: it says that as the polygons increase in number and get smaller, their combined area approaches the surface area of the cylinder.

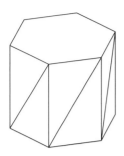

Figure 8.5
Triangulating the prism of Figure 8.2c.

Figure 8.6
The prism of Figure 8.5 twisted into an antiprism.

But rectangles aren't a terribly good choice for such big surface elements; for one thing, there's no guarantee that a rectangle is planar. So we can cut each rectangle into two triangles, as in Figure 8.5. The area of each triangle is half that of each rectangle, and there are $2m$ triangles, so the 2's cancel and the combined area works out to the same amount.

Note that we haven't proven that *all* choices of rectangles or triangles will approximate the cylinder, only this particular choice. Let's look at a slightly different way to go.

Everybody, Let's Twist

Suppose that you look at the cylinder of Figure 8.5 and you're concerned about how the silhouette's going to look when you get close to it. One way to try to smooth it out is to give the bottom part of the cylinder a bit of a twist. The same $2m$ triangles in Figure 8.5 end up as in Figure 8.6. Here we've moved one of the vertices of the lower m-gon directly under the midpoint of an edge above it; in other words, the lower ring has been rotated $2\pi/(2m)$ radians with respect to the upper ring. This figure is called an *antiprism*.

What's the surface area now? We need to be a little more careful here, because the height of the triangles is no longer the height of the cylinder. The new wrinkle is that they're tilted a little bit; this is going to cause us trouble later on.

Figure 8.7 shows the geometry. We want to find the area of triangle $\triangle A_1 B A_2$. A_1 and A_2 both lie on the cylinder, while C is their midpoint. D is

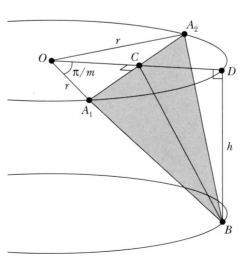

the point that we get by drawing a radius from the origin O of the upper disk through C to the edge of the cylinder, and B is the point on the lower disk directly beneath B. As a base we'll use the distance (A_1A_2), and the height will be (CB). So the area $A = bh/2 = (A_1A_2)(CB)/2$. We can find half the base length $(A_1A_2)/2$ by noting that this is just (A_1C). We found this length in Figure 8.3; it's $r\sin(\pi/m)$.

Figure 8.7
The geometry of one triangle of Figure 8.6.

The height (CB) is a bit more tricky, since it's not simply h anymore. We can turn to Pythagoras, and make some substitutions from the geometry in Figure 8.7:

$$(CB) = \sqrt{(DB)^2 + (CD)^2}$$
$$= \sqrt{h^2 + (OD - OC)^2}$$
$$= \sqrt{h^2 + (r - r\cos(\pi/m))^2}$$
$$= \sqrt{h^2 + \left(r\left[1 - \cos\frac{\pi}{m}\right]\right)^2}$$

This is starting to look unmanageable. To make things easier in the long run, I'll pull a rabbit out of my hat. You may recall the standard half-angle substitution:

$$\sin(\alpha/2) = \pm\sqrt{\frac{1 - \cos\alpha}{2}}$$

Cleaning up the right-hand side,

$$2(\sin^2(\alpha/2)) = 1 - \cos\alpha$$

We can use this to replace the right-hand term under the radical in the formula for length (CB). Setting α to π/m, we get

$$(CB) = \sqrt{h^2 + \left(r\left[2\sin^2\frac{\pi}{2m}\right]\right)^2}$$
$$= \sqrt{h^2 + 4r^2\sin^4\frac{\pi}{2m}}$$

Now we have both the width and height of the triangle. In symbols, the area of one triangle is

$$A = wh/2 = (CB)(A_1 A_2)/2 = r\sin(\pi/m)\sqrt{h^2 + 4r^2\sin^4\frac{\pi}{2m}}$$

We'll multiply that area by $2m$ to account for all the triangles, giving us the total surface area A_a (for antiprism):

$$A_a = 2mr\sin(\pi/m)\sqrt{h^2 + 4r^2\sin^4\frac{\pi}{2m}} \qquad \text{(I)}$$

I've labeled this as equation 1 because we'll come back to it later. Now that we have this monster, we'll repeat our previous steps and see what happens to its value as the number of triangles m goes to infinity:

$$A_a = \lim_{m \to \infty} (2r)\,[\,m\sin(\pi/m)\,]\sqrt{h^2 + 4r^2 \sin^4 \frac{\pi}{2m}}$$

$$= 2r\pi\sqrt{h^2 + 0}$$

$$= 2\pi rh$$

where we've noted that as m goes to infinity, $\pi/2m$ goes to 0, so $\sin(\pi/2m)$ goes to 0 as well, and thus the whole right-hand term under the radical goes to 0.

This is another happy result, since it means that the half-twist hasn't done anything to the quality of our approximation. Of course, we've only come this far because everything is about to go wrong.

The Schwarz Paradox

I'll now do something that appears completely innocent: I'll simply stack up n of these antiprisms to make the full cylinder. That is, I'll cut the cylinder perpendicular to its axis into n little cylinders, create a prism in each one, and then stack them together. Figure 8.8 shows the idea.

Figure 8.8
(a) A stack of two antiprisms. In this figure, $m = 6, n = 2$. **(b)** A shaded view.

(a)

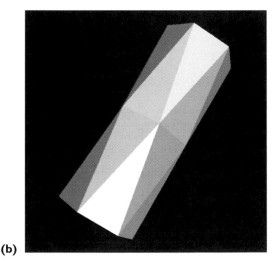

(b)

We only need to make two changes to our surface-area formula in equation 1. First, we need to compensate for the shorter height. The vertical leg used to compute height is now h/n rather than simply h. The base hasn't changed at all. The second change is that we need to multiply by a factor of n to account for the additional triangles. The new formula for A_s, the surface area of the stacked antiprisms, is then

$$A_s = 2mnr\sin(\pi/m)\sqrt{\left(\frac{h}{n}\right)^2 + 4r^2\sin^4\frac{\pi}{2m}}$$

$$= 2r[m\sin(\pi/m)]\sqrt{h^2 + 4r^2n^2\sin^4\frac{\pi}{2m}} \tag{2}$$

where in the second line I've moved n into the radical. I've labeled this equation 2.

Let's now examine what happens to the surface area as we try out different values of n. Notice that n only appears once, as a squared term under the radical sign. We'll begin gently, setting $n = m$:

$$A_s^{n=m} = 2r[m\sin(\pi/m)]\sqrt{h^2 + 4r^2m^2\sin^4\frac{\pi}{2m}} \tag{3}$$

This gives us equation 3. Let's look at the behavior of the right-hand term under the radical (we'll ignore the r^2 term for the moment):

$$\lim_{m\to\infty} 4m^2\sin^4\frac{\pi}{2m} = \lim_{m\to\infty} 4m^2\sin^2\frac{\pi}{2m}\sin^2\frac{\pi}{2m}$$

$$= \lim_{m\to\infty}\left[2m\sin\frac{\pi}{2m}\right]^2\sin^2\frac{\pi}{2m}$$

$$= \lim_{m\to\infty}\left[\pi\frac{\sin(\pi/2m)}{\pi/2m}\right]^2\sin^2\frac{\pi}{2m}$$

$$= \lim_{m\to\infty}\pi^2\cdot 0$$

$$= 0$$

where I've noted that as $m\to\infty$, $\sin^2(\pi/2m)\to 0$.

We can now plug in this result into equation 3:

$$A_s^{n=m} = 2r[m\sin(\pi/m)]\sqrt{h^2 + 4r^2 m^2 \sin^4\frac{\pi}{2m}}$$

$$= 2r \cdot \pi \cdot \sqrt{h^2 + r^2 \cdot 0}$$

$$= 2r\pi h$$

And everything is fine; the approximate surface area tends to the real surface area.

Well, heck, if setting $n = m$ worked, then let's chop up the cylinder into even littler pieces. Let's set $n = m^2$. This means that if we have, say, a six-sided hexagon at the top and bottom, then we'll chop the cylinder up into 36 little slabs, as in Figure 8.9. Now we're using lots more polygons, each one of which is smaller than before. More is better, right?

Okay, let's plug $n = m^2$ into our antiprism surface-area formula in equation 2 and watch what happens. Our only change will be that the n^2 term under the radical turns into m^4, so let's first examine the asymptotic behavior of that expression:

$$\lim_{m \to \infty} 4m^4 \sin^4\frac{\pi}{2m} = \lim_{m \to \infty}\left[2m\sin\frac{\pi}{2m}\right]^4 \frac{1}{4}$$

$$= \lim_{m \to \infty}\left[\pi\frac{\sin(\pi/2m)}{\pi/2m}\right]^4 \frac{1}{4}$$

$$= \lim_{m \to \infty}\frac{\pi^4}{4}\left[\frac{\sin(\pi/2m)}{\pi/2m}\right]^4$$

$$= \frac{\pi^4}{4} \cdot 1$$

$$= \frac{\pi^4}{4}$$

Uh-oh. I have a bad feeling about this. Let's actually use this in equation 2 and see what comes out:

$$A_s^{n=m^2} = \lim_{m \to \infty} 2r[m\sin(\pi/m)]\sqrt{h^2 + 4r^2 m^4 \sin^4\frac{\pi}{2m}}$$

$$= 2r\pi\sqrt{h^2 + r^2\frac{\pi^4}{4}}$$

Something is terribly wrong here. This says that as we use more and more polygons, the surface area goes to something that is larger than the surface area of the cylinder! If we set $r = h = 1$, the cylinder's surface area is 2π, but the approximated area is

$$2\pi\sqrt{1 + \pi^4/4}$$

which is an increase by a factor of about 32.

Maybe if we try setting $n = m^3$ we'll get some insight into the situation. That replacement means that we get an m^6 term under the radical in equation 2. Let's follow the limit as before:

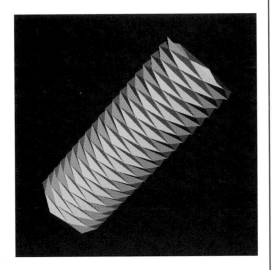

Figure 8.9
The triangles start to fold up like an accordion when $n = m^2$. In this example, $m = 6$, $n = 36$.

$$\lim_{m \to \infty} 4m^6 \sin^4 \frac{\pi}{2m} = \lim_{m \to \infty} \left[2m \sin \frac{\pi}{2m} \right]^4 \frac{m^2}{4}$$
$$= \lim_{m \to \infty} \frac{m^2 \pi^4}{4}$$
$$= \infty$$

Things are definitely looking bad. Plugging this into the surface-area formula in equation 2, we find

$$A_s^{n = m^3} = \lim_{m \to \infty} 2r[m \sin(\pi/m)] \sqrt{h^2 + 4r^2 m^6 \sin^4 \frac{\pi}{2m}}$$
$$= 2r\pi\sqrt{h^2 + r^2 \cdot \infty}$$
$$= \infty$$

Now we're in big trouble. This result says that if we chop the cylinder up into m^3 little pieces and triangulate them as antiprisms, then as m gets bigger and the triangles get smaller, the surface area goes up to infinity!

This result is called the *Schwarz paradox*. It's not really a paradox, because it's not a self-contradictory situation. Rather, it's just a disconcerting surprise: our old friends the polygons seem to have betrayed us. We have created an approximation that has a surface area that goes to infinity as we use smaller and smaller triangles.

What Went Wrong?

What the heck is going on here? In fact, there's nothing really wrong at all—we've simply chosen a really poor way of dicing up the cylinder. Because of the half-twist, the triangles are no longer following the surface of the cylinder but are folding in and out like an accordion. When $n = m$, the folding isn't too bad, but as the number of cylinder segments n increases to m^2, the triangles start mashing against each other very tightly. Figure 8.10 shows one view of the geometry. Finally, when n goes up with m^3, the triangles get so dense that the surface area just explodes. Figure 8.11 may give

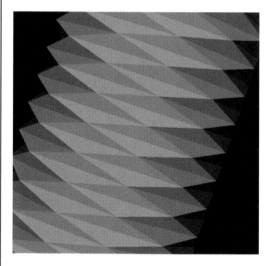

you a feeling for this. This also means that the cylinder is not going to look smoother and smoother with more and more polygons. Instead, it's going to get worse, and eventually those long thin triangles are going to cause some terrible aliasing problems.

Notice that I adhered to all the rules of thumb that we normally use for polygonal approximations: the polygons were triangles, they got ever smaller and more numerous, and the vertices always were located right on the surface of the mathematically smooth object.

Figure 8.10
A close-up of Figure 8.9.

The moral is that if you're going to use polygons to approximate a curved surface, the polygons themselves need to lie closer and closer to the surface as they become smaller and more numerous. Mathematically this means that we would have wanted to project these triangles out onto the surface of the cylinder.

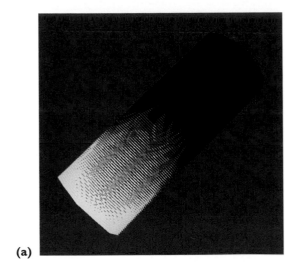 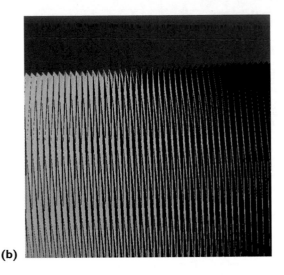

(a)   (b)

The surprise here is that we were able to find such a pathological failure of polygonalization in such a simple situation. Who knows what evils lurk behind other ways of chopping up surfaces? The lesson here is that it's not enough to just cut up a surface into polygons; you must make sure that your polygons lie ever closer to the surface they're approximating. That's not always easy to check, but it's worth the effort.

Further Reading

I first ran across the Schwarz paradox in *The Penguin Dictionary of Curious and Interesting Geometry* (David Wells, Penguin, 1992), which is a wonderful little book of many mathematical delights. My presentation of the phenomenon is based on the discussion given in *Calculus* (John F. Randolph, MacMillan).

Figure 8.11
(a) A cylinder with $n = m^3$, for $m = 6$, $n = 216$. The strange lighting pattern comes from the aliasing caused by the local light source and the closely packed triangles.
(b) A close-up. Note that the outer edge is still creased.

Inside Moiré Patterns

ANDREW GLASSNER'S NOTEBOOK
November/December 1997

9

Moiré patterns are very cool phenomena produced by the interaction of two overlaid regular patterns. You've seen moiré effects any time you've looked through two pieces of fine mesh screen and noticed the broad dark bands that appear as the meshes move or as you move your head.

When created deliberately, moiré patterns are a cheap special effect. Some children's books consist of many printed pages and a transparent sheet with a black pattern on it; by waving the transparent sheet over the pages, you can make waterfalls flow and clouds float by. But moiré patterns can creep in where they're undesired. When a photograph is scanned, the dot pattern used to originally print the image can interact with the digitizing dot pattern used by the scanner. The result can be bands or blocks of light and dark across the image. Badly registered color screens can also beat in a similar way, so what ought to be printed as a smooth field of color turns into something like a busy plaid. Moiré patterns also have a practical side. The field of moiré interferometry uses these patterns to measure very small displacements in surfaces and thin materials.

The principles behind moiré patterns aren't very complicated. With a little geometry, it's easy to understand where they come from and how to create and control them. To demonstrate most of the moiré effects, I'll use a very simple set of patterns: sheets of parallel lines. At the end of the chapter I'll show some examples of grids, dots, and circles creating moiré patterns.

Gratings

We'll begin with the *grating*. A grating is simply a sheet of parallel lines, as in Figure 9.1. In a grating, the black lines all have the same width, as do the white spaces between them. We can think of one adjacent pair of black and white bars as defining the fundamental region of the pattern—just rubber-stamping that pair of bars side by side creates the grating.

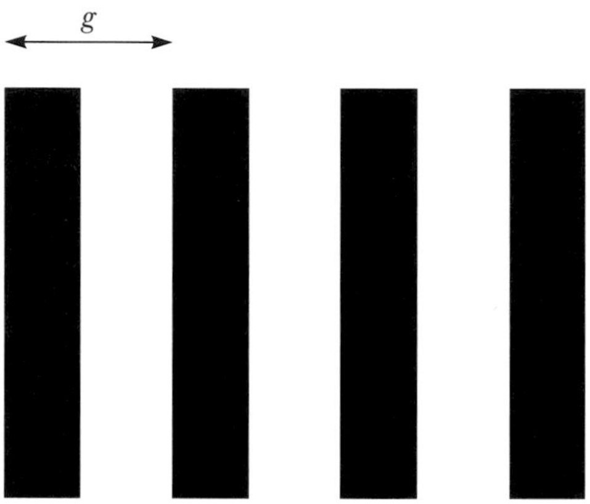

Figure 9.1
A grating is a set of alternating black and white bars. All of the black bars are the same width, as are all the white bars. The pitch *g* is the width of one pair of bars.

A grating is characterized by two numbers. The *pitch*, usually denoted by *g*, describes how closely packed the lines are. Now because these are real lines and not mathematical abstractions, they have some width. Referring to the vertical lines of Figure 9.1, I find it convenient to think of the pitch as the distance between the left-hand edge of neighboring black bars. The *ratio*, usually written *R*, is the fraction formed by the width of the black bar divided by the width of the white bar. A ratio of 1 means that the two bars have equal width.

EXTENSION

Let's create two gratings, each with a ratio of 1. The first grating, p_1, has more lines per inch than the second grating, p_2, so pitch g_1 is smaller than g_2. We'll pick the pitches so that they're nearly similar; let's say they're each within about 5% of each other. Let's overlap the two gratings, as in Figure 9.2, so that the lines are parallel. This kind of alignment is called *extension*.

You can see that a new pattern emerges, consisting of black bars that seem to represent a much wider grating. These bars are called *moiré fringes*, and they are, in fact, equidistant. The fringes come about because the two gratings "beat" against one another. What is the pitch *G* of this new pattern?

Figure 9.3 provides a way of answering this question. Here I've drawn a simple intensity profile of the bars as waves—a value of 0 means black and 1 means white. At the left edge of the figure, the two gratings are aligned.

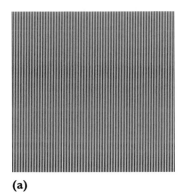
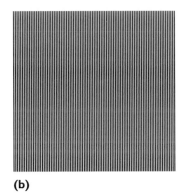
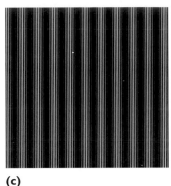

(a)   **(b)**   **(c)**

But after just one cycle of each, they've slipped a little. The finer (or more compact) grating p_1 is already starting into its second white bar before the coarser grating p_2 is finished with its first black bar. As we scan the pattern from left to right we see that p_2 falls farther and farther behind p_1, until eventually it falls one complete cycle behind and the two patterns are aligned again. It's just like one runner lapping another around a track.

How does this create the moiré pattern? Consider that the page you're reading this on arrives from the manufacturer completely white. The printing process deposits black ink to block the ambient light from reflecting off the page and into your eye. So anywhere we've printed black (due to either grating), the page will be black. Viewed the other way, it's only white where both gratings are white. We can find the white regions by simply taking the logical AND of gratings p_1 and p_2, producing the new pattern p_M. Notice that the black regions get wider as you scan from left to right, then narrower again. This composite pattern returns to where it started after one full cycle, which takes up a distance G.

Figure 9.2
(a) Grating p_1.
(b) Grating p_2.
(c) A moiré pattern created by pure extension by simply overlaying p_1 and p_2.

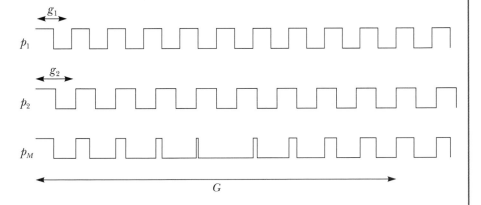

Figure 9.3
The two gratings of Figure 9.2 are shown in schematic form. The period of the resulting moiré pattern is G.

The cycle repeats when p_1 takes one more cycle than p_2. In symbols,

$$G = ng_2 = (n + 1)g_1$$

By noting that $1/g_2 = n/G$ and $1/g_1 = (n+1)/G$, we can eliminate n and write

$$\frac{1}{G} = \frac{1}{g_1} - \frac{1}{g_2}$$

Often it's convenient to speak of frequency rather than length of the cycles (or waves). Conventionally, frequency f is the inverse of wavelength. Let's suppose that we have some nice system of units, so that for any given grating pitch g, the corresponding frequency f is simply $1/g$. So we could write this equation equivalently as

$$F = f_1 - f_2$$

We've found that the frequency of the repeating black bars is simply the difference in the frequencies of the two gratings.

AMPLIFICATION

Now suppose that we move one of the gratings with respect to the other. What happens to the black bars? Well, we know that the distance between them doesn't change, since that depends only on the difference in the pitches (or the frequencies). But does the position of the bars move?

Suppose that grating p_2 is moved by some integer multiple of its pitch g_2. Then everything lines up exactly as before, and there's no change. But suppose that p_2 is moved to the right by $g_2/2$. Intuitively, we would expect that the fringes would move half their separation, or $G/2$. Similarly, if we move p_2 to the right by $g_2/4$, we'd expect the bars to move to the right by $G/4$. This is in fact exactly what happens, as illustrated by Figure 9.4.

This phenomenon of *fringe amplification* simply comes about because everything is linear—moving the grating some distance between its bars moves the moiré fringes by a similar amount. In symbols, if we move grating p_2 by a distance δ, the moiré pattern moves by a distance Δ, which is simply δ scaled by the ratios of the two patterns:

$$\Delta = \delta\left(\frac{G}{g_2}\right)$$

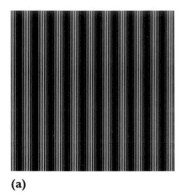

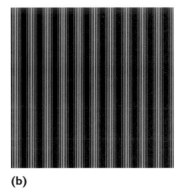

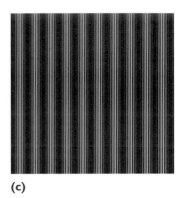

(a)   **(b)**   **(c)**

The term *amplification* here refers to the large movement of the fringes in response to the smaller movement of the underlying grating.

ROTATION

Let's return to our original two gratings, p_1 and p_2, with equal ratios and slightly different pitches. This time we'll superimpose them so that they're slightly tilted with respect to each other. To make things easy, we'll assume that the lines of p_1 are vertical and the lines of p_2 are nearly vertical; say they're within about 10 degrees of vertical. What happens?

Figure 9.5 shows the answer. The fringes reappear as black bars with spikes on their side, separated by white rhombuses. If you squint, the individual lines of the gratings disappear, and all you see are the thick bars of the fringes themselves. In practice, this is often the case—the gratings are all but invisible, but the moiré fringes reveal their relationship.

What is the pitch of these new fringes, created by pure rotation? The geometry of this pattern is shown in close-up in Figure 9.6. Each white space is a parallelogram whose dimensions are dictated by the pitches and ratios of the gratings and the angle θ between them. We will assume that both

Figure 9.4
The same gratings of Figure 9.2.
(a) The gratings are aligned at the left.
(b) Grating p_2 has been translated a distance $g_2/4$.
(c) Grating p_2 has been translated a distance $g_2/2$.

Figure 9.5
(a) A vertical grating.
(b) A slanted grating.
(c) The moiré fringes resulting from the overlay of the two.

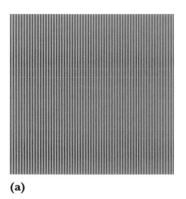

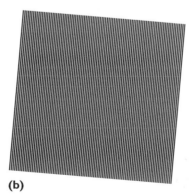

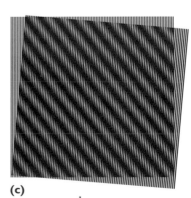

(a)   **(b)**   **(c)**

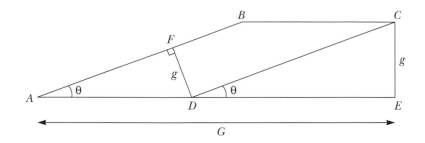

Figure 9.6
The geometry of a white parallelogram from Figure 9.5.

gratings have the same pitch g and the lines are very thin, so the black-to-white ratio R is nearly 0.

The parallelogram $ABCD$ is the white region; E is the point of intersection of line AD and the line through C perpendicular to BC. We know that distance CE is the pitch g. We know that $\tan \theta = (CE)/(DE)$, so distance $DE = g/\tan \theta$. If we erect a perpendicular on line AB such that it passes through D, the distance FD is also g (this is because it's the space created by the second grating). Since AD is the hypotenuse of right triangle $\triangle ADF$, we can see $g = AD \sin \theta$, or $AD = g/\sin \theta$. So the pitch of the fringe, G, is given by

$$G = (AD) + (DE) = \frac{g}{\sin \theta} + \frac{g}{\tan \theta} = g \left(\frac{1}{\sin \theta} + \frac{\cos \theta}{\sin \theta} \right)$$
$$= g(1 + \cos \theta)/\sin \theta$$

Now we assumed that the lines were very thin, but that doesn't change the analysis. If the lines get thicker, the parallelogram formed by the white space will get smaller, but the pitch G won't be changed.

However, if we're willing to assume that the angle θ is small and that the ratio is 1, we can make some simplifications. Figure 9.7 shows the reduced geometry. Since θ is small, we can pretend that the line BD is almost vertical (that is, perpendicular to both AD and BC).

Figure 9.7
Simplified geometry of Figure 9.6 for small angles.

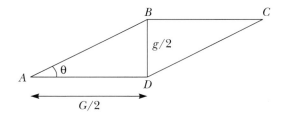

Then we can observe that $BD = g/2$ and $AD = G/2$, and write

$$\tan \theta = BD/AD = (g/2)/(G/2) = g/G$$

For small angles, $\tan \theta \approx \theta$, so using this and solving for G we find

$$G = g/\theta$$

which is the standard formula for the moiré pitch G for small rotation θ. In terms of frequency,

$$F = f\theta$$

which tells us that the fringes get closer together (and thus harder to resolve) as the angle gets larger. This argues for using smaller angles. But as we decrease the angle, the fringes can get very far apart. In practice, picking the right angle and the right pitches of the gratings is critical to getting useful results.

FRINGE SHARPENING

The fringes in Figure 9.5 are clear, but they're quite wide. It might be easier to locate their centers if the fringes were narrower. We can make this happen with a technique called *fringe sharpening*.

It's actually quite simple to sharpen the fringes. Think about their appearance for a second: the black fringe comes about when the two gratings are atop one another, and the long spikes are caused by the angled grating cutting across the white gaps in the vertical grating. If we keep the same pitch in the angled grating but make the black bars thinner (that is, we decrease the ratio), we will decrease the width of the spikes. At the same time, increasing the thickness (or ratio) of the vertical grating increases the area of the overlaps, strengthening the fringes.

The sweet spot occurs when the ratios are reciprocals of each other:

$$R_2 = 1/R_1$$

Figure 9.8 shows an example of fringe sharpening in the case of pure rotation.

Figure 9.8
Fringe sharpening.
(a) Original ratios.
(b) Reciprocal
ratios.

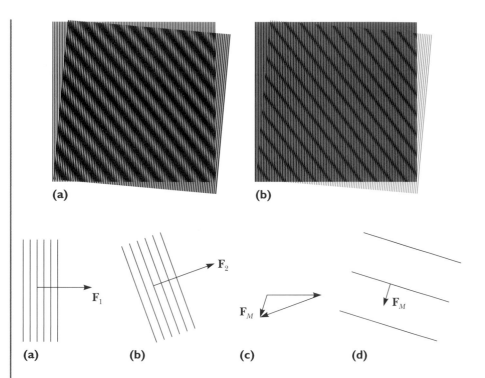

Figure 9.9
(a) Grating p_1 and
its vector $\mathbf{F}_1$.
(b) Grating p_2 and
its vector $\mathbf{F}_2$.
(c) Vector addition:
$\mathbf{F}_M = \mathbf{F}_1 - \mathbf{F}_2$.
(d) The resulting
moiré grating gen-
erated by $\mathbf{F}_M$.

VECTOR ADDITION

Another way to find the direction and interfringe distance of the moiré fringes is to use a little bit of vector addition. For each of our gratings, we can create a vector whose magnitude is equal to the frequency and whose direction is perpendicular to the lines of the grating. Figure 9.9 shows the idea where vectors $\mathbf{F}_1$ and $\mathbf{F}_2$ are built from gratings p_1 and p_2.

Then the resulting moiré fringes that we've been looking at are character-ized simply by a new vector $\mathbf{F}_M$, given by

$$\mathbf{F}_M = \mathbf{F}_1 - \mathbf{F}_2$$

Note that this short vector indicates a larger gap between the fringes than between black bars in the original gratings, which is the same phenome-non we've been seeing all along.

Grids, Dots, and Circles

So far, we've looked only at gratings, which are sheets of parallel lines. We've all seen moiré patterns created by wire meshes, which are simply two sets of gratings at right angles to one another. Everything that we've done

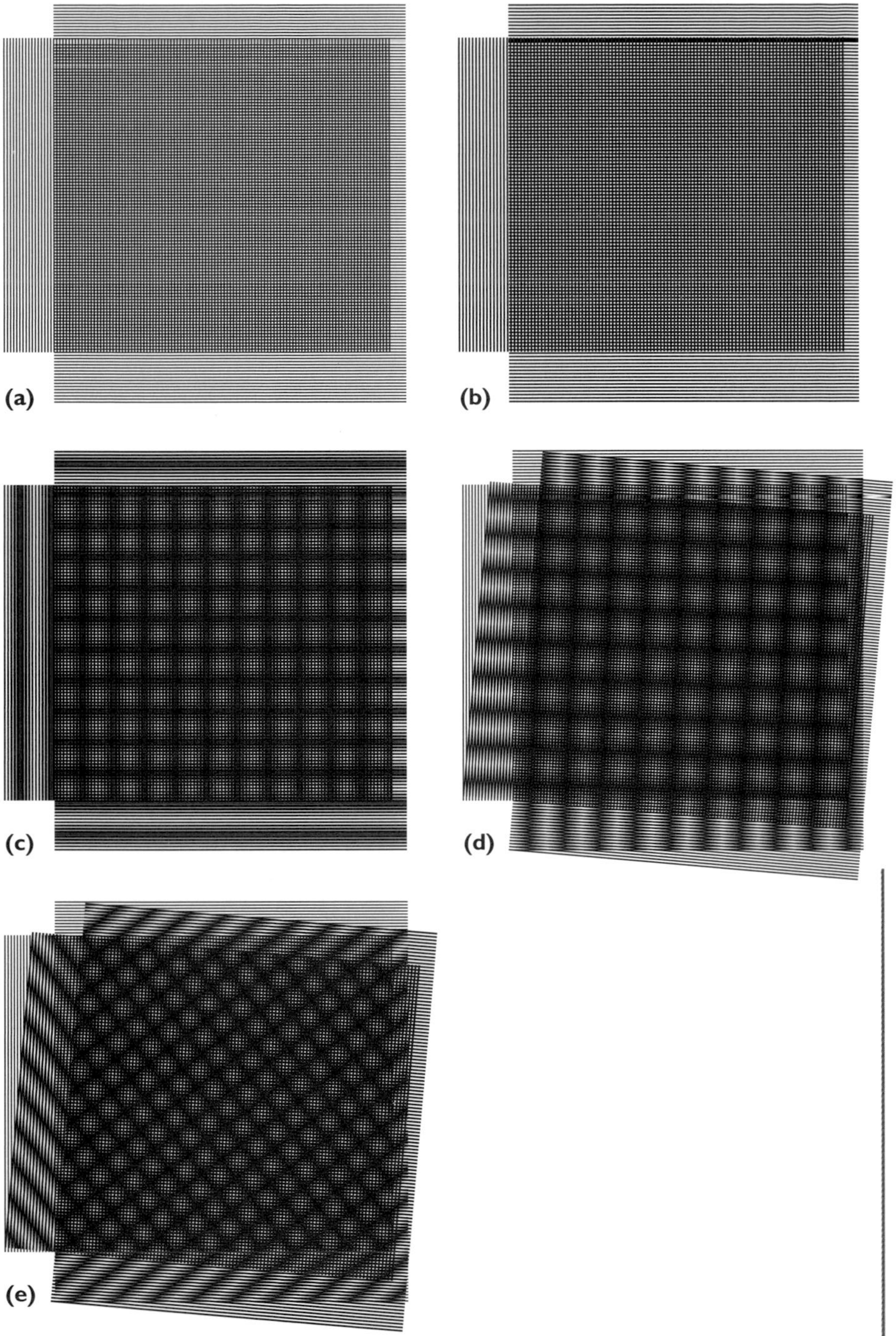

Figure 9.10
(a) Grid p_1.
(b) Grid p_2.
(c) Pure extension of the two overlaid grids.
(d) Pure rotation: a copy of p_1 has been placed over itself, rotated by 5 degrees.
(e) Combined rotation and extension: p_2 rotated 5 degrees and placed over p_1.

Figure 9.11
The same sequence
as Figure 9.10, only
using grids of dots.

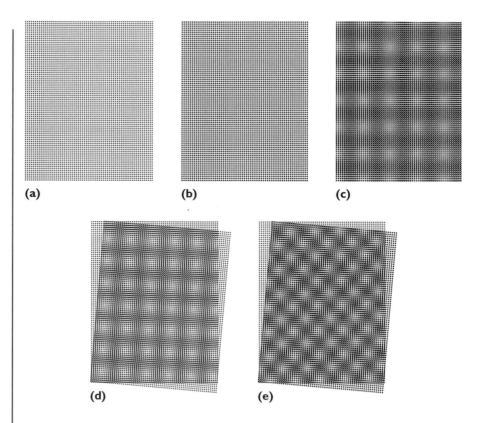

(a)   **(b)**   **(c)**

(d)   **(e)**

for gratings can be used to predict the interaction of two meshes (or grids), simply by superimposing the results. The fringes are much more interesting, though!

Figure 9.10 shows the result of two grids using pure extension, pure rotation, and combined extension and rotation. The two independent sets of gratings combine to produce the diamond fringes.

At the start of the chapter I mentioned that moiré patterns can pop up when the dot pattern of a scanner interacts with the dot pattern of a digitized photograph. Figure 9.11 shows our three canonical cases for two square patterns of dots. Of course, the dots are nothing but the points of intersection of the grid lines in the mesh case, so we would expect (and find) a lot of similarity between Figures 9.10 and 9.11.

A twist comes in when we start to work with nonlinear elements. Figure 9.12 shows the interaction of two circular gratings; here the pitch is the radial distance between the insides of two successive bands, or annuli. In Figure 9.12a I've overlapped two circular gratings with near-equal pitches over

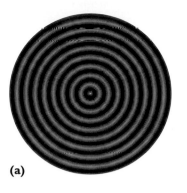
(a)

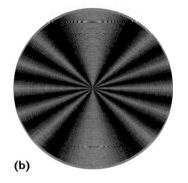
(b)

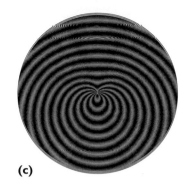
(c)

a common center. You can see the moiré fringes come and go just like the linear fringes in Figure 9.2. In Figure 9.12b I've used two circular patterns of the same pitch, but I've moved one of the circles with respect to the other. A very interesting set of curves arises. I suspect that there is a nice explicit formula for this family of curves, but I don't know what it is. Finally in Figure 9.12c I've combined the two effects, so the displaced second pattern also has a slightly different pitch.

Wrapping Up

We've only scratched the surface of moiré patterns here. It's interesting to look at the interaction of linear and circular patterns, elliptical patterns, and patterns of any other kind of geometry you'd like to invent. Once you get familiar with how to predict the effects of different patterns, you'll find that it's easy to create new ones on demand. You may also be able to cook up some strategies for removing moiré patterns in cases where they creep in uninvited.

Further Reading

Much of the material in this chapter comes from a book on moiré interferometry called *High Sensitivity Moiré* by Daniel Post, Bongtae Han, and Peter Ifju (Springer-Verlag, 1997).

Figure 9.12
Concentric circles.
(a) Different pitches (pure extension).
(b) Identical pitches, but offset centers.
(c) Different pitches and offset centers.

Upon Reflection

ANDREW GLASSNER'S NOTEBOOK

January/February 1998

10

In this chapter we'll take a look at the classic law of mirror reflection. As anyone who's written a ray tracer knows, this law tells us that the angle of incidence (the angle between the surface normal and the incoming light ray) equals the angle of reflection (the angle between the surface normal and the reflected light ray). It turns out that this little geometric truth can help solve another set of interesting problems called *billiard problems*, which describe the shortest path that can be taken by a billiard ball on a polygonal table.

We'll start out by looking at two different derivations of the law of reflection, one geometric and one analytic. It's always nice to see the same result come from two very different approaches. Then we'll look at the problem of finding the shortest circuit of a billiard ball around a triangular table. Before we get started, you might want to play around with pencil and paper and see if you can rederive the law of specular reflection yourself. You need to use only two laws of physics: in a vacuum, light will travel in a straight line unless interfered with, and light always seeks the shortest path.

The Geometric Approach

Figure 10.1 shows our basic setup. Light leaves a point P toward a mirror, represented by the line M, and ultimately arrives at point R. We want to

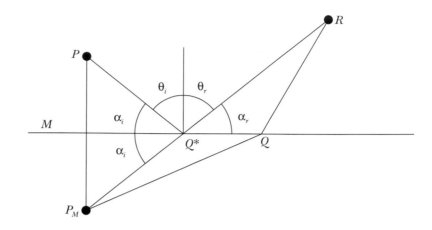

Figure 10.1
Light from *P* to *R*
bounces off of *M*
at some point *Q*.
The shortest path
is given when
Q = *Q**, located
on the line from P_M
to *R*.

find the point *Q* on *M* where the light does the bouncing; from that information we can deduce the law of reflection.

Are we ready to go? We know that three points determine a plane, so putting *P*, *Q*, and *R* all in the plane of the page seems reasonable. We'll use our straight-line law from above to prevent paths directly from *P* to *R*, though that might happen if *P* is radiating light directly along the line *PR*. Rather, we'll simply direct our attention to the path of light that actually does bounce off of *M* along the way.

There are a couple of subtleties we'll deliberately ignore. First, we'll stick completely with geometric optics—no wave effects such as diffraction will be considered. Second, we'll assume we're in a vacuum, so the index of refraction is a constant 1 everywhere. Finally, we'll assume that we haven't heard of Einstein yet, so light travels in perfectly straight lines all the time.

Now we're ready to search high and low, putting our point *Q* anywhere on *M*. The goal will be to find the placement of *Q* such that the time it takes the light to get from *P* to *Q* to *R* is minimized. Like water, light tries to find the quickest path from source to destination. So we want to find *Q* such that we minimize $|PQ| + |QR|$. In the figure, the angles θ_i and θ_r refer to the angles of incidence and reflection, and α_i and α_r refer to the complements of those angles.

We'll begin by creating point P_M, which is simply *P* reflected through *M*. Thus for all *Q* on *M*, $|P_M Q| = |PQ|$, and therefore $|PQ| + |QR| = |P_M Q| + |QR|$. So if we minimize the right-hand side of this equality, we also minimize the left.

We know from the triangle inequality that for any triangle with side lengths (a, b, c), $a + b \geq c$, achieving equality only when a, b, and c are colinear and in that order. So in ΔRQP_M, we can say $\left|P_M Q\right| + \left|QR\right| \geq \left|P_M R\right|$. As long as they're not colinear, the sum of the two steps from P_M to Q to R will be longer than the straight shot from P_M to R. Since P_M and R are both fixed, the only way to adjust the path is to move Q, and the shortest path is created when it's placed at that point on M that intersects the line $P_M R$.

So we now have the intersection of two lines, M and $P_M R$, which meet at Q. Thus $\alpha_i = \alpha_r$, therefore $\theta_i = \theta_r$, and we've proved the law of specular reflection.

The Algebraic Approach

We begin the algebraic solution by making two definitions. First, the *optical path length* (OPL) is the time it takes a photon to get from one point to another. Since in our simplified world we're in a vacuum, the OPL is simply the distance multiplied by the speed of light. For convenience, we'll ignore the speed of light since it's just a constant scaling factor (or we could say we're using a system of units where the speed of light is defined to be 1). Second, a *stationary point* in a 1D function is a point where the function has a derivative of 0; that is, the tangent is parallel to the X axis. As shown in Figure 10.2, that can be at a local maximum, a local minimum, or a flat spot.

One of the contributions to physics made by Pierre de Fermat was the proposal that a ray of light follows a path that corresponds to a stationary value in its OPL. In other words, if we look at a proposed candidate for the path taken by a ray of light, we should find that any other candidate path nearby

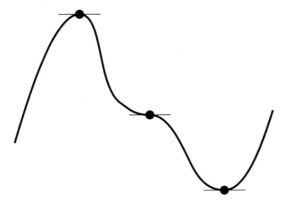

Figure 10.2
The black dots mark stationary points—locations where the function has a zero derivative.

Figure 10.3
Geometry for an
analytic solution of
specular reflection.

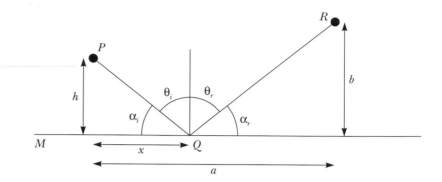

takes the same amount of time or more. You might enjoy thinking of a physical situation where a number of different rays of light all take the same time to get from one point to another.

Figure 10.3 shows the same geometry as in Figure 10.1, but I've relabeled some of the distances to make the calculations easier. The OPL is simply the sum of the distances:

$$\text{OPL} = |PQ| + |QR|$$
$$= \sqrt{h^2 + x^2} + \sqrt{b^2 + (a-x)^2}$$

To find the stationary points, we differentiate this with respect to x and set the result to 0:

$$\frac{d(\text{OPL})}{dx} = \frac{x}{\sqrt{h^2 + x^2}} - \frac{(a-x)}{\sqrt{b^2 + (a-x)^2}} = 0$$

From Figure 10.3, we can see that

$$\sin(\theta_i) = \frac{x}{\sqrt{h^2 + x^2}}, \text{ and } \sin(\theta_r) = \frac{a-x}{\sqrt{b^2 + (a-x)^2}}$$

Making these substitutions, we find

$$0 = \sin(\theta_i) - \sin(\theta_r)$$

or more simply, $\theta_i = \theta_r$, and we've come to the same conclusion.

Now that we're pretty much settled the law of specular reflection, we can prove a pretty little theorem about minimum inscribed polygons and billiard tables.

A Trio of Useful Observations

Before we plunge into the land of billiard balls, we'll make three observations that will make life easier later on. If you're geometrically inclined, these are probably old hat to you.

First, we note that any triangle inscribed in a semicircle has a right angle. Figure 10.4 shows what I'm talking about, using a triangle $\triangle ABC$ in a semicircle of radius r, or diameter $d = 2r$. Points A and C are at opposite ends of the diameter, and B is on the circle.

There are lots of ways to prove this. Let's use an algebraic proof. Assume the circle is centered at $(0, 0)$. Then $A = (-r, 0)$, $C = (r, 0)$, and $B = (x, y)$, where $r^2 = x^2 + y^2$, since B lies on the circle. Let's find the distance AC by assuming that angle $\angle ABC$ is a right angle (for the rest of this chapter, when there's only one angle at a vertex I'll write that vertex as an angle; so $\angle B$ here stands for $\angle ABC$). If $|AC|^2 = |AB|^2 + |BC|^2$, then Pythagoras is satisfied and $\angle B$ is a right angle.

We can prove this is so just by writing everything out and simplifying:

$$|AC|^2 = |AB|^2 + |BC|^2$$
$$= (r + x)^2 + y^2 + (r - x)^2 + y^2$$
$$= 2((x^2 + y^2) + r^2) = 4r^2$$

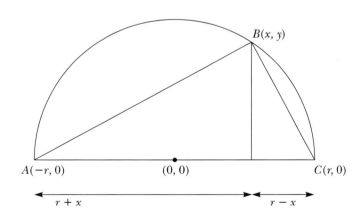

Figure 10.4
Because $\triangle ABC$ is inscribed in a semicircle, $\angle ABC$ is a right angle.

Taking the square root of both sides, $|AC| = 2r$, and therefore $\angle B$ is a right angle. When several points lie on a circle, such as A, B, and C in this example, we call them *concyclic*.

Second, an observation comes up when we reflect a point two times. If we reflect a point once, such as when we reflected P to P_M through the line M in Figure 10.2, we can say that P_M (the image of P as a result of reflecting through M) could have been created by simply translating P by the vector $P_M - P$. What happens if we create P_{LM} by reflecting P a second time through a different line, say L, that is not parallel to M?

Figure 10.5
The product of two reflections in intersecting lines is equivalent to a rotation through their point of intersection by twice the angle between the lines.

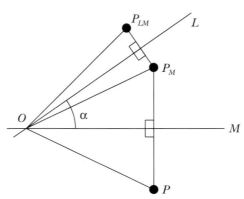

Figure 10.5 shows the situation. The result is that if the angle from M to L is α, then P_{LM} can be created either by translation of P (which isn't too interesting) or by rotation of P through an angle 2α, using the intersection point of L and M (labeled O) as the center of rotation.

There are lots of nice proofs of this, which is only one of the many pretty results that come from looking at isometries in the plane. However, we'll simply let Figure 10.5 speak for itself. There are two triangles, each cut into two equal halves. Since the sum of one of the halves from each is α, the other halves are also α, totalling 2α. If you like, you can consider cases where L and M are parallel, or where P starts inside their acute angle, or where P_M appears on the other side of M, and so on. You'll find that when L and M are parallel, the point P is translated along a vector perpendicular to them; when L and M intersect, the result is always a rotation of 2α around their intersection point.

Third, we will want to know that all inscribed angles that contain a common chord are equal. An *inscribed angle* is just a pair of lines that intersect at a point on a circle and contain a chord on that circle, as in Figure 10.6a. By comparison, a *central angle* is created by a pair of radii that contain a chord. We want to show that in this figure, if we keep the A and B fixed, the inscribed angle $\angle AJB$ is the same no matter where on the circle we place J (as long as it's outside the arc AB).

Let's really nail this one down. The approach I'll take is to prove that an inscribed angle is always half as large as the central angle that inscribes the same arc (or chord). Since there's only one central angle for any arc, this means that all the inscribed angles that contain that arc have the same size. The special case comes when the chord is a diameter, and that's exactly the case we just handled above.

To be very careful, I'll make sure to consider all the places J can go. This turns out to demand three cases, based on where the circle's center C falls with respect to the triangle $\triangle AJB$.

In case 1, illustrated in Figure 10.6b, C falls on the line JA. Note that since CJ and CB are radii, $\triangle BCJ$ is isosceles, and $\angle CJB = \angle CBJ$. Since ACJ is a diameter of the circle, $\angle ACB = \pi - \angle BCJ$. From $\triangle BCJ$, we find that $\pi - \angle BCJ = \angle CJB + \angle JBC$. Putting these together, $\angle ACB = \angle CJB + \angle JBC = 2\angle CJB = 2\angle AJB$, just as we hoped. In words, the central angle $\angle ACB$ is

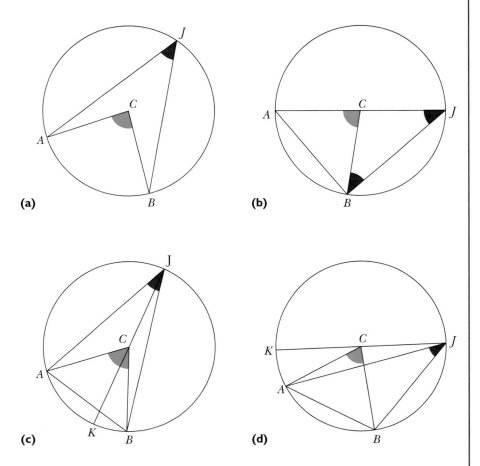

(a)

(b)

(c)

(d)

Figure 10.6
(a) The central angle (blue) is always twice the inscribed angle (red).
(b) Case 1: When the circle center C lies on the line AJ.
(c) Case 2: When C is inside $\triangle AJB$.
(d) Case 3: When C is outside $\triangle AJB$.

twice the measure of the inscribed angle $\angle AJB$. How about when J is located somewhere else?

In case 2, illustrated in Figure 10.6c, J is not on line CA, but point C is inside the triangle $\triangle AJB$. I'll use case 1 to figure things out, so I'll include the diameter from J through C; its other intersection with the circle is at K. The diameter JK cuts everything into two halves, each of which looks like case 1. On the A side, we find from case 1 that $\angle ACK = 2\angle AJK$. On the B side, $\angle KCB = 2\angle KJB$. Now the central angle $\angle ACB = \angle ACK + \angle KCB = 2(\angle AJK + \angle KJB) = 2\angle AJB$. So again we've found $\angle ACB = 2\angle AJB$.

Finally, case 3 is illustrated in Figure 10.6d, where J is not on line CA and point C is not in the triangle $\triangle AJB$. As before, we'll draw the diameter from J through C, creating point K. We can see that $\angle ACB = \angle KCB - \angle KCA$. These two right-hand-side angles are easily found from case 1. $\angle KCB = 2\angle KJB$ (where the enclosed arc is BK). And $\angle KCA = 2\angle KJA$. Subtracting these, $\angle ACB = 2(\angle KJB - \angle KJA) = 2\angle AJB$.

That wraps up the proof. So no matter where we put the vertex of an inscribed angle, it always has the same size, which is twice the size of the corresponding central angle.

Playing Billiards

When you bounce a billiard ball off a bumper, you expect the same sort of result as the ray of light we studied above: the reflection should be a perfect mirror reflection.

Let's ask the following question: what is the shortest path that a billiard ball can take, such that it bounces off of each table wall and returns to its starting point traveling in the same direction in which it started? If you're willing to discount friction, we could say that we want the ball to come back with the same position and velocity as when it started, so it could repeat the same circuit over and over forever. For simplicity, we'll use an acute triangular table in this discussion. At the end I'll mention what happens when we generalize our results to tables with more sides, or obtuse angles. Our answer will come from studying the reflections of the ball as it bounces around. The technique of the proof was developed by H. Schwarz, who lived from 1843 to 1921.

Let's begin with $\triangle ABC$ as shown in Figure 10.7. Since we want one complete cycle, we'll say that the ball follows the inscribed triangle $\triangle PQR$. The point P lies strictly within edge BC—that is, it is on the line between those points and not right on top of either vertex. Similarly, Q is inscribed in edge AB and R in edge AC. Just where should these points lie?

To get started, let's assume that we've already found the ideal locations for P and Q. We might expect that the shortest path from P to Q via line AC would come from similar reasoning that we used to find the shortest path of light above. This would come from placing R so that it forms a perfect mirror reflection from P to Q. We would expect the same property from P and Q as well.

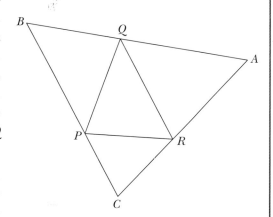

Figure 10.7
A triangle $\triangle ABC$ and an inscribed triangle $\triangle PQR$.

That's a nice intuitive start, but hardly a proof. If we're willing to commit to this line of reasoning, we have to answer two questions: Can we in fact construct a triangle that creates a perfect specular reflection at each edge? And is that in fact the shortest path that forms a repeating circuit? We'll take these two questions—existence and optimality—in turn. First, we'll analyze the construction of $\triangle PQR$ to see if we can in fact make the beast. If we can, we'll have created what is called a *light polygon* (in this case a light triangle), because of its close relation to the reflection of light.

Questions of Existence

If you'd like, you can take a break here and try to devise a construction scheme for making a light triangle $\triangle PQR$. I'll cut to the chase and propose a method, then show that it works.

The proposed technique is pretty simple: P, Q, and R are the feet of the altitudes of $\triangle ABC$. Recall that the altitudes are the perpendiculars of each edge that pass through the opposite vertex, as shown in Figure 10.8. The three altitudes meet at point H, called the *orthocenter*. Our goal is to show that these points form a light triangle with respect to the outer triangle $\triangle ABC$. This means that each pair of edges supports the mirror-reflection law. In Figure 10.9, I've indicated this with colored dots—each pair of angles that shares a similarly colored dot should be the same size. I'll now

Figure 10.8
The green triangle
△PQR is formed by
the altitudes of
△ABC.

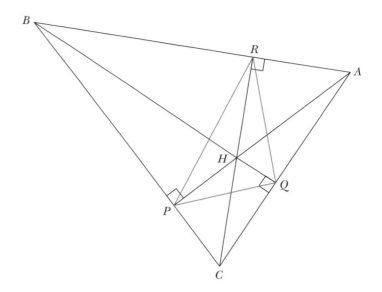

focus exclusively on point *R*, where θ*ᵢ* = ∠*QRH* and θ*ᵣ* = ∠*HRP*. So showing θ*ᵢ* = θ*ᵣ* requires showing ∠*QRH* = ∠*HRP*.

No problem. We'll do this in three steps, as shown in Figure 10.10. First,
we'll show that ∠*QRH* = ∠*QAH* (the red wedges), then ∠*QAH* = ∠*HBP*
(the green bands), and then ∠*HBP* = ∠*HRP* (the lavender wedges).
Putting these together, ∠*QRH* = ∠*QAH* = ∠*HBP* = ∠*HRP*, so ∠*QRH* =
∠*HRP*, which will conclude the proof.

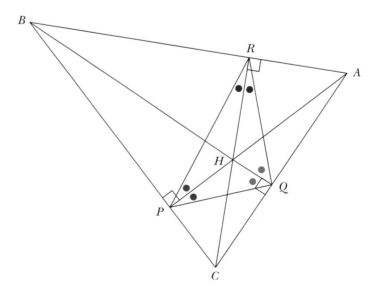

Figure 10.9
If △*PQR* is a light
triangle, then each
pair of like-colored
angles is equal.

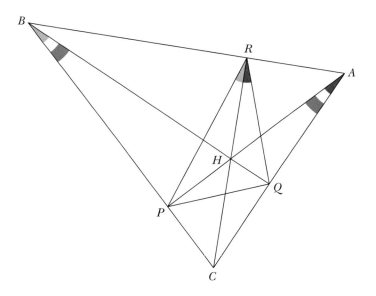

Figure 10.10
The proof strategy
for showing that
ΔPQR is a light
triangle. Step 1
(red wedges):
∠QRH = ∠QAH.
Step 2 (green
bands):
∠QAH = ∠HBP.
Step 3 (lavender
wedges):
∠HBP = ∠HRP.
Thus ∠QRH =
∠HRP.

For the first step, we note that Q, H, R, and A are concyclic—they all lie on a circle, as shown in Figure 10.11. Think of AH as the diameter of a circle; since $\angle AQH$ is a right angle, we know that Q lies on that circle. Similarly, R lies on the same circle, since it has the same diameter and $\angle ARH$ is also a right angle. Note that $\angle QRH$ forms an inscribed angle enclosing the chord QH, and $\angle QAH$ does the same. As we saw above, this means the angles are equal: $\angle QRH = \angle QAH$.

Figure 10.11
Proving $\angle QRH =$
$\angle QAH$, since both
are inscribed in the
same circle and
both contain arc
QH.

Figure 10.12 shows the second step, involving $\triangle ACP$ and $\triangle BQC$. In $\triangle ACP$, since $\angle P$ is a right angle, $\angle CAP = \angle QAH$ is equal to $(\pi/2) - \angle C$. In $\triangle BQC$, $\angle Q$ is a right angle, so $\angle QBC = \angle HBP$ is equal to $(\pi/2) - \angle C$; that is, $\angle QBP$ is also the complement of $\angle C$. Thus $\angle QAH = \angle HBP$.

In step 3, we'll play the same game as in step 1. Note from Figure 10.13 that points P, H, R, and B are concyclic, since they share the common diameter BH, and $\angle BRH = \angle HPB = (\pi/2)$. And as before, we note that $\angle HRP = \angle HBP$, since they both contain the common chord HP. Therefore $\angle HBP = \angle HRP$.

Figure 10.12
Proving ∠QAH =
∠HBP, since both
△CAP and △CBQ
contain ∠C and a
right angle.

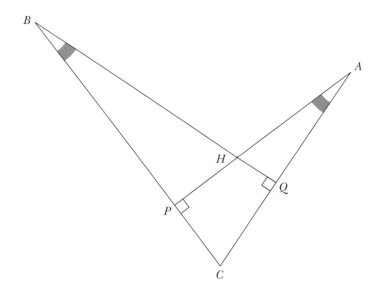

That's it! As promised this chain of reasoning has led to ∠QRH = ∠HRP, which was our goal. We have shown that if a billiard ball leaves Q and strikes R as we've constructed it, and then bounces just like light bounces off a mirror, the ball will travel to P. Since there was nothing special about our choice of R, the same argument goes through for the other two points. The complete set of relationships is shown in Figure 10.14. Thus △PQR is a light triangle for △ABC—we have proven that such a triangle indeed exists.

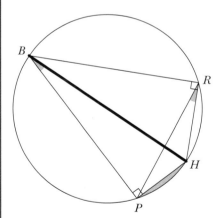

Figure 10.13
Proving ∠HBP =
∠HRP, since both
are inscribed in the
same circle and
both contain arc
HP.

Proving that it's the fastest route for the ball is another matter, but reflection will be our ally again in that proof.

Smaller Is Better

Now we want to show that △PQR is the smallest (or fastest) light triangle. Writing $p(\triangle PQR)$ to denote the perimeter of a triangle, we want to show that $p(\triangle PQR) \leq p(\triangle UVW)$ for any other light triangle △UVW. In fact, we can prove something even stronger: △PQR has the smallest perimeter of

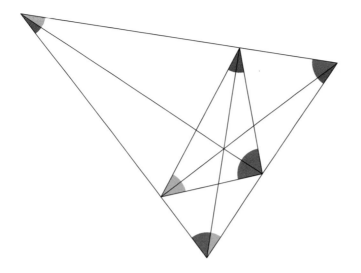

Figure 10.14
The light triangle and its relationship to the triangle it's inscribed in. All angles with the same color are equal.

any triangle inscribed in $\triangle ABC$, whether it's a light triangle or not. This is actually even a little easier to prove, since we don't have to prove that our contender $\triangle UVW$ is a light triangle.

Let's begin with our original triangle $\triangle ABC$ and our light triangle $\triangle PQR$, as shown in Figure 10.15. Here we've also drawn some other triangle $\triangle UVW$. We won't say anything specific about $\triangle UVW$ except that it's inscribed in $\triangle ABC$. We'll now show that the perimeter of $\triangle UVW$ will always be larger than the perimeter of $\triangle PQR$, unless they're the same triangle.

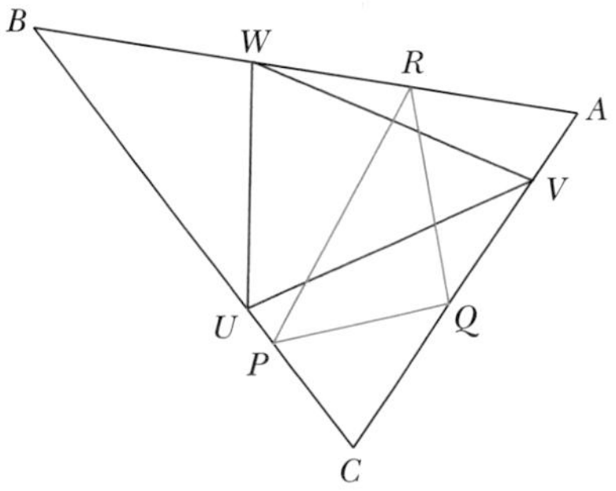

Figure 10.15
Our original triangle $\triangle ABC$, the light triangle $\triangle PQR$ in green, and a possible shorter inscribed triangle $\triangle UVW$ in red.

First, we'll reflect $\triangle ABC$ through side AC, as in Figure 10.16. I'll use superscripts to refer to the images of points after reflection. So A and C stay fixed, but B flips to B^1. Note that P, Q, and R^1 are colinear, as are R, Q, and P^1, because of equal angles at AC. In general, U, V, and W^1 will not be colinear, nor will W, V, and U^1.

Now we'll reflect the new triangle $\triangle AB^1C$ through edge AB^1, creating $\triangle AB^1C^2$. Continuing, we'll reflect through B^1C^2, then C^2A^3, and finally through A^3B^4, giving us the chain shown in Figure 10.17.

Figure 10.16
Reflecting △*ABC*
around edge *AC* re-
sults in two
reflected inscribed
triangles.

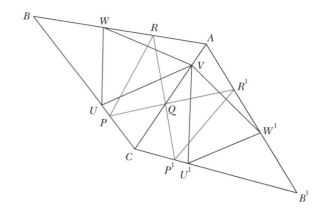

Figure 10.17
Reflecting △*ABC*
five times about
different edges cre-
ates the straight
polyline (P, P^5). Edge
B^4C^5 is parallel to
BC. Polyline (U, U^5)
will always be lon-
ger than (P, P^5).

We'll stop here after five reflections, because now edge B^4C^5 is parallel to its original position *BC*. To see this, consider that on the first reflection, edge *BC* is rotated around point *C* by a clockwise angle $2\angle C$. On the second reflection, it's rotated around point B^1 by the same amount. The third reflection is in B^1C^2 itself, so that edge stays fixed. Then that edge gets rotated by $-2\angle C$ around C^2 (that is, it's rotated counterclockwise), then again by another $-2\angle C$ around B^4. Adding these up, we find $\angle C(2 + 2 + 0 - 2 - 2) = 0$, so the total angle of rotation is 0 and B^4C^5 is now parallel again to *BC*.

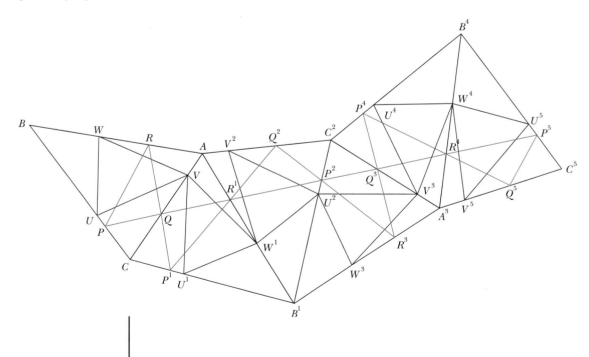

Consider the polyline P, Q, R^1, P^2, Q^3, R^4, P^5. This is equivalent to two copies of $\triangle PQR$ unfolded and straightened out. Each edge in $\triangle PQR$ is accounted for twice, so the length of this polyline, which we will denote as simply (P, P^5), is $|(P, P^5)| = 2p(\triangle PQR)$. Note that this polyline is in fact a straight line because of construction.

Now consider the polyline created by our potentially shorter triangle $\triangle UVW$. This polyline is given by U, V, W^1, U^2, V^3, W^4, U^5. Again we find that we have the three sides of $\triangle UVW$, each counted twice, so $|(U, U^5)| = 2p(\triangle UVW)$. Since BC and B^4C^5 are in the same orientation, U^5 is in the same relative position to P^5 as U is to P, so the straight line from U to U^5 is parallel to the straight line from P to P^5. Now we can ask if it's possible that $p(\triangle UVW) < p(\triangle PQR)$. Visually, the answer is clear from Figure 10.17: there's no path from U to U^5 shorter than the straight line from P to P^5. Writing $|(P, P^5)|$ for the length of the straight line from P to P^5, and similarly for $|(U, U^5)|$, we summarize this as

$$|(U, U^5)| = 2p(\triangle UVW) \geq |U, U^5| = |(P, P^5)| = 2p(\triangle QPR)$$

So the perimeter of $\triangle UVW$ will always be greater than that of $\triangle PQR$, except when they're the same triangle (and then of course they have the same lengths).

We can see from Figure 10.17 that $\triangle PQR$ is the only triangle that can be reflected five times and have its pieces lie on a straight line from P to P^5; any other triangle will necessarily have kinks in the path, and this will make it longer. Thus we have proven that $\triangle PQR$ is a light triangle, and that this light triangle has the smallest perimeter of any inscribed triangle.

More of Everything

The next step is to think about generalizing this approach to polygons with obtuse angles, or more than three sides. It turns out things get rather more complicated. I'll summarize the results here; you can find proofs in the references in the Further Reading section.

Let's begin with obtuse angles. Suppose $\triangle ABC$ has an obtuse angle at A (that is, $\angle A$ is more than 90 degrees). Clearly the other two angles must be acute. The minimum-perimeter inscribed polygon has one vertex at the foot of the altitude from A through BC and the other two vertices at A itself.

This is a little unfortunate. First, this degenerate triangle hardly seems like a triangle at all. Secondly, it's not strictly inscribed, since at least one (and in fact two) of the vertices do not lie strictly on an edge of the original triangle. And finally it brings up the question of what happens when a ball strikes the vertex of a polygon—after all, there's no well-defined normal or tangent plane there, even though we fake one all the time in graphics to do smooth shading on polygons.

Mathematicians shrug off this problem of reflection at a vertex by basically defining it away—the general idea is that it happens infrequently enough that it can be ignored when studying the larger problem of general billiard trajectories. After all, to hit the vertex exactly right you have to hit that point exactly, which is likely to be pretty infrequent. Even if you think of real balls on real tables, it's going to be rare that a ball will strike two sides of the table at precisely the same moment. Of course, that doesn't answer the question of what happens at such an occurrence, but it allows you to look the other way for a while without feeling that you've left a big hole in your theory.

What if you have more than three sides to your polygon? Here are a few things that are true of billiard trajectories in general. Any convex polygon has a least-perimeter inscribed polygon, which may contain vertices of the original polygon. Any strictly inscribed least-perimeter polygon is a light polygon. Conversely, any light polygon has the minimum perimeter of any strictly inscribed polygon.

If your convex polygon has an odd number of sides, then there is a unique minimum-perimeter inscribed polygon, and if that polygon is strictly inscribed, it is a light polygon. So break out the heptagonal tables! On the other hand, if your convex polygon has an even number of sides, and it has at least one light polygon, then it will have an infinite number of light polygons. There are some necessary and sufficient conditions that you can check to see if you have any (and thus an infinite number) of light polygons, but they're too complicated for us to cover here.

The billiard-ball problem is not completely solved in general. Suppose you're playing billiards on a circular or elliptical table, or one shaped like a lima bean or the letter R. Can you always find a starting point and trajectory such that the ball will return to the same point and trajectory? When such starting conditions exist, can you actually find them?

Further Reading

The billiards discussion here was based on the presentation of that method by Dan Pedoe in *Geometry* (Dover Publications, 1988). You can find more information on the method there. You can also find proofs of the billiard theorems, and some starting points on related theorems, in *Geometry I* by M. Berger (Springer-Verlag, 1987).

Circular Reasoning

ANDREW GLASSNER'S NOTEBOOK
March/April 1998

11

Here I'll talk about two interesting relationships between circles and lines. The first topic is a pretty simple but cool property, and I suspect there's a computer graphics application out there that can use this to run faster or better. The second topic is Ptolemy's theorem, which is a generalization of the triangle inequality. I'll show how it can be used to derive the angle-addition formulas (which I always forget). Then I'll extend Chapter 10's topic of reflection and show how Ptolemy's theorem can be used to prove that Snell's law and Fermat's principle of least time both lead to the same geometry of refraction.

Ptolemy's theorem is an elegant little relationship that does for quadrilaterals what Pythagoras' theorem does for triangles. It's not much more complicated to prove and just as easy to apply.

Circular Powers

We'll begin with an important property of lines and circles that I haven't seen mentioned before in the graphics literature. Figure 11.1 sets the stage: we have a circle with center C and radius r, a point P not on the circle, and a line s through P that intersects the circle at points Q and R. We'll write $C_r(P)$ for the value of point P in the implicit formula for the circle.

Figure 11.1
The circle (C, r)
and a point P. The
line s through P in-
tersects the circle
at Q and R.

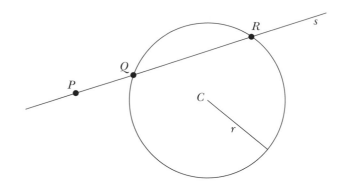

I'll demonstrate the remarkable fact that $C_r(P)$ is the product of the distances $|PQ|$ and $|PR|$; in symbols, $C_r(P) = |PQ||PR|$.

To see this, we only need to write out the standard intersection of a ray and circle—this is the familiar algebra that appears in every ray-tracing program. I'll use vector notation for two reasons. The first reason is that it's a lot less messy than writing out all the coefficients. The second reason is sneaky, as you'll discover in a moment. Writing out the value of the circle at an arbitrary point A, its value $C_r(A)$ may be written in vector notation as

$$C_r(A) = (A - C) \cdot (A - C) - r^2$$
$$= A \cdot A - 2C \cdot A + C \cdot C - r^2$$

We'll write the line s as a parameterized ray with origin P and direction vector $\mathbf{V} = (Q - P)$. This means that points L on s are given by various values of t in the formula $L = P + \mathbf{V}t$. Plugging this into the circle equation to find $C_r(P + \mathbf{V}t)$ and then gathering terms of t, we find

$$0 = (P + \mathbf{V}t) \cdot (P + \mathbf{V}t) - 2C \cdot (P + \mathbf{V}t) + (C \cdot C) - r^2$$
$$0 = t^2(\mathbf{V} \cdot \mathbf{V}) + t[2\mathbf{V} \cdot (P - C)] + [(P - C) \cdot (P - C) - r^2]$$
$$0 = at^2 + bt + c$$

The roots t_0 and t_1 of this quadratic equation are the values of t that generate points where the ray intersects the sphere. Let's find the product p of the two roots; this will come in handy in a moment. Writing d for the discriminant $d = \sqrt{b^2 - 4ac}$, we find

$$p = t_0 t_1 = \left(\frac{-b + d}{2a}\right)\left(\frac{-b - d}{2a}\right) = \frac{b^2 - d^2}{4a^2}$$

If we plug in the value for d, expand, and simplify, we find

$$p = \frac{b^2 - (b^2 - 4ac)}{4a^2} = \frac{c}{a}$$

This is a nice general relationship to keep in mind for quadratic equations.

Now back to business. Let's assume that our direction vector $\mathbf{V}$ is normalized, so $\mathbf{V} = (Q - P)/|Q - P|$. This means that the values of t corresponding to the roots of the equation are exactly the same as the distances from P to Q and P to R. That is, if t_0 and t_1 are the two roots (and t_0 is the lesser one), $t_0 = |PQ|$, and $t_1 = |PR|$. Since $\mathbf{V} = 1$, then $a = \mathbf{V} \cdot \mathbf{V} = 1$, and thus $p = c/a = c$. Using our value of c from the quadratic formula above,

$$p = t_0 t_1 = c = (P - C) \cdot (P - C) - r^2$$

which is simply $C_r(P)$, the value of point P in the circle equation!

So we have proven that the product of the distances is the same as the value of P in the circle's equation; that is, $C_r(P) = |PQ||PR|$, as promised. Notice that nowhere did we actually use the fact that we were in 2D. The vector notation that I used doesn't care how many dimensions we're in. That's the sneaky reason I used vectors—I was working with lines and circles in the plane, but the result is equally true for lines and spheres in space.

Ptolemy's Theorem for Cyclic Quadrilaterals

Our second topic is Ptolemy's theorem. Claudius Ptolemy (AD ~87–150) was an astronomer, mathematician, and geographer who lived in Alexandria, Greece. He wrote an early atlas, remarkable for the fact that not only did he describe the places listed, but he also included their latitude and longitude. His other major work was a set of books called *The Mathematical Collection*. This was later translated into Arabic where it was titled *Al Magiste*, or *The Greatest*. This title was later corrupted, and the books are now often called the *Almagest*.

The Almagest consisted of 13 books giving early algorithms for 2D geometry as well as an astronomical system for the motion of the stars and planets. The Sun and Moon had their orbits centered on Earth, while everything else revolved around those centers. Such geocentric systems remained popular until the Copernican Revolution in the sixteenth century.

Ptolemy also gave an approximate value of π as 377/120 ≈ 3.141666, which is accurate to one part in ten thousand—accurate enough to sail a ship for a few weeks and then find port by eye!

One of the still-influential pieces in the Almagest is a proof of what is now called *Ptolemy's theorem*. This can be considered an extension of the tri-

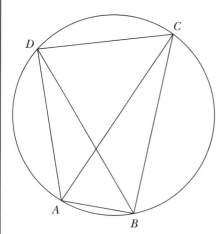

angle inequality. Recall that the triangle inequality states that for any three points *A*, *B*, and *C* in the plane, *AB* + *BC* ≥ *AC*. Ptolemy's theorem gives a similar result for *cyclic quadrilaterals*.

A cyclic quadrilateral is a figure created by four unique points on a circle. Figure 11.2 shows a generic cyclic quadrilateral, which I've labeled counterclockwise as *A*, *B*, *C*, *D*. Ptolemy's theorem says that if you multiply the lengths of opposite sides and add the products, this will equal the product of the diagonals. In fact, equality only holds if the points are on a circle (just as the triangle inequality is only equal when the points are colinear). We will stick with the cyclic equality version here.

Figure 11.2
A cyclic quadrilateral *ABCD*.

To prove Ptolemy's theorem, we'll create an additional point *K* on line *DB*, such that ∠*KCD* = ∠*BCA*, as in Figure 11.3. Without loss of generality, we will assume that *K* is closer to *D* than the intersection of *CA* and *DB*. We will find two sets of similar triangles to find the relations that lead to the

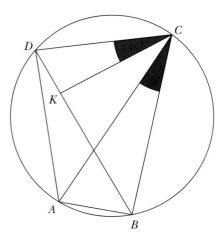

Figure 11.3
Point *K* is placed so that ∠*KCD* = ∠*BCA*.

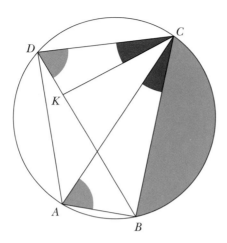

Figure 11.4
Both of the in-
scribed angles
∠CAB and ∠CDB
include arc BC;
therefore they are
equal.

theorem. We will use unsigned distances, so that $|DB| = |BD|$. Further-
more, to reduce clutter I will leave the vertical bars off of the distance measures. Unless I specifically refer to a pair of letters as something like "arc
AB," AB will mean $|AB|$.

We first observe that $\angle CAB$ and $\angle CDB$ are both inscribed angles that include arc BC, as in Figure 11.4. As we saw in Chapter 10, this means that
these two angles are equal. Thus, as shown in Figure 11.5, triangles $\triangle CAB$
and $\triangle CDK$ are similar, since both have two common angles. Because the
two triangles are similar, we can write

$$\frac{AC}{AB} = \frac{DC}{DK}$$

or $AC \cdot DK = AB \cdot DC = AB \cdot CD$.

For the second set of triangles, we note that $\angle BCA = \angle KCD$ by construction. Adding $\angle ACK$ to both, we have $\angle BCA + \angle ACK = \angle KCD + \angle ACK$,
or $\angle BCK = \angle ACD$, as shown in Figure 11.6. Furthermore, both $\angle DBC$ and
$\angle DAC$ are inscribed angles including arc CD, which means they are also
equal, as shown in Figure 11.7. And $\angle KBC = \angle DAC$. Thus triangles $\triangle BCK$

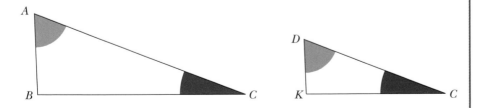

Figure 11.5
Similar triangles
$\triangle CAB$ and $\triangle CDK$.

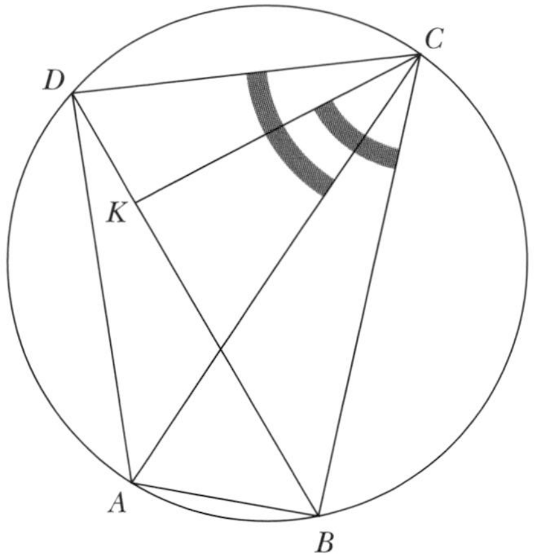

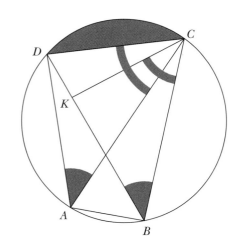

Figure 11.6
Equal angles ∠BCK
and ∠ACD.

Figure 11.7
Angles ∠DBC and
∠DAC are both in-
scribed and include
arc CD, so they are
equal.

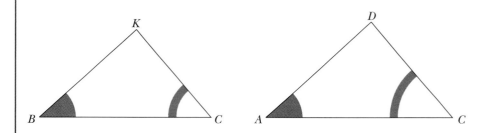

Figure 11.8
Similar triangles
△BCK and △ACD.

and $\triangle ACD$ are similar. Figure 11.8 shows them side by side. We can write a similar pair of ratios as last time:

$$\frac{BC}{BK} = \frac{AC}{AD}$$

or $AC \cdot BK = BC \cdot AD$. Now we'll add these two equalities together:

$$AC \cdot KD + AC \cdot BK = AB \cdot CD + BC \cdot AD$$
$$AC \cdot (KD + BK) = AB \cdot CD + BC \cdot AD$$
$$AC \cdot DB = AB \cdot CD + BC \cdot AD$$

This last line is the cyclic form of Ptolemy's theorem. As promised earlier, it tells us that for a cyclic quadrilateral, the product of the lengths of the diagonals is equal to the sum of the products of the lengths of opposite sides.

All of this discussion has taken place with respect to four cyclic points. In fact, there is a form of Ptolemy's theorem that holds for noncyclic points, which we will find useful. We'll look at that next.

Ptolemy's Theorem for General Quadrilaterals

If the four points are not on a circle, then Ptolemy's theorem replaces the equality sign with a less-than sign. This is a generalization of the well-known *triangle inequality*. For any triangle with points A, B, and C,

$$AB + BC > AC$$

unless the triangle is degenerate (that is, a line segment with A and C at the ends and B somewhere between them). In a degenerate triangle, the greater-than sign becomes an equal sign.

The first step in deriving Ptolemy's theorem for the quadrilateral is to define a useful geometrical operation known as *inversion* (which has lots of other uses), and then see what happens to lengths under inversion. Then Ptolemy's theorem falls out with no fuss.

Inversion treats points as though they passed through a special circular mirror. When a point is reflected in a linear mirror (that is, about a line segment), we draw a line perpendicular to the line through the point, then mark off a distance on the other side of the line equal to the original

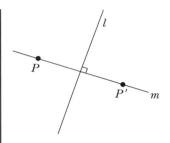

distance from the line to the point. Take a look at Figure 11.9. Here I've marked a line l and a point P. The reflected point P' is found by drawing line m perpendicular to l and through P, which intersects l at Q. We then find point P' on m, such that $|P'Q| = |PQ|$, and $P' \neq P$.

Figure 11.10 shows what happens under inversion. Instead of a line, we have a circle $C = (A, r)$ with center A and radius r. Given any point P, we draw a line m through A and P. We now find the point P' on the line m such that $AP \cdot AP' = r^2$. Clearly one point is inside the circle, and the other is outside. The two points are uniquely related; if we start with point P' instead, we find P as its inverse. We say that P' is the inverse of P with respect to circle C.

Now if we invert a line segment with respect to a circle, we get an arc, as shown in Figure 11.11. But it will be useful for us to find the distance between the two endpoints of the segment (or arc) before and after inversion.

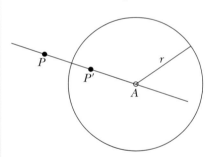

sion. Suppose that we have two points, P and Q, and their inverses, P' and Q'. What is the relationship between lengths $|PQ|$ and $|P'Q'|$?

Figure 11.12 shows the setup. The important thing to note is that triangles $\triangle APQ$ and $\triangle AQ'P'$ are similar triangles. Proving this would take us pretty far astray from our main topic, so I'll leave it as an exercise for you. If you just want to see it proven, take a look at Chapter 22 of Pedoe's book, mentioned in the Further Reading section.

If we accept that these are similar triangles, then we can simply write down some ratios and monkey with them algebraically.

$$\frac{P'Q'}{PQ} = \frac{AP'}{AQ} = \frac{AP \cdot AP'}{AP \cdot AQ}$$

where on the right I just multiplied top and bottom by AP. Solving for $P'Q'$, and remembering that by definition, $AP \cdot AP' = r^2$, we find

$$P'Q' = \frac{r^2 PQ}{AP \cdot AQ}$$

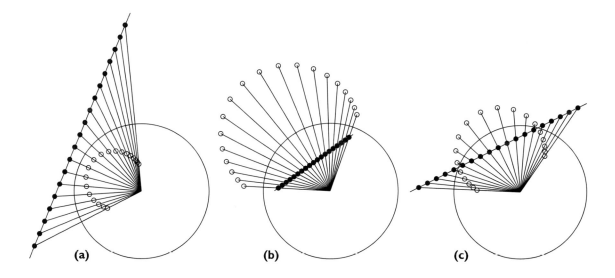

(a)   (b)   (c)

We can of course also solve for PQ, finding

$$PQ = \frac{r^2 P'Q'}{AP \cdot AQ'}$$

So now let's return to the noncyclic form of Ptolemy's theorem, which I promised would come easily at this point. Consider Figure 11.13, showing a circle (A, r) and three points B, C, and D, not on the circle. We invert all three points with respect to the circle to find B', C', and D'. Now we know from the triangle equality that

$$B'D' < B'C' + C'D'$$

unless the three points lie on a line, in which case the less-than sign becomes an equal sign. In general, they won't. The exception is when A, B, C, and D all lie on a circle. This may suggest to you a way to prove Figure 11.11, which asserts that the inverse of a circle is a line, and vice versa.

We'll assume the more general case of the inequality. Now using the inversion formula from

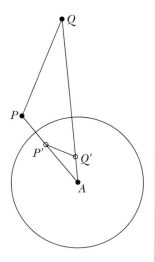

Figure 11.11
The inverse of a line is a circular arc.
(a) A line of black dots is outside the circle; their inverses shown as hollow dots form an arc.
(b) The line is inside the circle.
(c) The line crosses the circle.

Figure 11.12
Inverting points P and Q gives us points P' and Q'. Triangles $\triangle APQ$ and $\triangle AQ'P'$ are similar.

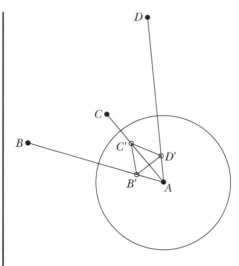

above, we can substitute for the three lengths in terms of the original points A, B, C, and D:

$$\frac{r^2 BD}{AB \cdot AD} < \frac{r^2 BC}{AB \cdot AC} + \frac{r^2 CD}{AC \cdot AD}$$

Factoring out the common r^2 term and rearranging, we find

$$AC \cdot BD < AB \cdot CD + AD \cdot BC$$

which matches our earlier statement of Ptolemy's theorem, except that it's an inequality. So Ptolemy's theorem sets the two sides equal when the four points are cyclic, and otherwise the product of the lengths of the diagonals is strictly less than the sum of the products of the lengths of the opposite sides.

Angle Addition

To get some experience with Ptolemy's theorem, we can derive the formula for finding the sine angle-addition formula $\sin(\alpha + \beta) = \sin\alpha\cos\beta + \cos\alpha\sin\beta$.

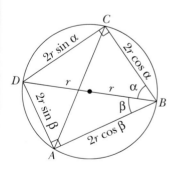

We'll start with a cyclic quadrilateral of radius r, as shown in Figure 11.14, with $\alpha = \angle DBC$ and $\beta = \angle ABD$. Points B and D are at opposite ends of a diameter, thus $BD = 2r$. Recall that the law of sines tells us that for a triangle $\triangle ABC$, $a/\sin A = b/\sin B = c/\sin C = 2r$. We use this law to find $AC = 2r\sin B$, where angle $\angle B = \alpha + \beta$. Note that angles A and C are both right angles, because they're inscribed in the semicircles made by diameter BD; thus we can label the edge lengths with the sines and cosines as shown.

Now we just write out Ptolemy's theorem, replacing each length with its value from Figure 11.14, and simplify:

Figure 11.13
Inverting points B, C, and D in the circle. The inverted triangle satisfies the condition $B'D' < B'C' + C'D'$.

Figure 11.14
A cyclic quadrilateral where DB is a diameter of length $2r$.

$$AC \cdot DB = AB \cdot CD + BC \cdot AD$$

$$2r \sin(\alpha + \beta) \cdot 2r = 2r \cos \beta \cdot 2r \sin \alpha + 2r \cos \alpha \cdot 2r \sin \beta$$

$$\sin(\alpha + \beta) = \cos \beta \sin \alpha + \cos \alpha \sin \beta$$

This is the standard formula for $\sin(\alpha + \beta)$. I love it when these things work out so nicely. The other variations, e.g., $\cos(\alpha - \beta)$, can all be found by plugging in standard trig identities. Now we can move on to a more challenging application.

From Snell to Fermat via Ptolemy

Refraction is an important part of our visual world. Almost every transparent object bends light to some degree as that light passes through. This phenomenon gives rise to everything from multicolored prisms to the ability for our eye to focus at different distances.

In Chapter 10 I wrote about proving the law of mirror reflection by using the mathematical technique of reflection. The two had a lot in common, which probably wasn't too surprising. Now I'll show how to use Ptolemy's theorem to prove that Snell's law (an algebraic relationship) leads to Fermat's principle of least time (a physical hypothesis).

The law of specular reflection tells us what happens to a ray of light when it passes from one medium to another. When light passes through the boundary, or interface, from an incident medium i (say, air) to a transmitted medium t (say, glass), its speed v changes from v_i to v_t. This causes the light ray to bend, as illustrated in Figure 11.15. We won't discuss the mechanics of that bending here; it's covered in detail in most optics and computer graphics texts.

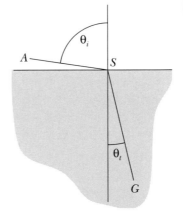

Figure 11.15
The basic geometry of refraction from air to surface to glass.

There are two laws that people generally use to compute the transmitted angle θ_t: Fermat's principle of least time and Snell's law. We encountered Fermat's principle in Chapter 10 when we looked at reflection: it says that light takes the least amount of time to get from one point to another. As then, we'll assume a world where light travels in straight lines. Suppose the light travels from air point A, to surface point S, and then to glass point G. Fermat's principle tells us that the time it takes to get from A to S to G must be a minimum. Given A and G, our job is to find S.

Note that S is not simply on the line AG. Remember that we're looking for the least time of flight, which is not necessarily the shortest path. We want to travel less distance where the material is denser, even if it means we travel farther in the more rarified medium.

In terms of Figure 11.15, we can observe that the time it takes light to get from A to S is the distance divided by the speed in the incident medium, or AS/v_i, and similarly the time from S to G is SG/v_t. Thus we want to minimize $AS/v_i + SG/v_t$. In symbols, for any other S' on the surface, we want to show that the path $AS'G$ takes longer than ASG:

$$\frac{AS'}{v_i} + \frac{S'G}{v_t} > \frac{AS}{v_i} + \frac{SG}{v_t}$$

Snell's law is a famous geometrical relationship that tells us where S is located. In terms of the geometry of Figure 11.15, Snell's law says

$$v_t \sin \theta_i = v_i \sin \theta_t$$

We will show that Snell's law and Fermat's principle are equivalent. The approach will be to assume Snell's law, then show that Fermat's principle is automatically satisfied. Figure 11.16 shows the basic setup. We've drawn a circle (C, r) through points A, S, and G. We've also drawn a vertical line v perpendicular to the horizontal interface h and found the point B where v intersects the circle (C, r) below line h.

Our first goal will be to find the lengths BA and BG. We note that $\angle ASB$ forms an inscribed angle in the circle. Recall that in Chapter 10 we showed that an inscribed angle of θ is equivalent to a central angle of 2θ. Figure 11.17 shows how to find the length of a chord UW in a circle (C, r); if V is the midpoint of UVW, then angle $\angle VCW = \theta/2$, and $VW = r \sin(\theta/2)$, so $UW = 2VW = 2r \sin(\theta/2)$.

Returning to BA, the inscribed angle $\angle ASB$ is $\pi - \theta_i$, so the central angle is $2(\pi - \theta_i)$, and therefore the length of the chord is

$$BA = 2r \sin[2(\pi - \theta_i)/2] = 2r \sin(\pi - \theta_i) = 2r \sin \theta_i$$

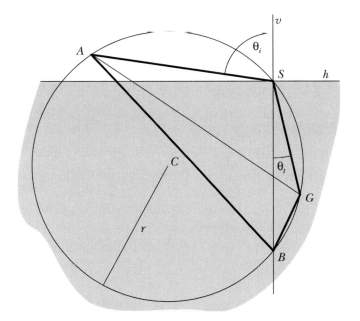

Figure 11.16
The inscribed
quadrilateral *BGSA*.

By similar reasoning, $BG = 2r \sin \theta_t$. Writing out our chord lengths and using Snell's law, we find

$$BA = 2r \sin \theta_i = 2r \frac{v_i \sin \theta_t}{v_t} = \frac{k}{v_t}$$

$$BG = 2r \sin \theta_t = 2r \frac{v_t \sin \theta_i}{v_i} = \frac{k}{v_t}$$

where $k = 2rv_i \sin \theta_t = 2rv_t \sin \theta_i$.

Now we'll use Ptolemy's theorem. Since A, S, G, and B are all on a circle, in that order, we have

$$AG \cdot BS = AS \cdot BG + SG \cdot BA$$

Substituting our lengths for BG and BA from above,

$$AG \cdot BS = AS \frac{k}{v_i} + SG \frac{k}{v_t} = k \left(\frac{AS}{v_i} + \frac{SG}{v_t} \right)$$

This is the critical result; we'll use it in a moment to complete the proof.

Figure 11.17
Finding the length
of a chord.

For a moment, imagine some other point S' on the line h between the two media; is it possible that this point, in violation of Snell's law, could lead to a shorter time of flight from A to G? Since S and B are both on v, which is perpendicular to h, $BS' > BS$ for all $S' \neq S$ on h. Multiplying both sides by AG, we get

$$AG \cdot BS' > AG \cdot BS$$

Now we use the result from above. We'll replace both sides of this inequality with their equivalent formulae from Ptolemy's theorem. Taking the right-hand side first, since the four points are cyclic, we find

$$AG \cdot BS = k \left(\frac{AS}{v_i} + \frac{SG}{v_t} \right)$$

The left-hand side represents an arbitrary quadrilateral, so we use the inequality form:

$$AG \cdot BS' < k \left(\frac{AS'}{v_i} + \frac{S'G}{v_t} \right)$$

Note the inequality sign; it means that the right-hand side is strictly larger than the left; it's never equal to it or smaller. This is a slightly tricky point: we're safe plugging this into our inequality, because all we're saying is that we know that $AG \cdot BS'$ is larger than $AG \cdot BS$, so any other value larger than $AG \cdot BS'$ will also be larger than $AG \cdot BS$. In symbols, and removing the common factor k, we find

$$AG \cdot BS' > AG \cdot BS$$

$$\frac{AS'}{v_i} + \frac{S'G}{v_t} > \frac{AS}{v_i} + \frac{SG}{v_t}$$

which was what we had hoped to find. So if we choose S in accordance with Snell's law, then no other point S' on the interface h can form a path $AS'G$ with a shorter time of flight than ASG.

Thus we used Ptolemy's theorem to show that if we assume Snell's law, we have also satisfied Fermat's principle of least time for refraction.

Wrapping Up

I'm surprised that I haven't seen more on Ptolemy's theorem; it seems like a very useful general tool. There are often lots of ways to prove these nice little theorems, and after I worked out one to my own satisfaction I hunted around on the Net for something better. I found one! The nice little proof that I used in this column follows the proof given at *http://www.cut-the-knot.com/proofs/ptolemy.html*. The triple play using Ptolemy's theorem for refraction, as well as the relationship between line distances under inversion, is based on the discussion by Dan Pedoe in *Geometry* (Dover Publications, 1988).

There are probably ways of using these bits of circle-and-line geometry to accelerate ray-tracing, but I'm not sure how. I'd be happy to hear from any of you who manage to use these techniques in practice.

Aperiodic Tiling

ANDREW GLASSNER'S NOTEBOOK
May/June & July/August 1998

12

I love patterns. I think that as people we're really good at spotting patterns. We can find recurring patterns everywhere we look: in the structures of rocks, the personalities of our friends, and the cycle of seasons. Theme and variation have been a staple of creative invention since time immemorial, spanning every form of creative endeavor. I think that theme and variation represent a balance between the extremes of regularity and sheer randomness.

Imagine a million grains of sand, placed one next to the other in a straight line. Dullsville, man. Now imagine those grains of sand scattered at random over a rocky surface. That's just as dull as before. But take those grains and stack them up, let the wind play over them and shape them into dunes, and you've got something beautiful and interesting. Balancing repetition and randomness can lead to patterns that draw us in and keep our interest. In this chapter, we'll talk about some interesting patterns, how to make them, and what you might do with them.

Tiling the Plane

Let's look at some interesting ways of assembling small units along one of the lattices that make up crystals. In this chapter I'll live entirely in a 2D world, so our "crystals" will be nothing but collections of polygons in the

Figure 12.1
The three regular tilings. Each is made of many copies of a single regular polygon.

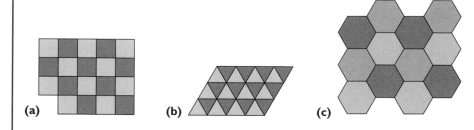

(a)   **(b)**   **(c)**

plane. It's well known that if we limit ourselves to regular polygons, there are only three ways to tile the plane, shown in Figure 12.1. Here the verb *tile* means covering the infinite plane with a set of polygons so that there are no gaps or overlaps among the polygons. Each polygon is called a *tile,* and the composite pattern is called a *tiling.*

The tilings of Figure 12.1 are theoretically interesting, but because they are so perfectly repetitive they're pretty boring to look at. Usually when we use one of these patterns to cover a wall or floor we decorate the tiles with colors or shapes to make the whole thing a little more interesting—again balancing the regularity of the tiling with the variation in the tiles themselves. I've done this in Figure 12.1 by using two or three colors, but it doesn't help very much. We can get a little more interest by allowing more than one regular polygon in the game, resulting in the *semiregular* tilings in Figure 12.2. This is better, but the regularity is still pretty dominant.

We can control our tiling patterns by adopting *matching rules*. These describe the permitted ways that tiles can be placed next to one another. Figure 12.3 shows a few examples for assembling such a tiling from a single piece. All the examples in this figure share a matching rule that says tiles may only be placed so that the shared edge is of the same length (that is, we can't push a short edge up against a long one). I've also distinguished the two short ends. In Figure 12.3a, I've used a matching rule that says that matching vertices must have the same color. Figure 12.3b enforces the same result by modifying the common edge into a mountain, so the tiles can only interlock in the desired way. In Figure 12.3c the rule is that colored bands must be continuous across tile edges. Whether described as vertex, edge, or face rules, the result is the same pattern.

The patterns in Figures 12.1, 12.2, and 12.3 are *periodic*. Essentially this means that you can find a group of tiles that you can pick up and use as a rubber stamp. In other words, the pattern is created by a single patch—the *fundamental cell*—that repeats by translation to cover the plane. The

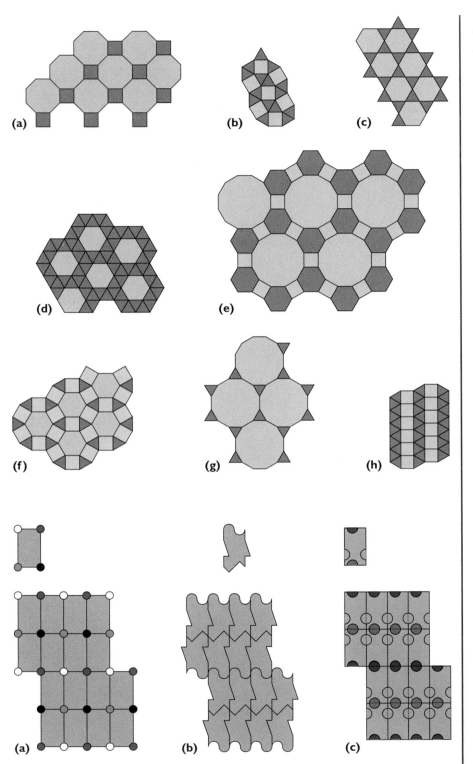

Figure 12.2
The 8 semiregular tilings. Each is made of one or more regular polygons, and every vertex contains the same kinds of polygons meeting in the same order.

(a)

(b)

(c)

(d)

(e)

(f)

(g)

(h)

Figure 12.3
Matching rules.
(a) Vertex rules. Corresponding colors must overlap.
(b) Edge rules. The deformed edges must link together.
(c) Face rules. The decoration on the faces must be continuous.

(a)

(b)

(c)

Figure 12.4
(a) Isosceles triangles can tile the plane periodically. **(b)** The same triangles can create a radial tiling that is not periodic.

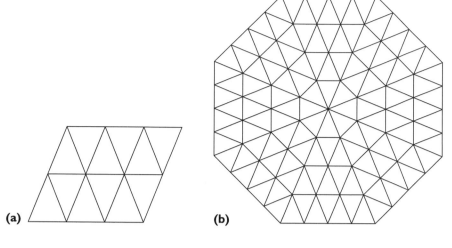

(a)　　　　　　　　**(b)**

distance from one copy to the next is called the *period* of the pattern. The translational part of the definition is important. Figure 12.4a shows a periodic tiling built from an isosceles triangle. Figure 12.4b shows a rotationally symmetric pattern built from the same triangle, but this one isn't a periodic tiling, even though there's obviously a great deal of internal structure.

In any periodic tiling there are typically an infinite number of fundamental cells, but often there's only one smallest such cell. For example, in Figure 12.1a the smallest fundamental cell is a single square, but you could use two squares adjacent horizontally or vertically, or a 2-by-2 square of squares, and so on.

There are surprising ways to create tilings. Figure 12.5 shows a spiral tiling (it's also nonperiodic) inspired by a construction by Heinz Voderberg. I found that the easiest way to construct a cell for this sort of tiling is to start with an acute isosceles triangle, as shown in Figure 12.6. The tiling works if the acute angle goes into 360 degrees an even number of times; I used 16 for this figure, so the acute angle is 360/16 = 22.5 degrees. First create a parallelogram from the triangle. Draw a curve, and then rotate that curve by 180 degrees to get it to match up with the opposite corner. Now take another copy of the triangle, and move its acute point to the lower-right corner of the parallelogram. Make a copy of the curve, and rotate it around the lower-right corner of the parallelogram by the acute angle. Now join up the sides of the curves, and voilà. Making sure the curves don't intersect each other is the only tricky part.

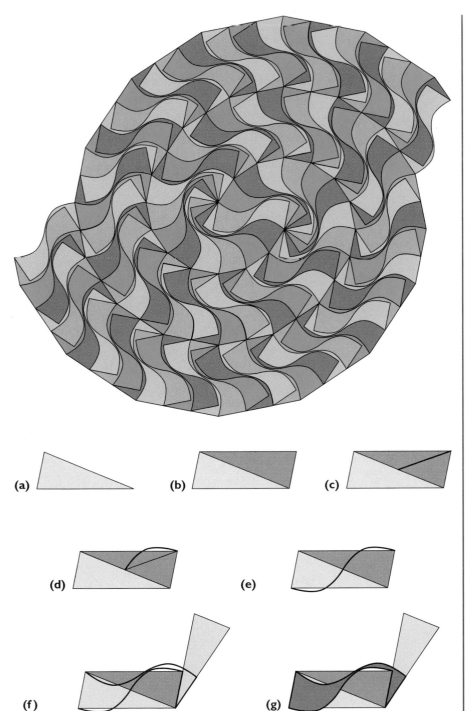

Figure 12.5
A spiral tiling made of a single tile. The tiling can be extended to cover the entire plane.

(a)   **(b)**   **(c)**

(d)   **(e)**

(f)   **(g)**

Figure 12.6
Creating a tile for Figure 12.5.
(a) Start with an isosceles triangle with an angle of $360/n$ degrees (here $n = 16$).
(b) Make a parallelogram.
(c) Find the midpoint.
(d) Draw a curve from the upper-right corner to the midpoint.
(e) Rotate the curve 180 degrees.
(f) Rotate around the lower-right corner of the parallelogram by an angle equal to the acute angle of the triangle.
(g) Join up the edges.

Figure 12.7
(a) The tile made in Figure 12.6.
(b) This tile fits into itself by rotation.
(c) The tile also fits into itself by a vertical reflection, making a block that can tile the plane periodically.

(a)   **(b)**   **(c)**

Figure 12.7 shows that a tile produced this way has two important properties: it fits into itself both by a small rotation equal to the acute angle of the original triangle and by a full 180-degree rotation. You'll notice that the spiral tiling in Figure 12.5 uses both properties: the two centers use slightly rotated copies of the tile, and they join each other with a half-rotated pair. From there it's pretty straightforward to add tiles and follow the spiral outward, though notice that the pattern changes slightly each time it wraps around 180 degrees.

It's easy to build *nonperiodic* tilings, simply by being careful enough not to repeat yourself. Figure 12.8a shows a periodic tiling of rectangles, and Figure 12.8b shows the same rectangles in a nonperiodic tiling. Theoretically we could extend the pattern of Figure 12.8b, always mixing things up, so that the final result is not periodic. But is it possible to create tiles that can *only* tile the plane nonperiodically? The rectangles of Figure 12.8 don't fill the bill, since they can be coerced into a periodic pattern. Let's investigate further.

From 20,000 to 2

If there's a set of one or more tiles that fit together to create *exclusively* nonperiodic tilings, that set of tiles—and the resulting pattern—is called *aperiodic*. To my eye, aperiodic tilings made of a small number of distinct tiles fit into that desirable class of patterns that balance regularity—because of the recurring instances of just a few tile shapes—and randomness—because the pattern never repeats.

Figure 12.8
(a) The rectangle can tile the plane periodically.
(b) The rectangle can also tile nonperiodically.

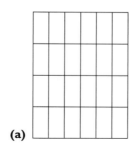
(a)

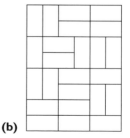
(b)

The question of whether there were any aperiodic sets of tiles at all was unanswered until recently. In 1961 Hao Wang put forth the conjecture that in fact there were no aperiodic tiles; that is, any set of tiles that could tile the plane aperiodically could also do so periodically. In 1964 Robert Berger disproved this conjecture by inventing a theoretical, aperiodic set of dominoes. The only problem was that Berger's solution required more than 20,000 dominoes.

Once aperiodic tilings were proven to exist, many people set about to find smaller sets. Berger later found a set of 104 tiles, and Donald Knuth found a set of 92 tiles. Robert Ammann and Raphael Robinson independently found several different aperiodic sets of six tiles. The current record for the smallest set is held by Roger Penrose, whose sets contain only two tiles.

It's interesting that the Ammann tiles and the Robinson tiles are both based on squares. This is great for computer graphics, where we deal with square grids in everything from sampling grids to texture patterns. So we'll kick things off with a look at the square-based Robinson tiles.

ROBINSON TILES

One set of Robinson's tiles is shown in Figure 12.9. Following Grünbaum and Shephard, who wrote the fundamental reference on tiling, I've used edge modifications to show how the tiles lock together. I've included labels a through f on each tile, to show the tiling sequence, as well as the letter F, to show the orientation of the tile.

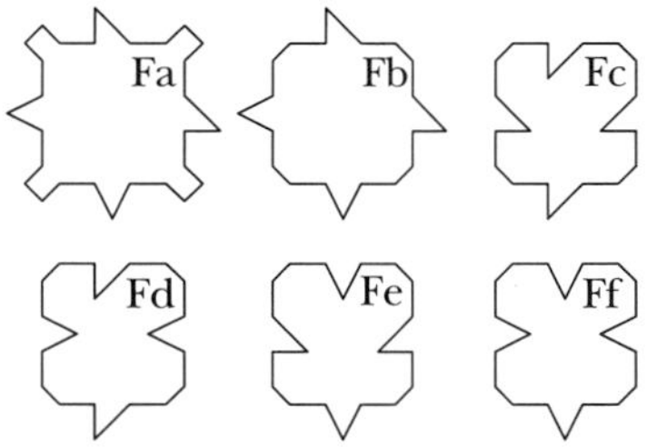

Figure 12.9
The Robinson tiles. Pieces can only go together so that the tabs fit the slots, and the corners are covered.

You'll notice that tile Fa has a little tab in each corner, while the other tiles have that corner sawed off. This means that exactly one Fa tile must appear at each vertex of the tiling. To assemble the pattern, you only need to put the pieces together so that they fit. These tiles may be rotated and flipped over as needed.

Starting with a single Fa tile, you can build up the 3-by-3 block in Figure 12.10. You might want to try to create other such blocks; you'll find that except for some choices of orientation, this is the only 3-by-3 block that you can make with these tiles.

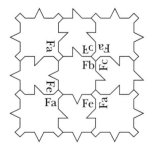

Figure 12.10
Building a 3-by-3 Robinson block.

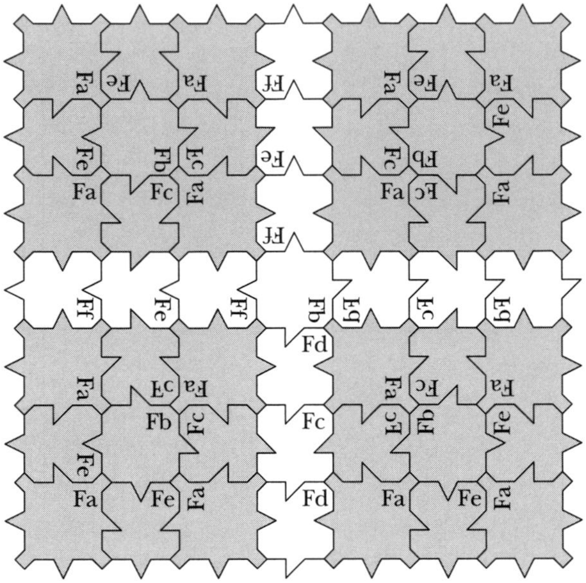

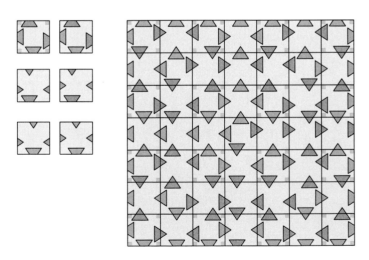

Figure 12.11
A 3-by-3 Robinson block (here shaded gray) is in each corner of this 7-by-7 pattern. The glue tiles make a large plus sign.

To grow the pattern, you can run a new row of tiles above it and to its right. Then rotate the 3-by-3 block and affix copies of it to the right and top of the 4-by-4, and then place a fourth rotated copy into the upper-right corner. The resulting 7-by-7 grid is shown in Figure 12.11. You can then run a new row of tiles above and to the right of the 7-by-7 grid to grow a 15-by-15 block, and so on.

Part of the fun of working with aperiodic tilings is decorating the tiles so that you get interesting-looking visual patterns. There are two ways to

Figure 12.12
A decoration of Figure 12.11. The top of row tiles are Fa and Fb, the second row Fc and Fd, and the third row Fe and Ff.

Figure 12.13
A decoration of
Figure 12.11.

approach these decorations. One is to come up with designs that enforce the matching rules, so you can dispense with the edge modifications. In this case, you'd simply draw designs on six square tiles, then build the pattern so that the designs are continuous across tile edges. I found this difficult to achieve with the Robinson tiles, because I couldn't find a decoration that would force one and only one copy of the Fa tile at each vertex. The other approach is to decorate the tiles that have edge modifications and then assemble the pattern according to the edge rules. In this case the decoration does not force the rules but simply comes along for the ride. I found this to be much easier for this set of tiles.

Figures 12.12 through 12.16 show three different decorations for the Robinson tiles. In all cases, the 7-by-7 block is exactly the one in Figure 12.11,

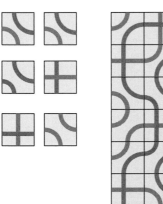

Figure 12.14
A decoration of
Figure 12.11, and a
variation of Figure
12.13.

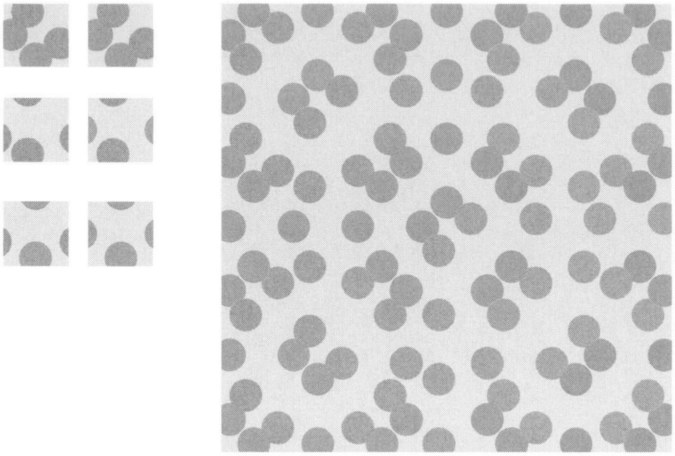

Figure 12.15
A decoration of
Figure 12.11.

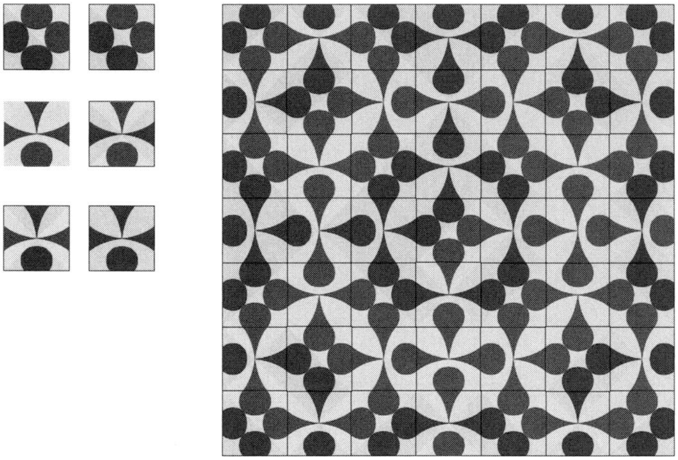

Figure 12.16
A decoration of
Figure 12.11.

except I've used the indicated patterns on the tiles. It's surprising how much variation you can get out of the completed pattern just by changing the decoration a little bit.

An interesting variation on the basic Robinson tiling pattern is shown in Figure 12.17. Here I've grayed out the pattern of Figure 12.11 and placed to its left two *fault lines*. These are strings of identical tiles that can knit together two larger patterns. Notice that this also gives us the chance to break the regular pattern of the tiles with corners: each time we hop over one of these infinite lines, we can displace the corner tiles by one unit. A decorated example of this fault-ridden tiling is shown in Figure 12.18, using the decoration of Figure 12.13. The fault-tiling technique might be useful to tile a polygonal model. You can pave each polygon with Robinson

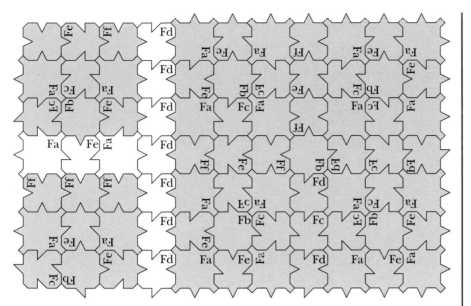

Figure 12.17
Introducing a fault into a Robinson tiling. The fault lines are in white; the gray tiles are sections of the 7-by-7 block in Figure 12.11.

tiles, then use the fault lines on the edges to stitch individual polygons together.

Now that we know how to build patterns with these tiles, we can reasonably ask if they're actually aperiodic. Remember that the decoration I've used here can be misleading, since it doesn't necessarily force the conditions of tiling. A simple example of the problem is a decoration consisting of a single circle in the center of each tile. Even if the matching rules were followed out exactly, the resulting pattern would be nothing but a perfectly

Figure 12.18
A decoration of Figure 12.17, using the tiles of Figure 12.13.

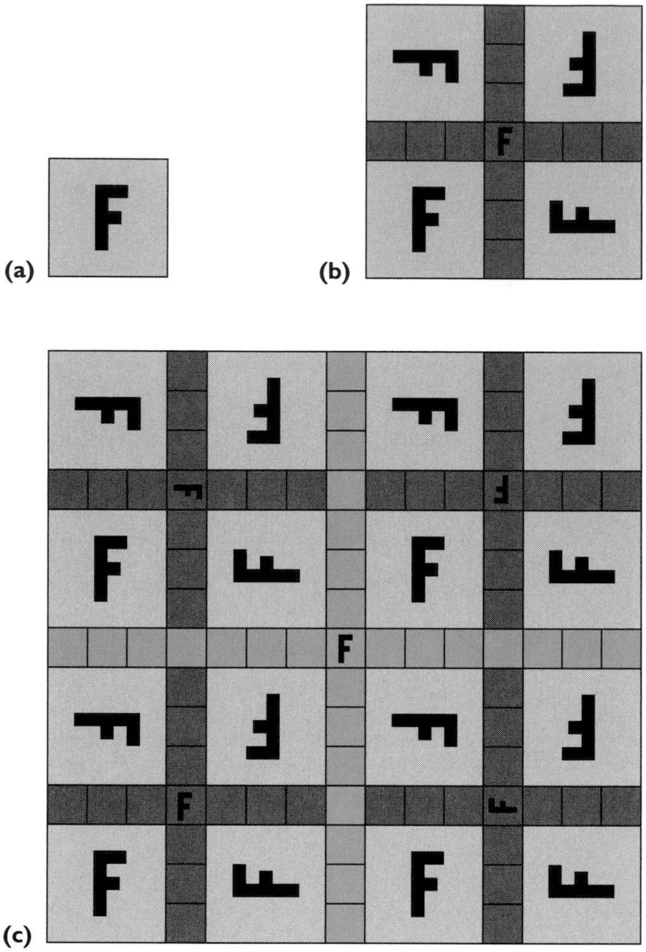

Figure 12.19
(a) A single 3-by-3 Robinson block.
(b) A 7-by-7 block is formed by gluing together four 3-by-3 blocks. Notice that they rotate when assembled.
(c) A 15-by-15 block made by rotating and gluing together 7-by-7 blocks.

regular grid of circles. So we need to look at the geometry of the tiles rather than their decorations.

The insight into the periodicity of the pattern rests on the construction of the basic 3-by-3 block (we'll ignore fault lines in this discussion). Rather than get bogged down in the nitty-gritty, I'll give the general idea here. Basically the trick is based on extending the construction we saw in Figures 12.10 and 12.11. Schematically, it's shown in Figure 12.19. I've used my favorite orientable symbol, the letter F, to represent one of the 3-by-3 blocks. Figure 12.19 shows our construction of the 7-by-7 grid from four copies of the 3-by-3 grid plus a row and column of glue tiles to hold them together. Clearly there's no single rectangular unit that will generate this whole pattern—the rotating red and blue glue tiles get in the way.

To see the big picture, consider it this way: the construction builds up blocks of ever-greater size, built from sub-blocks. None of the sub-blocks will work, since they get rotated by the step that glues them together. So however large a block you choose as your unit tile to stamp out the pattern, there's going to be a rotated copy, or some glue tiles, that get in the way. I hope I've suggested to your intuition that the Robinson tiles are aperiodic, but I certainly haven't proven anything. You can find a complete proof in Grünbaum and Shephard's book.

The Robinson pattern isn't periodic, but it is *almost periodic*. Again ignoring fault lines, you'll notice that each 3-by-3 block repeats with period 8, and the 7-by-7 blocks repeat with period 16. Basically each block that is 2^{n-1} on a side repeats with a period of 2^{n+1} tiles. So you can easily find huge repeating patterns, even though the whole pattern never repeats. Furthermore, this implies another property call *local isomorphism,* which states that any patch of tiles (without fault lines) will repeat infinitely often in the pattern. These traits seem to be shared by many aperiodic sets of tiles.

AMMANN TILES

A closely related set of tiles was independently developed by Ammann in 1977. Figure 12.20 shows the tiles themselves: once again there are six tiles based on squares, with one tile marked as having special corners that fill in the gaps left by the other tiles. While the Robinson tiles had only two kinds of notches (one symmetrical and one asymmetrical), the Ammann tiles use three different matching conditions on the edges.

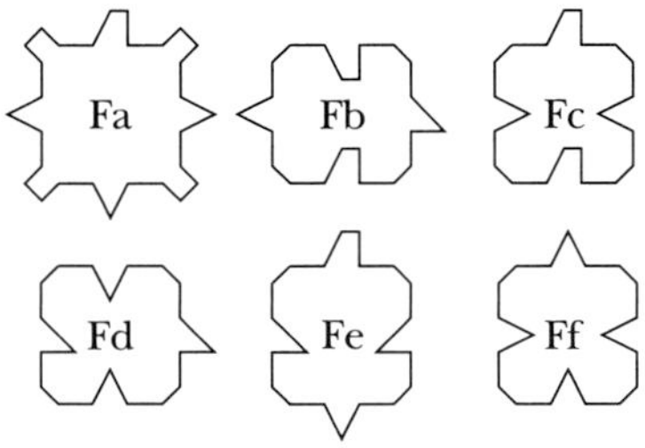

Following Grünbaum and Shephard, I've again marked these tiles with edge deformations that force them to link up correctly. Here we have a symmetrical point, an asymmetrical wedge, and a blunted asymmetrical wedge. Each tab may only go into its correspondingly shaped slot, though tiles may be rotated and flipped over as needed.

We can build up patterns from these blocks using the same strategy as for the Robinson tiles. Figure 12.21 shows a 3-by-3 block of Ammann

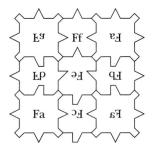

Figure 12.20
The six Ammann tiles. Note the three edge modifications.

Figure 12.21
Assembling a 3-by-3 Ammann block.

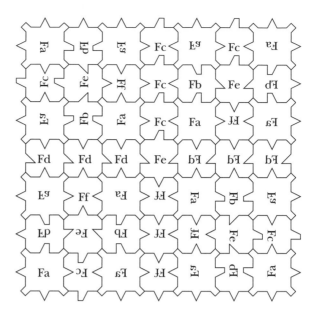

Figure 12.22
Assembling a 7-by-
7 Ammann block
from 3-by-3 blocks.

tiles, and Figure 12.22 shows a 7-by-7 block. These tiles can also be decorated, as shown in Figures 12.23 through 12.26.

PENROSE TILES

Perhaps the most famous sets of aperiodic tiles were invented by Roger Penrose. I'll talk about two versions of them here, and I'll also talk about making them, decorating them, and using them.

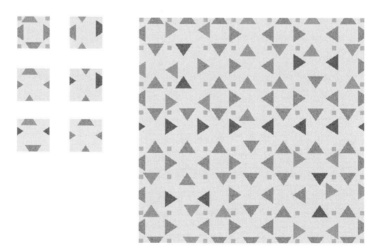

Figure 12.23
A decoration of
Figure 12.22.

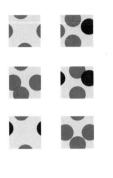
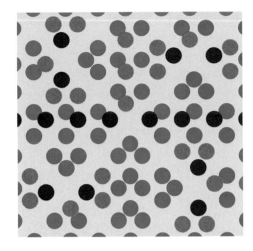

Figure 12.24
A decoration of
Figure 12.22.

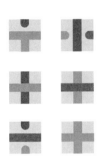
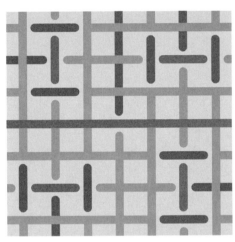

Figure 12.25
A decoration of
Figure 12.22.

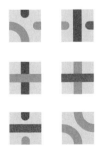
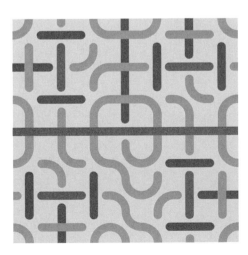

Figure 12.26
A decoration of
Figure 12.22, and a
modification of Fig-
ure 12.25.

Penrose Kites and Darts

One version of Penrose tiles is the kite and dart shown in Figure 12.27. The *kite* (the larger tile) and the *dart* (the smaller, pointed one) may be assembled only by placing them so that edges of similar length are adjacent and the colored bands are continuous. The names "kite" and "dart," and this decoration of the tiles, were conceived by John Conway. Figure 12.28 shows an example of a pattern created by these tiles.

These tiles are indeed aperiodic. A full proof would take more room than we have, but a general outline of the approach conveys most of the key ideas. I'll use a construction technique that's based on substitution rules. Like the rules of a formal grammar in computer science, or an L-system used in botanical simulations, we take each tile and replace it, in position, with another set of tiles.

Let's simplify the problem for a moment and look just at 1D patterns. Suppose that you had an infinite string, and you wanted to fill it up with an aperiodic pattern of white and black beads. We'll use two production rules to do the job. First, every white bead will be replaced with one white and two black beads in that order. We write this W → WBB, as shown in Figure 12.29a. Similarly, we'll replace each black bead with the rule B → BWW, as in Figure 12.29b.

Let's start with a single white bead and then apply these rules to start filling up the string. The first few steps are shown in Figure 12.29c. Each time you apply the rules, you take the original string of beads and apply all the rules at once. So the first generation is simply WBB. Now the new W goes to WBB, and each of the two B's independently goes to BWW, giving us the

Figure 12.27
(a) The geometry of the Penrose kite and dart.
(b) A decoration that forces the matching rules. ϕ is the golden ratio: $(1+\sqrt{5})/2$.

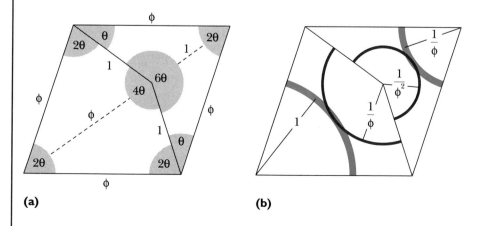

(a)　　　　　　　　　　　　　**(b)**

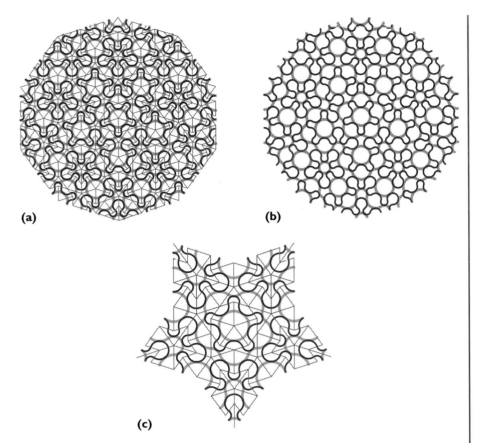

(a)

(b)

(c)

Figure 12.28
A pattern created
by Penrose kites
and darts.
(a) With kites and
darts outlined.
(b) Just the deco-
ration.
(c) A close-up of
the center region.

new string WBBBWWBWW. Let's run the process forever, so that we have (theoretically) filled up the infinite string with beads.

If the pattern generated this way is periodic, then we could find some chunk of beads—perhaps short, perhaps enormously long—that repeats. We could then take one of these chunks and glue it together into a super-bead, then match the original pattern by simply filling another string with an infinite number of copies of this single superbead. If we can't find such a superbead, the pattern is either nonperiodic or aperiodic. You may be

Figure 12.29
Creating an
aperiodic bead se-
quence.
(a) The rule
W → WBB.
(b) The rule
B → BWW.
(c) Three steps
starting with a
white bead.

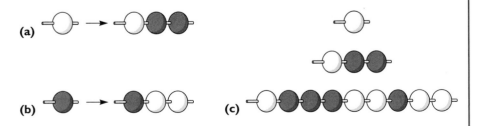

(a)

(b)

(c)

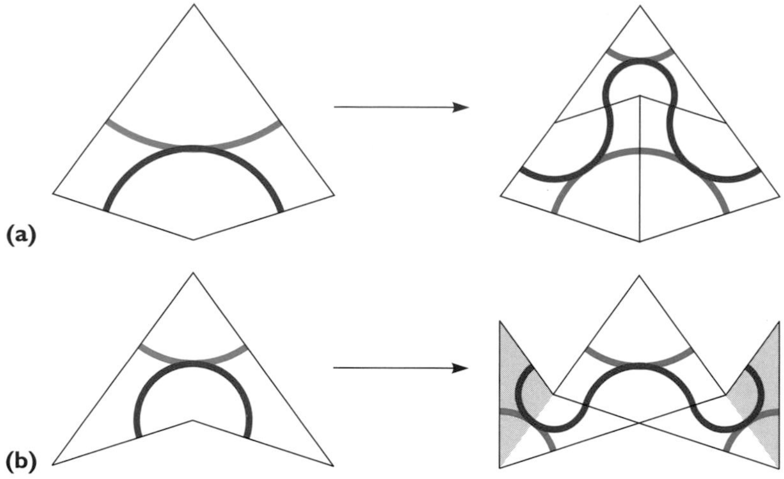

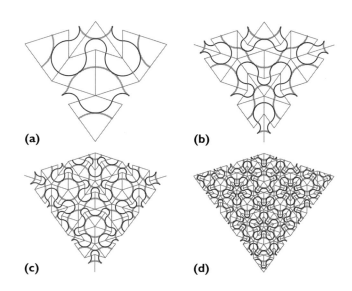

Figure 12.30
(a) Inflating a kite turns it into two kites and a dart.
(b) Inflating a dart turns it into a kite and two half-darts.

able to convince yourself that in this example we would never be able to find such a superbead.

We follow a similar process in 2D for Penrose tiles. The technique is typically called *inflation* since we're increasing the number of tiles. Figure 12.30 shows the inflation rules for the kite and the dart. Notice that two of the newly created darts in the dart rule fall off the side of the tile. The matching rules come to rescue here; you can prove that each half-tile is exactly completed by each of its legal neighbors when that neighbor tile is inflated. If you run the process back the other way and reduce the number of tiles in a tiling, it's called *deflation*.

Figure 12.31
A Penrose "Ace" inflated four times.

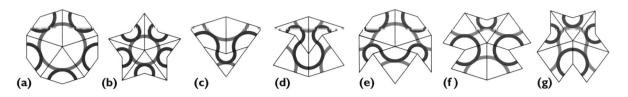

(a)   (b)   (c)   (d)   (e)   (f)   (g)

Figure 12.31 shows a few inflation steps applied to a small starting pattern of Penrose tiles. You may notice that some configurations of tiles seem to appear several times in these tilings, because there are only a limited number of ways to assemble tiles around a vertex. For example, take the vertex at the tip of the dart and enumerate all the ways that other kites and darts can be assembled around that vertex while obeying the matching rules. Then repeat the process for the other vertices on the dart and then for the kite. If you run through this process and keep track, you'll find that there are only seven different kinds of clusters that can be formed. These clusters taken together are called the *atlas* of the tiling. The atlas for the Penrose kites and darts is shown in Figure 12.32. Each of these clusters repeats an infinite number of times throughout any Penrose tiling and can serve as a good starting point for a tiling process. Figure 12.33 gives analytic expressions for the locations of all the points in the atlas.

Figure 12.32
The atlas for kites and darts.
(a) Sun.
(b) Star.
(c) Ace.
(d) Deuce.
(e) Jack.
(f) Queen.
(g) King.

Growing a Penrose Tiling

Now that we've seen something about Penrose tilings, how do we generate them? It is very difficult to "grow" a covering of the plane using kites and darts. Suppose that you start with just a single tile and place new ones that are always in accordance with the matching rules. After a while, you'll probably find yourself in a state where you can't add any new tiles. What went wrong wrong in this process?

Nothing actually went wrong; it just didn't go right enough. As an analogy, suppose you were writing a limerick, and you got this far:

There once was a penguin named Bryce

Who lived in a house made of ice.

He painted it orange,

Now what? There's nothing technically wrong with this limerick (the third line is kind of clunky, but let's overlook that). The major problem here is that you just can't rhyme with "orange"—you're stuck and it's nobody's fault. You just have to back up a line or two and try again. It's the same thing with building Penrose tilings. You can follow all the rules and find

Figure 12.33
Analytic expressions for vertices in the atlas of Figure 12.32. In these expressions, $k^2 = 1 + \phi^2 - 2\phi\cos(2\pi/5)$, $d^2 = 1 + \phi^2 - 2\phi\cos(\pi/5)$, and $R_y(D)$ means the reflection of point D around the Y axis (i.e., if $D = (D_x, D_y)$, then $R_y(D) = (-D_x, D_y)$).

Sun

A	$(0, 0)$
B	$(0, \phi)$
C	$(0, \phi + k)$
D	$(\cos(\pi/10), \sin(\pi/10))$
E	$\phi\,(\sin(2\pi/5),\, 1 - \cos(2\pi/5))$
F	$(k\sin(2\pi/5),\, \phi + (k\cos(2\pi/5)))$
G	$(\cos(\pi/10),\, \phi + k - \sin(\pi/10))$
H	$R_y(D)$
I	$R_y(E)$
J	$R_y(F)$
K	$R_y(G)$

Star

A	$(0, 0)$
B	$(0, \phi)$
C	$(0, \phi + 1)$
D	$(\cos(3\pi/10), \sin(3\pi/10))$
E	$\phi\,(\sin(2\pi/5),\, 1 - \cos(2\pi/5))$
F	$(\sin(2\pi/5),\, \phi + \cos(2\pi/5))$
G	$(\cos(\pi/10),\, \phi + 1 + \sin(\pi/10))$
H	$R_y(D)$
I	$R_y(E)$
J	$R_y(F)$
K	$R_y(G)$

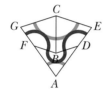

Ace

A	$(0, 0)$
B	$(0, 1)$
C	$(0, \phi + 1)$
D	$\phi\,(\cos(3\pi/10), \sin(3\pi/10))$
E	$\phi\,(\cos(\pi/10),\, 1 + (\phi(1 - \sin(\pi/10))))$
F	$R_y(D)$
G	$R_y(E)$

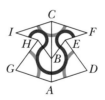

Deuce

A	$(0, 0)$
B	$(0, 1)$
C	$(0, \phi + 1)$
D	$\phi(\cos(\pi/10), \sin(\pi/10))$
E	$\sin(\pi/5),\, 1 - \phi(\cos(\pi/5))$
F	$(\phi\cos(\pi/10),\, 1 + \phi(1 - \sin(\pi/10)))$
G	$R_y(D)$
H	$R_y(E)$
I	$R_y(F)$

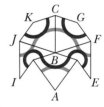

Jack

A	$(0, 0)$
B	$(0, k)$
C	$(0, \phi + k)$
D	$\phi\,(\cos(3\pi/10), \sin(3\pi/10))$
E	$k(\cos(\pi/10), \sin(\pi/10))$
F	$(\phi\cos(\pi/10),\, k + \phi\sin(\pi/10))$
G	$(\cos(\pi/10),\, \phi + k - \sin(\pi/10))$
H	$R_y(D)$
I	$R_y(E)$
J	$R_y(F)$
K	$R_y(G)$

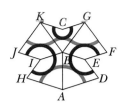

Figure 12.33
(continued)

Queen		King	
A	$(0, 0)$	A	$(0, 0)$
B	$(0, \phi)$	B	$(0, 1)$
C	$(0, \phi + d)$	C	$(0, 1 + d)$
D	$\phi\,(\cos(\pi/10), \sin(\pi/10))$	D	$(\sin(\pi/5), -\cos(\pi/5))$
E	$k\,(\cos(3\pi/10), \sin(3\pi/10))$	E	$(\sin(\pi/5) + (\phi\,\cos(3\pi/10)), -\cos(\pi/5) + (\phi\,\sin(3\pi/10)))$
F	$(\sqrt{2(1- \cos(4\pi/5))}, \phi)$	F	$(\cos(\pi/10), d + \sin(\pi/10))$
G	$(k\,\cos(3\pi/10), k(1 + \sin(3\pi/10)))$	G	$(\cos(\pi/10), 1 + d + \sin(\pi/10))$
H	$R_y(D)$	H	$R_y(D)$
I	$R_y(E)$	I	$R_y(E)$
J	$R_y(F)$	J	$R_y(F)$
K	$R_y(G)$	K	$R_y(G)$

yourself unable to add any more tiles. You need to take some tiles away and try again, in a process of trial and error.

Obviously if we want to create and use Penrose tilings on a regular basis, we need a more reliable approach to generating the patterns. We saw one approach above: start with a single tile and inflate it over and over, producing an ever-denser (or ever-larger) tiling. Any finite region can be covered with a finite number of inflations, and the infinite plane can be covered if we inflate forever. This is fine mathematically. A problem occurs, though, when we try to use this structure to explain the physical phenomenon of *quasicrystals*.

In 1984, Dan Shechtman and his colleagues at the National Institute of Standards melted together samples of aluminum and manganese. They then quenched, or quickly cooled, this molten metal by squirting it at a rapidly spinning wheel, causing the temperature of the metal to drop by about a million degrees Kelvin per second. When they examined the structure of the resulting material using electron diffraction, the pattern looked like one typical of crystalline structures, except that it had fivefold rotational symmetry.

This was very, very strange. Fivefold symmetry is disallowed by all the laws of standard crystallography. Just try to put five regular pentagons together at a single point—you can't do it unless you let them flop over on one another. This alloy seemed to be a crystal by most measures, but it had this bizarre, and disallowed, internal symmetry. The discoverers called this perplexing structure a *quasicrystal*. Since then, many other compounds have been discovered that fit into the quasicrystal category, including materials with five-, eight-, ten-, and twelvefold symmetries.

One of the first papers that tried to explain the internal structure of quasicrystals was written by Levine and Steinhardt in 1984. They showed that a 3D generalization of the Penrose tiles matched the diffraction results of the real material and thus seemed to be a plausible model for the internal structure of the quasicrystal. This explanation worked mathematically, but in practice it posed three problems. First, the traditional way to think of crystal formation is that it begins with lots of copies of a single atomic configuration; the Penrose model requires two building blocks. Second, the Penrose matching rules are straightforward on paper, but it's hard to imagine how simple atomic structures would cooperate in order to pull them off. Third, as we've seen, it's hard to grow a Penrose tiling without getting into a situation where you can't grow any more; this would make it very difficult for large crystals to form. So the Penrose techniques we've seen so far don't look like a good explanation for quasicrystals.

A number of alternative theories have been put forth to explain quasicrystal structures, but Penrose tiles have always been in the running, despite their problems. The challenge to those who believed in the Penrose explanation was to simplify the matching rules and deal with the puzzle of two basic units, rather than one. And closer to the topics in this chapter, such rules would also help us build new patterns of arbitrary size without getting stuck.

A breakthrough in this quest came in a 1996 paper by Petra Gummelt. She showed that a particular decagon, shown in Figure 12.34, could be used to

Figure 12.34
The Gummelt decagon.

grow a Penrose tiling by overlapping. The overlap rules were only that overlap actually occurred (that is, decagons could not sit simply side by side) and that colors had to match in the overlapped region. Figure 12.35 shows the

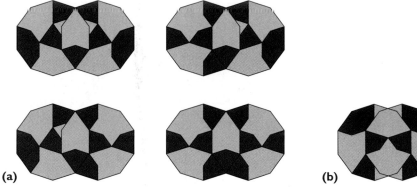

(a) **(b)**

Figure 12.35
The five possible
ways that Gummelt
decagons can over-
lap.
(a) Overlaps with
small shared area.
(b) The overlap
with large shared
area.

five possible ways that a decagon can overlap. You can break down any Penrose tiling into a collection of these overlapping decagons.

This work showed that a single structure, albeit a complex one, could be used to create the aperiodic Penrose tilings in the plane. This addressed the problem of requiring multiple building blocks. But the matching rules were still a problem: how do you imagine random atomic clusters, floating around in a soup, obeying complicated overlap assembly rules? (On a technical note, observe that the Gummelt decagons do not strictly tile the plane, because they overlap: a true tiling creates no overlaps and leaves no holes. Gummelt suggested that this be called a *covering* rather than a tiling.)

In their 1997 paper, Jeong and Steinhardt discuss Gummelt's decagon and simplify her original proof that it generates a valid Penrose tiling. They then go on to present a second technique, also based on overlapping clusters of Penrose tiles. Figure 12.36 shows one of these clusters. Jeong and Steinhardt prove through a compli-  cated argument that if many copies of this cluster are overlapped (as in Figure 12.37) so that the complete til- ing has the highest possible density, the result is a Penrose tiling. They point out that the maximal possible overlap corresponds to the minimum possible energy.

Figure 12.36
The Jeong and
Steinhardt cluster.

This approach addresses the two chief difficulties with using the Penrose model to explain 2D quasicrystal formation and structure: we're now down to a single structure, and we have eliminated the matching rules in favor of a more physically plausible juggling about for minimal energy. Whether

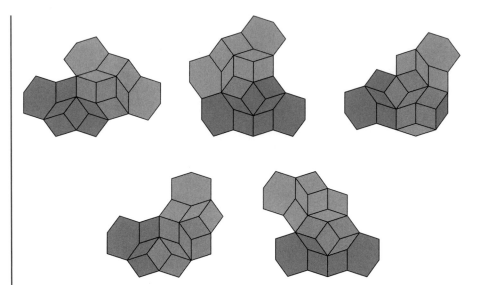

Figure 12.37
The five ways that
the cluster of Fig-
ure 12.36 can over-
lap with itself.

this cluster argument can be extended to 3D, and whether it accurately predicts new quasicrystals yet to be found, only time will tell.

Materials scientists and engineers are excited by quasicrystals and developments such as these that seek to explain them. Such understanding can lead to new materials, which can exhibit new properties that have commercial and technical value.

Penrose Rhombs

In addition to the kites and darts, Penrose also came up with another pair of aperiodic tiles, shown in Figure 12.38. These are usually called the *Penrose rhombs,* and the two tiles are simply named *thin* and *thick*. The figure

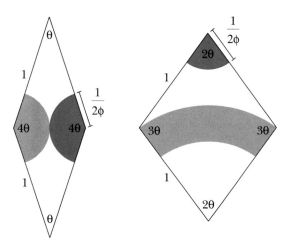

Figure 12.38
The geometry of
the Penrose
rhombs.

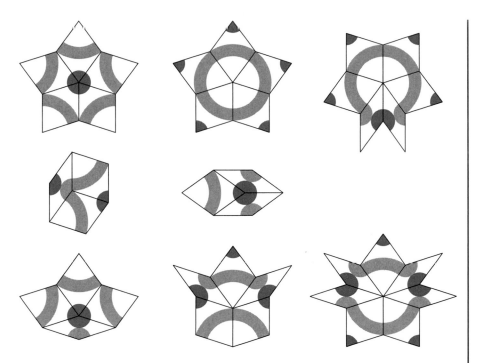

Figure 12.39
The atlas of
Penrose rhombs.
Top row: Dotstar,
Ringostar, and
Medal.
Middle row: Fat
cube and Thin
cube.
Bottom row: Bud,
Leaves, and Flower.

also provides the matching rules; as before, the color bands need to be continuous. The edge-length conditions are easier here, since all sides have the same length. The atlas for the rhombs is shown in Figure 12.39. There's no set of shorthand names for these that I know of, so I've suggested a set of names for the shapes in the figure caption.

You can inflate rhombs directly, just like kites and darts. Figure 12.40 gives the recipe. It's interesting to note that you can in fact convert a kites-and-

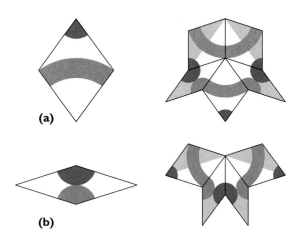

(a)

(b)

Figure 12.40
How to inflate a
thin and thick
rhomb.

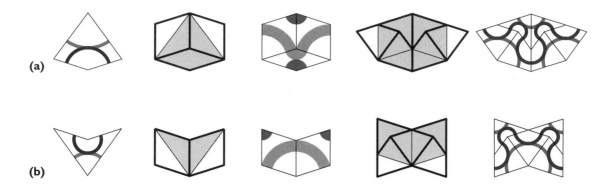

(a)

(b)

Figure 12.41
How to convert rhombs into kites and darts, and vice versa.

darts tiling into a rhomb tiling, and vice versa. Figure 12.41 shows the basic idea. Figure 12.42 shows the rhomb equivalent of Figures 12.28 and 12.31. There's clearly a lot of common ground between the two kinds of tiles and their decorations; Figure 12.42c shows what they look like when both versions are drawn together.

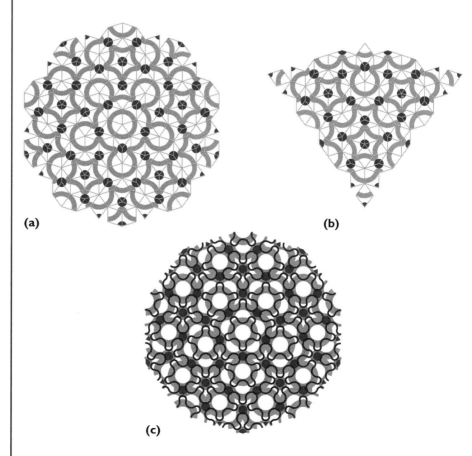

(a)

(b)

(c)

Figure 12.42
(a) The rhomb version of Figure 12.28.
(b) The rhomb version of Figure 12.31.
(c) The two decorations for the inflated Sun pattern overlaid.

Tiling without Decoration Rules

All of the tiles we've seen so far require some kind of matching rules to ensure aperiodicity. I was surprised to learn that Ammann discovered a way to modify the Penrose rhombs to create an aperiodic set that avoids this restriction. Specifically, he found how to build a set of three convex tiles that don't require any matching rules beyond just making sure that adjacent edges are of the same length.

Figure 12.43 shows how to build this set of tiles. In Figure 12.43a we begin with a pair of Penrose rhombs, sharing an edge in a legal configuration. In Figure 12.43b I've drawn a circle around point *A* and a circle of a different radius around point *D*. Their intersections are marked *F* and *G* in Figure 12.43c. Now in Figure 12.43d I've drawn a circle centered at point *E*, with a radius of length *EF*. In Figure 12.43e you can see I've placed a copy of that circle over point *B* and also a copy of the circle we built earlier around *D* at point *C*. In Figure 12.43f I've marked their intersection as point *H*. The only rule on this construction that I haven't mentioned yet is that radii of the circles must be chosen so that line segments *FA, FD, FE,* and *GH* are all of different lengths. If they're not, then the resulting tiles won't be aperiodic.

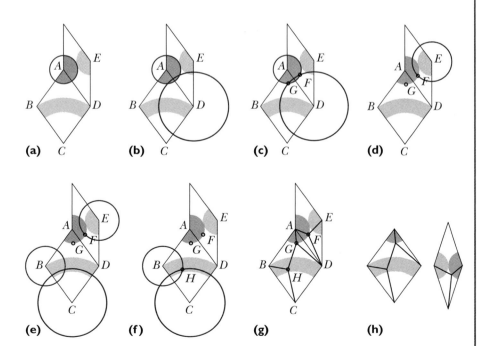

(a)   (b)   (c)   (d)

(e)   (f)   (g)   (h)

Figure 12.43
Creating the Ammann construction lines.
(a) Two Penrose rhombs and a circle at *A*.
(b) A circle at *D*.
(c) Points *F* and *G* are the intersections of these two circles.
(d) A new circle at *E* that passes through *F*.
(e) Copying the circle from *E* over to *B* and copying the circle from *D* to *C*.
(f) Their intersection is point *H*.
(g) The Ammann construction lines.
(h) The thin rhomb must be flipped over before it can be used for tiling.

That completes the construction. Figure 12.43g shows the new lines that we draw to define the new tiles. We're almost ready to use these to create the Ammann tiles, but one critical step remains: the thin rhomb needs to be reflected first. Remember that this isn't just a rotation but rather a left-right flip of the whole tile. The resulting pair of modified rhombs is shown in Figure 12.43h.

To create the set of Ammann tiles, I've built a flower cluster of Penrose rhombs in Figure 12.44a using the enhanced rhombs of Figure 12.43h. Figure 12.44b shows how to build each of the Ammann tiles by combining regions of the rhombs. There are two pentagons (marked in gray and yellow) and one hexagon (marked in red).

These three polygons will tile the plane as long as touching edges are of the same length. You can decorate them if you want, but you don't need to. This makes them very attractive if you're planning to lay out a tiled floor, or you want to automatically generate tiled texture of unpredictable size. To give you a feeling for how they look, Figure 12.45a shows a tiling of Penrose rhombs, Figure 12.45b shows those rhombs with the Ammann construction lines, and Figure 12.45c shows the corresponding tiling by the aperiodic Ammann set. Of course, you don't need to start with the rhomb pattern—that's the whole point of making these tiles! You can be assured of creating an aperiodic tiling of the plane as long as you simply lay down the tiles so that touching edges are of equal lengths.

Implementation

How might we write a program to create Penrose tilings? In this section I'll concentrate on kites and darts; you can use Figure 12.41 to adapt these ideas to the rhombs.

Figure 12.44
Building the Ammann tiles.
(a) A flower cluster of Penrose rhombs with Ammann markings.
(b) The three Ammann tiles— two pentagons and one hexagon.

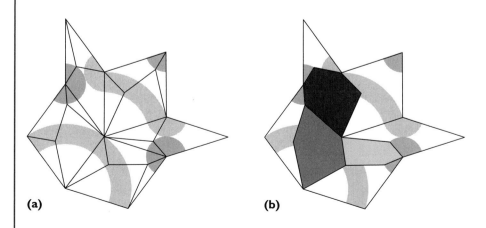

(a)　　　　　　　**(b)**

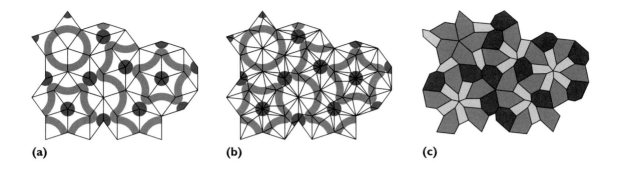

(a)   **(b)**   **(c)**

The simplest method is to apply inflation rules to a starting tile, or set of tiles. The easiest way to inflate a pattern is to first turn it into triangles. Each kite and each dart can be split into two congruent triangles along the dashed line in Figure 12.27a. Each of the dart triangles contains an obtuse angle (of 4θ = 144 degrees) while the kite triangles don't, so they're typically referred to as *obtuse* and *acute* triangles, respectively.

The inflation process is now simply a matter of running through the list of triangles, replacing each one with the appropriate set of new triangles as shown in Figure 12.46. The new triangles can be reassembled into kites and darts if desired, or they can go through the substitution process again immediately.

If you don't choose to draw the black lines around each kite and dart, it doesn't matter how you store the triangles. But if you do want to draw the composite tiles, you want to make sure that when you draw each triangle, you don't draw a line down the edge that's internal to the kite or dart to which the triangle belongs. You can see the effect of these suppressed lines

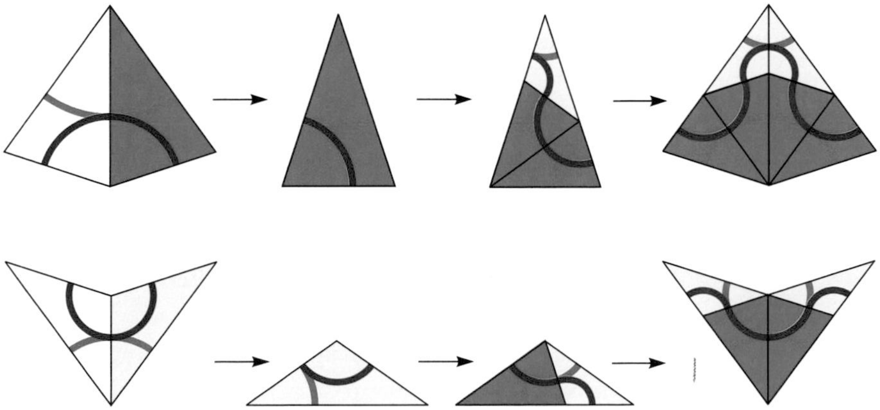

Figure 12.45
How the Ammann tiles correspond to the Penrose rhombs.
(a) A tiling by Penrose rhombs.
(b) The Ammann markings.
(c) The corresponding Ammann tiling.

Figure 12.46
Using triangles to inflate the kites and darts. I've color-coded the triangles for clarity: blue triangles are acute and yellow triangles are obtuse.

around the perimeter of Figure 12.31. You can use some conventional scheme to identify that edge, such as always making it the first one in the list.

Programming this process can be very easy. Simply maintain a list of triangles, each containing its three points and a flag indicating whether it's obtuse or acute. Then run through the list, building up a new list. When you're done, go through the list again, drawing the appropriate decoration on each triangle.

To convert to rhombs, use Figure 12.41 to build a new list of thin and thick rhomb triangles from the obtuse and acute kite and dart triangles.

Uses

Now that we know how to make Penrose tilings, what good are they to us in graphics? The most obvious answer is to use them to create endless aperiodic texture on surfaces. Simply draw some interesting face decoration that obeys the matching rules, pick an initial tile and orientation, and then inflate until the surface is covered with tiles. You can use this to create a nice big texture on a flat surface, such as the side of a building or a floor.

If you're careful you can carry this construction across polygons so you don't get a seam where two polygons adjoin. But how could you apply this technique to a sphere, or simpler yet, a cube? Of course, formally you can't do this at all. If you followed the pattern from the front face, say, around to the right face, then in back, then to the left, and then back again to the front face, you've completed a loop: the pattern is periodic in the distance covered by the lengths of the four faces. And since Penrose tilings are by definition aperiodic, you can't use them to cover a cube, a sphere, or even trickier surfaces like donuts or Möbius strips.

There may be modifications of the tilings that will match up around the surfaces of these objects. I haven't been able to find any such instances, but that doesn't mean that they're not out there. Other uses of these tilings include generating nonuniform sampling patterns for stochastic sampling, such as that used in distribution ray tracing.

Another use of Penrose tilings is to create image maps that control models. For example, suppose you want to lay out a city that wasn't planned out in advance, but rather grew up. You could decorate your tiles with building bases and create a tiling of the plane. Then use the result as a blueprint upon which you erect office towers, homes, apartment buildings, and so on. They will have a visible large-order structure, but they won't be on a regular, boring grid. You could use such blueprints to specify geometry, materials, density of flowing lava, or whatever else you'd like to create with some large-scale but nonrepeating structure.

Decoration

Inventing new face decorations for the Penrose tiles is fun, but there are two important rules to keep in mind: each of the tiles must be symmetrical across the edge marked with a dashed line in Figure 12.27a. I haven't seen this restriction discussed anywhere, but it's not too hard to find the reason. Consider the Sun pattern in Figure 12.32. Let's assume that the long edges are different; we'll call them types 1 and 2. We'll see that assuming we actually have these two distinct edges leads to a contradiction.

The proof is easy. Pick any radial spoke of the sun and label it 1. Then label its clockwise neighbor 2, then the next clockwise neighbor 1 again, and so on, around the Sun. You'll find that you have the sequence 12121, which means that the last 1 is up against the first 1, which violates our assumption that the kite had two distinct edges. You can prove the same thing for the long sides of the dart using the Star pattern.

The restriction on the short sides follows the same process. Surround a Sun with darts, and assume that the short sides are different. By simply alternating the two side labels you can see that we again reach a contradiction.

Of course, there's no reason not to create tile patterns that are asymmetric on the inside, as long as the edges match up. Or for fun, you could have a variety of different internal designs (as long as the edges are all the same) and mix them up. You can choose the decoration of each tile at random, or according to a procedural scheme. If you're going for a complicated texture, this is an easy way to make the resulting pattern more complicated. Remember that introducing complexity in the picture moves you away from pattern and toward randomness, so you'll want to approach this process with caution.

To create allowable and attractive decorations, I found it useful to make a chart of the legal and illegal configurations. Figure 12.47 shows all eight pairings of kite and dart edges, split into legal and illegal pairs. I still like to cook up designs using paper and colored pencils. I've found it useful to make a little cluster, as in Figure 12.48, that shows all the legal configurations in one unit so I can get a general idea of how the decorations look.

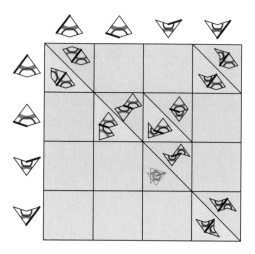

Figure 12.47
Dart and kite configurations. Illegal pairs are surrounded with red; legal pairs are in green. The bold segment at the edge of each row and column shows the segment being matched. The lower-left corner of the grid is symmetrical to the upper-right corner, so I've left it empty. The four gray squares in the upper-right corner indicate illegal pairs, because the edges are not the same lengths.

Figure 12.49 shows a pair of tiles that I made from a photo of a starfish; note that these are symmetrical across their central axis. In Figure 12.50 I've lovingly hand-assembled these into a Penrose tiling. To show the value of asymmetrical designs, Figure 12.51 shows the tiles after I've changed them to make them asymmetrical, and Figure 12.52 shows the resulting pattern.

Figure 12.48
A single cluster that tests all of the legal kite/dart edge combinations.

Of course, if you want a really random look, you can generate some kind of random pattern on the tiles using fractal noise, diffusion-reaction patterns, or any other pattern generator you like, then enforce the boundary conditions programmatically.

WANG TILES

Although it's a bit off the subject of aperiodicity, there's another important tiling topic that I can't resist mentioning briefly. The subject is the close connection between tiling and computing. Recall that a *Turing machine* is a

Figure 12.49
A symmetrical kite and dart decoration.

Figure 12.50
A Penrose tiling made from the tiles of Figure 12.49.

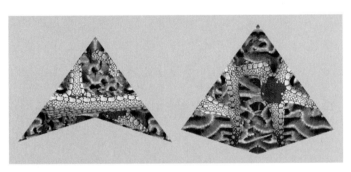

Figure 12.51
An asymmetrical modification of the tiles of Figure 12.49.

Figure 12.52
A Penrose tiling made from the tiles of Figure 12.51.

conceptual machine that is made up of an infinite piece of tape, a read/write head, a state marker, and a collection of transition rules. When the machine is running, it looks at the current value on the tape (typically either a 0 or 1) and then looks up its current state. The machine then rummages through its rules until it finds one that matches these inputs. This rule tells the machine what number to write back onto the tape, what state to consider itself in next, and whether the read/write head should be moved one step left, right, or not at all.

Although you'd never want to write a big program on a Turing machine, it's not too hard to write little programs. The remarkable thing is that Turing machines are powerful enough, in theory, to execute any computable algorithm. They might be slow and clunky, but anything that can be done by the biggest computer imaginable can also be done by the humble Turing machine.

In 1975, Wang showed that Turing machines could be simulated by tilings. Rather than go through the theory, I'll show an example of the idea. I've chosen a simple operation inspired by something that we do all the time in computer graphics: Z-buffering. An essential Z-buffer step is finding the minimum of two numbers. To make things simpler, I'll pose the problem this way: find the smaller of two positive integers, each larger than 2. Figure 12.53 shows a set of tiles to accomplish this goal and the computation. For convenience, I've also numbered the columns of the tiling. The origin

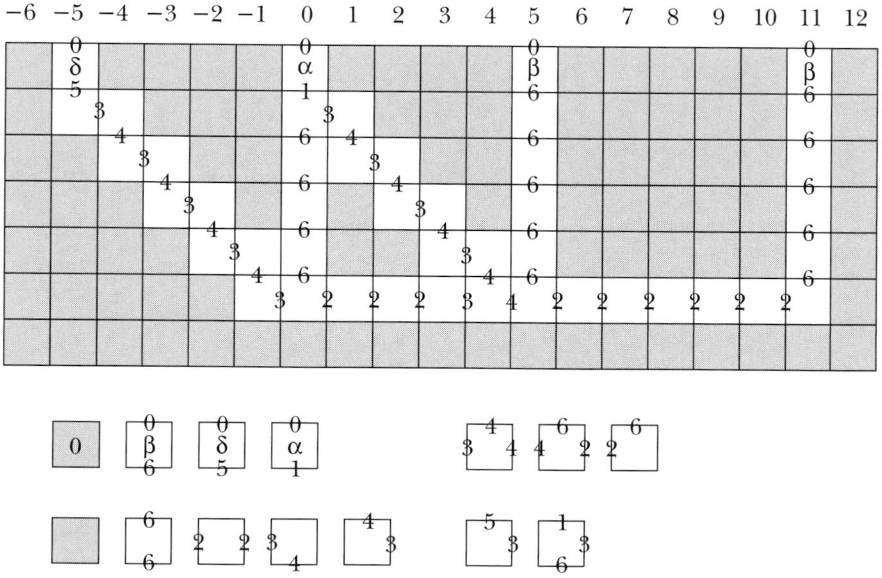

Figure 12.53
A Wang tiling that finds the minimum of two numbers. All unmarked edges are assumed to have the value -1. The tile marked α is the origin. The tile marked δ is to the left of α by the same distance as the closer of the two tiles marked β: $\delta = -\min(\beta_1, \beta_2)$.

of the number line is fixed at 0 by the tile marked α. Two other tiles, marked β, mark the two numbers we want to compare; in this example they're placed at 5 and 11. Their minimum appears to the left of the origin at a tile marked δ, located at −5. This tiling puts δ at −min(β₁, β₂). How does this work?

As always, tiles can only abut if their sides match; here I've marked the sides with numbers, so the numbers have to be the same across each edge. Edges that are unmarked are implicitly numbered −1, so most of the infinite plane is filled with tiles that are −1 on all four edges. For convenience, the plane is only half infinite; the upper boundary is marked with edges 0. The tiles in gray are assumed to match along the marked edges and have labels of −1 on the others. I've shown the indices of the number line above the grid to make it easier to see what's happening. α is located at 0, and our two input β's are at 5 and 11.

Another representation of the identical tiling is shown in Figure 12.54. I'll refer to this figure from here on, since I believe the color coding and interlocking shapes make the discussion clearer. The little bumps at the top of the tiling capture the top row; imagine that they fit up against an infinite row of half-circle concavities. Rather than add gray to every colored tile and make things much more complicated, I've adopted the convention that any straight edge is implicitly colored gray.

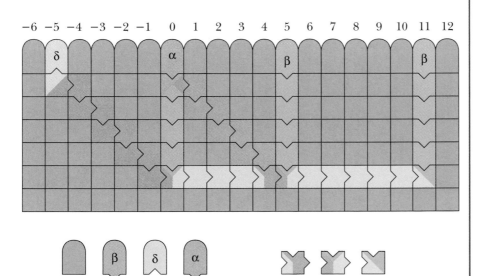

Figure 12.54
A color-and-shape version of Figure 12.50.

Let's start with the β tiles. Each one connects to the upper border with a half-circle, and generates a downward-heading column of red tiles. These columns will continue downward forever unless something interferes. Of course, I've set things up to create interference!

Now look at the α tile, marked in green. It sends down a tile that forks off into a downward-heading red column and into a blue diagonal that heads down and to the right. The blue diagonal continues until it reaches the nearer of the red columns created by the β tiles. A couple of multicolored glue tiles mediate the collision. At this point of intersection, two new rows are created, marked in yellow. One row moves to the right, where it eventually reaches the outermost red column and stops it (using a multicolored glue tile). The other row moves to the left, until it encounters the red column sent down from the origin. That collision, again handled by a multi-colored tile, signals a new blue diagonal up and to the left. Eventually this gets to within one square of the top border, where the pink tiles take over. The δ tile then connects the diagonal to the top of the grid.

Because the two blue diagonals are the same length, and both start directly underneath the origin, the distance from δ to α is the same as the distance from α to the nearer β, and we're finished. Note that although I spoke of columns "moving" in one direction or another, that was just to help analyze how the pattern came together. This computation is represented by a single, static tiling.

Simply by creating the right set of 14 tiles, we've computed the minimum of two positive integers. Wang showed that this process could be carried out in general, so that any Turing-machine program could be converted into a set of tiles and connection rules. Now, I'm not suggesting that you run out and sell your workstation for some tiles and a big checkerboard, but it's worth knowing that theoretically any program, its inputs, its computation, and its results can be represented by one of these tiling patterns—though admittedly anything beyond a toy problem would be enormous.

You may notice a similarity in spirit between this form of computation and cellular automata. Notice, though, that these tiles are static—the act of simply creating a stable and consistent tiling pattern *is* the computation, unlike automata, which themselves are little processors that run local programs.

I really like the idea of using a computational Wang tiling to decorate a kitchen or bathroom floor. It would be quite an in-joke, of course, but it would also be personally satisfying to occasionally be gently reminded of the fact that the humble geometrical mosaic is capable of any computational task, from predicting weather and understanding speech to rendering 3D images.

An Aperiodic Tile

I'll end this chapter with an open question: Is there a single aperiodic tile? That is, is there a single shape that can cover the plane with no gaps or overlaps and creates a pattern that cannot be also created by translation of a subset of the pattern? Nobody knows. The trend from 26,000 to 2 seems to suggest that the step to 1 might be possible.

I've fantasized that this would be a terrific one-page doctoral thesis. Simply titled "An Aperiodic Tile," it would contain a one-line abstract, a picture of the tile, a picture of the inflation rule(s), and a single reference to Grünbaum and Shephard. I hope somebody writes it!

Further Reading

The fundamental reference on tiling of all sorts is *Tiling and Patterns* by Grünbaum and Shephard (W. H. Freeman, 1987). It's a beautiful book in addition to being the standard reference work on the subject. A very good book on the mathematics of quasicrystals and aperiodic tilings is *Quasicrystals and Geometry* by Marjorie Senechal (Cambridge University Press, 1995). A popular account of Penrose tiles appears in Martin Gardner's book *Penrose Tilings to Trapdoor Ciphers* (W. H. Freeman, 1989). Gardner discusses many fascinating properties of these patterns that I haven't had the space to cover here. There are also some interesting discussions in *Connections* by Jay Kappraff (McGraw-Hill, 1990).

Textures have long been used as periodic patterns in computer graphics. A discussion of aperiodic texturing appears in "Aperiodic Texture Mapping" by Jos Stam (available from the European Research Consortium for Informatics and Mathematics, report ERCIM-01/97-R046).

In the text, I've referred to "Penrose Tilings as Coverings of Congruent Decagons" by P. Gummelt (*Geometriae Dedicata,* 62:1–17, 1996) and "Constructing Penrose-like Tilings from a Single Proto-tile and the Implications for Quasicrystals" by Hyeong-Chai Jeong and Paul J. Steinhardt, *Physical Review B,* 55(6):3520–3532. There are some great online references; a good place to start is the QuasiTiler page at the University of Minnesota's Geometry Center Web site, located at *http://www.geom.umn.edu/apps/quasitiler/.*

Know When To Fold

ANDREW GLASSNER'S NOTEBOOK

September/October 1998

13

In the woods of Snoqualmie there's a tale that is told

When the daytimes are balmy and the night stars turn cold,

Of a bear that roamed freely, making campsites a wreck,

Thwarting trappers from Greeley, New Orleans, and Quebec.

'Til a gal with red hair and a trained 3D brain

Said, "I'll capture that bear in a folded-up plane."

She cut and she scored, and made a sight to behold:

An old sheet of board that was ready to fold.

When the job was complete, she made bait from old fish.

The bear thought it smelled sweet: "Les Poissons! Très delish!"

Then sproing, slip, and slap! As quick as a fox

She flipped the last flap, and caught the bear in the box.

They set the bear free, far north in the wood,

Where he let campers be and ne'er again ate their food.

The lesson we've learned is to question brute force,

And you've no doubt discerned that I had to work in some reference to this chapter's topic of cardboard boxes, though I did have to stretch—just a little, of course.

Boxes made out of corrugated cardboard are ubiquitous but often overlooked. Some boxes are remarkable because they are made of a single piece of cardboard that is neither glued nor taped. Yet they are capable of great strength, rigidity, and longevity, protecting fragile items during international shipping, or holding a set of favorite pens and pencils for many years.

In this chapter I'll share a few box designs and talk a little about how I like to think about them. My goal is not so much to present specifics, but to get your 3D visualization skills fired up. Once you make the models and play with them, and start to think about where the pieces fold and where the clearances need to be, then you can start to really see the entire shape in your head. The simple 2D layout transforms into a potential 3D object: the template seems to want to jump up and fold itself into a box, and you can see in your mind's eye just how cleanly everything fits and how strong and stable the result will be.

A Long Time Ago . . .

Corrugated cardboard is a relatively recent invention that began life as something called *fluted medium*. This is simply paper that has been shaped into an extruded sine wave, shown in Figure 13.1a. Fluted medium was originally used as a sweatband in men's hats. I suspect that this had two advantages. First, the crinkled paper could give a little bit, thus ensuring a snug and comfortable fit for slightly different head shapes and sizes. Second, like a fractal, this design increased the available surface area, so that the ring could absorb more sweat than a simple cylinder.

In 1871, Albert L. Johnes received a patent on using fluted medium to protect bottles when they were stored and shipped. One drawback to fluted medium at this point was that with enough pressure, it could flatten out again and lose its shock-absorbing abilities. This changed in 1874, when Oliver Long received a patent for gluing a sheet of paperboard to both sides of the fluted medium, creating the corrugated cardboard we know today. The paper served to keep the fluted medium curved, maintaining its ability to absorb shock. The original fluted medium is today called *unlined*. With a paperboard liner on one side (as in Figure 13.1b), it's called *single-face corrugated board*. The most common variety is covered on both sides; it's shown in Figure 13.1c and called *double-face* or *single-wall corrugated board*.

Figure 13.1
Making corrugated
cardboard.
(a) Fluted medium.
(b) Single-face cor-
rugated board.
(c) Double-face or
single-wall corru-
gated board.

The idea of selling individual products in their own package directly to the individual came a few years later. In 1879, Robert Gair was a Brooklyn printer and packaging material manufacturer. During a press run of seed packets, one of the printing plates was incorrectly placed on the press and ended up slicing a package. While looking at the ripped package, Gair had the idea of replacing the printing plates with cutting plates, and the die-cut package was born. It first hit the shelves in 1896, when the National Biscuit Company started to sell Uneeda crackers in their own boxes (along with an inner sleeve to retard spoiling). As little as 25 years later there were hundreds of manufacturers of cardboard cartons in the United States alone.

Building Better Boxes

Designing a cardboard box is not trivial work: it requires balancing aesthetic demands and practical efficiency. A designer needs to wield a relatively small set of design techniques with imagination to come up with a design that is economical, practical, and attractive.

When a designer wants to show a proposed box to a client, he or she prepares a *cutter diagram;* this is simply a drawing of the layout of the unfolded box, showing where cuts need to be made, pieces punched out, and folds scored (along with the direction of the fold). The conventions for these diagrams are very much like those in origami. A solid line indicates a cut, a dotted line means the pieces on both sides of the fold are pushed away from you (creating a mountain), and a line of alternating dashes and dots means the pieces are folded up toward you (creating a valley). From the cutter diagram the designer makes a *blank,* or a plain cardboard mock-up of the design. If the client approves, then the artwork is designed and registered to the box.

The blanks are generally created in one of three ways. First, you can shape a piece of metal into the desired outline of the box and use it like a cookie cutter to stamp the box from the cardboard sheet. This is called *hollow die cutting,* a technique used exclusively for labels and envelopes. Second, you can shape one or more metal steel rules into shape, then push them into precut grooves in a piece of 3/4-inch plywood. This technique of *steel-rule die cutting* can be used with both flat and cylindrical presses. If the steel rule is blunted, then it can be used to press grooves and thereby score folds. This is by far the most common technique. A recent innovation is *laser cutting.* The advantage here is efficiency and accuracy, though it's used less often than steel-rule die cutting.

Once cut and scored, the blanks are delivered to the client in *knock-down form,* which simply means that they're flat but ready to be assembled (this involves folding, and perhaps gluing, taping, and adding extra pieces such as rubber bands or springs).

Many cutter diagrams can be made at home with traditional tools: straightedge, ruler, compass, calipers, etc. I find that although there's a certain aesthetic appeal to the paper-and-pencil route, I can work a lot more quickly on the computer using an off-the-shelf 2D drafting program. Then it's easy to make a variation on a design, which can be printed, rubber-cemented to a piece of manila folder, and then cut out and scored. I find that a metal straightedge and X-ACTO knife work fine for making cuts. An empty ballpoint pen can be used for scoring, but you have to be careful not to rip through the paperboard. One iteration of the loop from printing the diagram to holding the final box takes only about 15 minutes for the boxes I describe here.

Hexagonal Envelope

Before we get into major 3D mental-visual calisthenics, let's warm up with a simple workout: a flat hexagonal envelope. This is made from light board such as a manila folder; because this material is quite thin, we can pretty much treat it as infinitely thin when designing the diagram, and things will still line up pretty closely. This envelope is meant to contain something thin and small, such as a party announcement, photograph, or blueberry pancake.

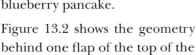

Figure 13.2 shows the geometry behind one flap of the top of the envelope. Figure 13.3 shows the template for the entire hexagonal envelope, and Figure 13.4 shows the result. The top stays closed because the curved bit on the side of each triangle holds down its neighbor. Since the lid is circular, each flap simultaneously contributes both to the tension pulling the envelope open and to the mutual pressure to keep it closed.

In Figure 13.5 I've added walls to create a squat hexagonal box; the principle is the same. The triangular flaps tuck inside their neighbor to prevent cracks at the edges. You could still use manila folders for a short box; corrugated cardboard would be better for a tall one. This is a good box

Figure 13.2
The geometry of a flap of the hexagonal envelope. Equilateral triangle $\triangle ABC$ sits next to 30-60-90 triangle $\triangle ADC$. E is the center of a circle that lies anywhere on the line joining A and the bisector of side BC. When E is chosen, the radius is determined by the distance to B (or C). The heavy line shows the flap.

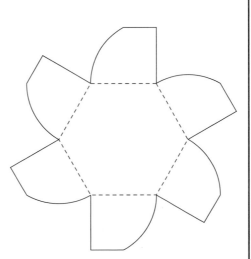

Figure 13.3
The cutter diagram for the hexagonal envelope.

for collections of things, such as buttons, rubber bands, or stacks of blueberry pancakes.

Construction Techniques

Now we're ready to get into thicker, stronger materials, such as corrugated cardboard. I'm not an expert in this subject; I don't have any firsthand knowledge of how these boxes are professionally designed and built. But from examining a lot of boxes, and playing with them on my own, I've come to recognize a few techniques that appear over and over. The description of the boxes will be much easier if we cover these techniques first.

Figure 13.4
The hexagonal envelope made from a manila folder.

To see them, let's start with a simple cube; Figure 13.6 shows one of many possible cutter diagrams for the six square faces. To build a cube from this we'd need to tape the edges, since it can't hold together by itself. And even then it will be structurally weak and prone to wobbling and crushing. For practical use, we'd want to improve two things about this cube. First, it should be stronger, so anything placed inside (such as a handful of pudding) won't be squashed. Second, it should be more rigid, or stable, so that it doesn't wobble around. These two properties of a strong box are closely related, but before passing judgment on a design we should check it for both criteria.

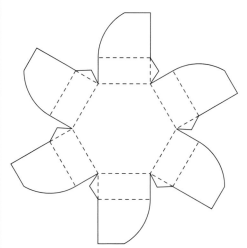

Figure 13.5
The cutter diagram for the hexagonal box.

Let's now look at some techniques for improving this simple box.

FLAPS AND LOCKING

One of the most elegant answers to both strength and rigidity is the use of *flaps*. Flaps can be used to create walls several layers

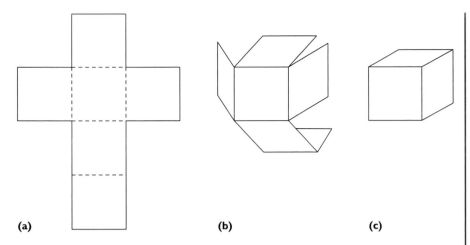

(a)   **(b)**   **(c)**

Figure 13.6
A cubical box.
(a) The cutter diagram.
(b) Folding it up.
(c) The resulting box, which will only hold together if taped or glued.

thick, which strengthens them. And flaps can hold in place other flaps, helping the structure maintain its designed shape. There are all sorts of ways to use flaps to do these jobs, but they all have something in common: somewhere, something has to lock into place.

Figure 13.7 shows one approach using a tab and a hole: a flap has a tab at the end, and that end goes into a hole elsewhere. The tab doesn't come out the other side; it's only as long as the cardboard is thick. The only pressure on the tab is sideways, which pushes it against the side of the hole. The rest of the box is usually arranged to keep the tab in the slot when the box is closed.

A cheaper version of the same device is shown in Figure 13.8, except in this case we don't even make the hole. The flap is shorter and the tab pushes

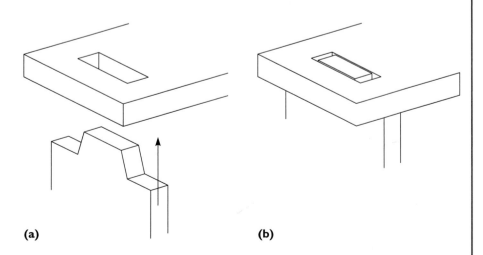

(a)   **(b)**

Figure 13.7
(a) The tab fits into the hole.
(b) But it doesn't extend out the other side.

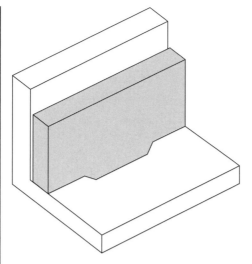

against the board where a hole would be. By making the tab slightly too long to fit in the box, if you jam the tab down into the board it will crush a little, and the pressure will keep the tab from sliding around. This is weaker than using a slot, but cheaper to manufacture (since you don't have to cut a hole). You can make this device stronger on a long edge by using several tabs side by side.

Another useful device keeps the box shut. Figure 13.9 shows the idea: a tab on the front face pushes into a hole in the edge between the top and inside-front faces. If the cardboard is just a little thicker than the hole, it will be squeezed a little by the bottom edge of the hole against the top. If

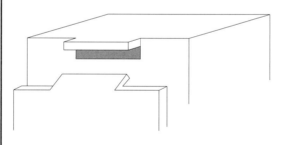

the grain of the cardboard is parallel to the hole, then the bottom piece can actually move into the dips of the inner corrugated layer, as in Figure 13.10. This friction helps keep the tab in place, and this keeps the top closed. A U-cut in the tab creates the smaller piece that you grip in order to

Figure 13.9
The tab fits into the slot along the edge.

pull the larger tab out. As we'll see with the shoe box below, a particularly elegant touch is that the hole is cut so that the top face protrudes a little forward; this gives you something to grip with your thumb when pulling the top of the box open.

PARAMETERIZATION

The thickness of the cardboard is imperative to the success of tabs. The tab technique just doesn't do you much good with thin card, because there's nothing for the tab to push against. The size of any locking device (tab or hole) needs to be matched to the thickness of the card.

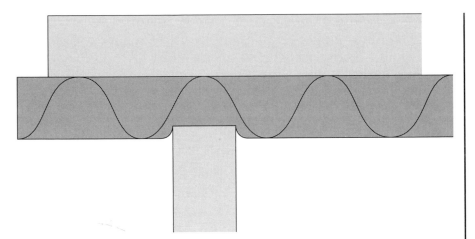

Figure 13.10
The tab in Figure
13.9 is held in place
by the slightly too
narrow slot.

Thus we are naturally led to parameterizing the templates, which is a good idea anyway. All of the sizes of the template should be in proportion to the four numbers that describe the box. These are length L, width W, depth D, and thickness T. I found it convenient to define T as one-half the thickness of the board; thus a sheet of cardboard has thickness $2T$.

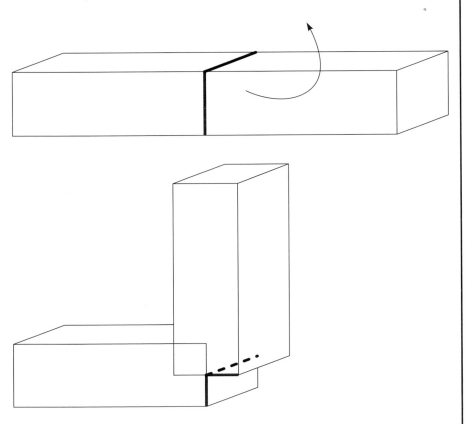

Figure 13.11
The fold is mod-
eled as though two
separate pieces of
cardboard shared a
centered hinge.

The box's measurements denote its outermost dimensions, including the thickness of the cardboard. So if you have a hole in a piece of concrete with dimensions L, W, and D, then a box made with those numbers will exactly fit in the hole.

Naturally, this isn't exactly true in practice. The big question is what happens when the board folds. I spent some time folding corrugated cardboard and examining the process, and I came up with the model in Figure 13.11. Basically I assume that the board folds around a hinge in the middle of the card. The paper on the inside of the hinge compresses, and the paper on the outside stretches. This is obviously an approximation, but it seems to fit what I see when I fold a sheet, and it matches the way most boxes seem to be cut when I open them up and measure the pieces.

Figure 13.12 shows how to analyze a U-fold, such as at the bottom of a box. The rule of thumb is that at a 90-degree fold, the folded cardboard sticks out a distance T beyond the base (and extends T inward as well). So if the U is meant to be W units wide, the fold lines are drawn a distance of $W - 2T$ apart; when the ends are folded upward, the distance T sticking out on both sides brings the total width to W. This is why I use T for the half-thickness of the cardboard and $2T$ for the full thickness.

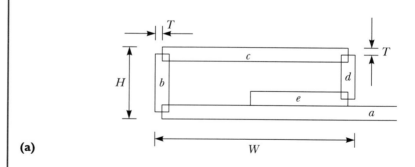

(a)

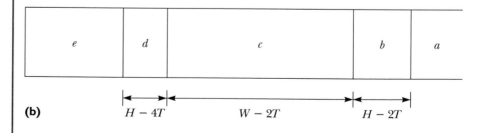

(b)

Figure 13.12
(a) A U-fold as part of a wrapped-up tube.
(b) If the total width is W, the distance between fold lines for section c is $W - 2T$.

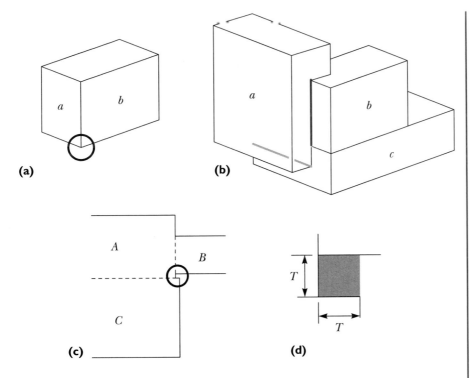

(a)

(b)

(c)

(d)

Figure 13.13
A corner fold.
(a) The corner of
a box.
(b) A close-up of
the fold.
(c) The diagram
for the corner.
(d) A close-up of
the diagram.

IDIOMS

We've already seen one common feature of corrugated boxes: folds extend
T units over their base. Another common idiom is the 3D corner.

Figure 13.13a shows the corner of a box; Figure 13.13b shows how to analyze the construction. Notice two features. First, the bottom of b is above
the bottom of a; this is because c folds around hinge AC and will extend T
units above the hinge line. Thus b needs to be cut short by T units. Similarly, the side of c has to be wider than a, so it can line up with b. So c extends beyond a by T units. Figure 13.13c shows how this looks in a diagram.
The little notch is a characteristic feature of many corners.

You can cheat sometimes and leave the notch out. The safest place to do
this is if one of the sides is an internal flap, not an actual outside of the
box. Then it will scrunch up against the other piece, which can provide it
with a little side-to-side strengthening.

Lockbox

Figure 13.14 shows a box that I call a *lockbox,* because it locks up tight. I got
this design from a box full of books that I recently received. I knew it had

Figure 13.14
A photo of a
lockbox.

to be very reliable if it carried such precious cargo without damage. I took the box apart and studied it, resulting in the diagram in Figure 13.15. I've labeled some spots in Figure 13.15—the other half of the diagram is symmetrical (as such templates often are).

The first trick is set up by the side flap f. When folded in, it provides another layer of thickness against wall h, strengthening it and keeping it from moving. The payoff comes with the flap made of p and r. p pops up on the outside, which is fine. Then the little bit between them rolls over the top and r goes back down inside, locking into the base with a tab. This is a huge win in stability and strength. With this trick we have tripled the thickness of the side wall, making it strong and stable. We've also added stability to the front and back sides s and t, because they are now prevented from rotating around their hinges.

As if this weren't enough, the top fits inside this thick wall and adds a fourth layer. Then the front tucks into the front of the wall, reinforcing the corner against dents while adding a fifth layer to the wall (though it only covers a bit of the wall). Figuring out the parameterizations and hinge axes

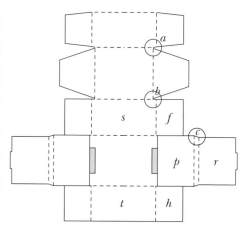

for this box is enormously aided by having the real box there to work on.

I've made special note of three interesting spots, marked a, b, and c; these are enlarged in Figure 13.16. The things to note here are the extra clearance in the notches of thickness T in a and b, and how the width of flap r is reduced by $2T$ in c. I origi-

Figure 13.15
The diagram for
the lockbox.

nally wrote a few paragraphs to explain these details, but decided this is one case where experience is worth a thousand explanations. I highly encourage you to build this box (or disassemble one like it) and see for yourself why these little adjustments are not just useful, but elegant.

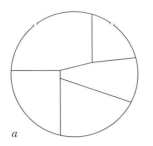
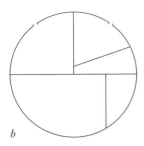
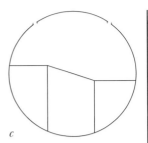

Figure 13.16
Close-ups of regions *a*, *b*, and *c* in Figure 13.15.

Shoe Box

I bought some new sneakers last week, and I selected one model in particular because they were tough and strong. The manufacturer played off this reputation by printing locks and chains on the shoe box, as though what was inside was so powerful that it required that kind of force to keep it contained. Wow—that's a lot of promise for a sneaker!

Figure 13.17
A photo of a shoe box.

The package would be a joke if it were made of flimsy, thin board. This shoe box is *solid,* contributing to the notion of something strong inside. I squeezed hard on the walls of this box, and it didn't buckle or give. A photo is shown in Figure 13.17, and the diagram is in Figure 13.18. A close-up appears in Figure 13.19.

This strength starts with a medium-thickness board (about 3 mm). We then see a couple of variations on the lockbox trick. The side flaps reinforce the base rather than the sides, but then other flaps make the sides triple-thick. We then use a tab and a slot to keep the sandwich on the sides together. The front flap doesn't tuck into the front as we saw before. Instead, there's a flap that sticks into a slot in the top front. This is very important: if

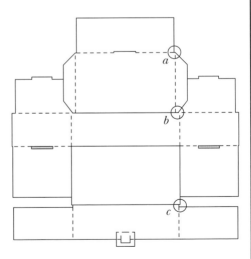

Figure 13.18
The diagram for the shoe box.

Figure 13.19
Close-ups of re-
gions *a*, *b*, and *c* in
Figure 13.18.

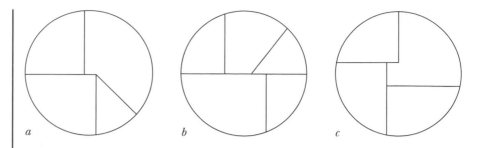

this additional locking device had not been included, then the top would stay on only as a friction fit, and the dangerous sneakers could escape at any time.

Figure 13.20
A photo of an easel
display.

Again, I've noted three interesting details in the diagram and enlarged them in Figure 13.19; if you build the box you may be as impressed as I was with how the designer made the right adjustments in the right places.

Display Easel

A nice example of a display made out of corrugated board is shown in Figure 13.20. This little display easel is made from a single sheet, yet it provides a stand with thickness (for many sheets of paper, or a thin product), a short base, and a solid, locking support. The diagram is in Figure 13.21.

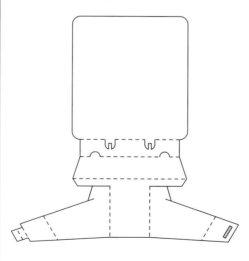

Figure 13.21
The diagram for
the easel.

CD-ROM Package

A lot of software is sold today on CD-ROM. But CD-ROMs are pretty small, and I've gotten the feeling that manufacturers like to sell things in big boxes—it implies that you're getting a lot of stuff for your money. So they include some documentation, a registration card, and perhaps advertisements for other products. Now they have the problem of keeping the CD-ROM from flopping around in the much larger box.

Typically designers create a light, eye-catching cardboard sleeve around a corrugated sheet that cradles the CD-ROM and keeps the documentation together. Figure 13.22 shows an example. The diagram is shown in Figure 13.23.

I included this example because it is so elegant. The CD is held safely in the middle of the box, protected and buffered on all sides, and the printed materials are all kept in their own compartment. The downside of this design is that it is wasteful; the package could be much smaller and use less material. I'm guessing that marketers and retailers have a minimum-sized package in mind, large enough to contain arresting graphics and to suggest that it's full of good stuff.

Figure 13.22
A photo of a partially folded CD and documentation holder.

Pizza Box

I recently bought a refrigerated pizza in my grocery store. The pizza was packaged in a strange cardboard container. The pizza and the packaging are the product of Testa Rossa, a local Seattle pizzeria. On the bottom of the box, they say that in order to protect the pizza, they spent "oodles of time" inventing the box. I think they did a pretty good job.

Figure 13.24 gives the template. It's probably pretty obvious how it works: the pizza sits on the circular piece, and the straps wrap up around it. Each strap has a short segment in it, just the height of the pizza. Each strap is attached to the base at both ends, and the straps are connected together where they cross. Thus neither of the straps can slip sideways with respect to the other. The pizza is protected at the outsides, and the only place it can really get crushed is in the middle.

These pizzas are displayed in the supermarket tilted upward slightly. The packaging keeps them protected from each other, and from the other food in your cart, bag, and refrigerator.

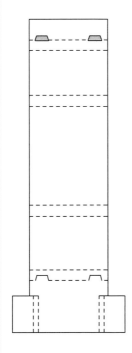

Figure 13.23
The diagram for the CD and documentation holder.

Folding Up

I encourage you to build the models, play with the pieces, and try out variations. Or disassemble some boxes on your own and see how they're built.

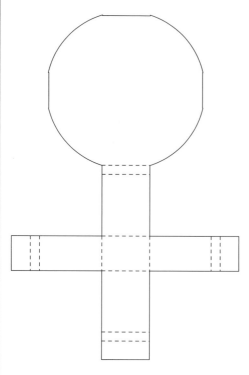

Figure 13.24
The diagram for the pizza box. Note the small notches in the circular base that are one thickness deep.

Some good advice on studio tips for making boxes is contained in *Card Engineering* by Ian Honeybone (Outline Press, 1990). The hexagonal box in this chapter was taken from that book. Most of the history section (excluding my conjectures) came from *The Packaging Designer's Book of Patterns* by Lászlo Roth and George L. Wybenga (Van Nostrand Reinhold, 1991).

I recommend starting out with thin card for your designs until you get the hang of things; it's easier to cut and quicker to try out new ideas. Then you can go to double-sided corrugated cardboard for structures with a lot of strength, rigidity, and durability.

Incidentally, box knowledge can have great practical value. Every few years, the Siggraph conference hosts the Siggraph Bowl. This is a contest in which three-person teams compete to answer questions about computer graphics trivia and lore. I was part of Team Seattle at Siggraph '98 in Orlando, along with my teammates David Salesin and Michael Cohen. Against some great teams, we somehow won Siggraph Bowl III.

As a first-place prize, we each received an inscribed Luxo desk lamp. One member of the team—who shall remain forever nameless—opened up his box on the spot to admire his prize, only to discover when putting it away that the lamps had been creatively packed in tricky cardboard boxes. Only through our knowledge of boxes and packing techniques were we able to get the lamp safely repacked in its original box and shipped back to Washington unharmed, where it now sheds its light of triumphant victory through the rainy Seattle days and nights.

The
Triangular
Manuscripts

ANDREW GLASSNER'S NOTEBOOK
November/December 1998

14

Last week I got a call from my old friend, Professor Stan Conversion. He'd just bought a new boat, the *Wave Interference,* and invited me to a cruise on Lake Washington. That Saturday the weather was beautiful. As we sailed around the islands of Puget Sound, he handed me a letter.

"This arrived recently from a former student," he said. "What do you think?" I settled back in the deck chair and read. "Dear Stan," it began.

"A month ago my husband and I were shopping for antiques in Port Townsend when we found a wonderful old dresser in a dusty, out-of-the-way shop. It was kind of beat up, but Dan agreed that with some work it could look lovely. When we asked the store owner how much it cost, he suddenly looked very frightened and said that he thought he'd gotten rid of the dresser long ago. Not 'sold,' but 'gotten rid of.' He seemed quite upset.

"Then he told us to leave, and to forget about the dresser. He said it was haunted! He told us that when the spirits were angered, the drawers wouldn't close properly, and if you pushed harder, you could hear the sound of their withered, ghostly bones cracking in agony. Well, of course Dan and I laughed it off and insisted that he let us buy it from him. He warned us again, but we persisted. I think he finally sold it to us just to get it, and us, out of his store.

"We started in on it that afternoon, and sure enough we found that after removing the bottom drawer, we couldn't push it all the way back in again. And we actually did hear a strange crunching sound when we tried to force it shut! Taking off the back of the dresser, we found a large brown envelope full of old papers, caught on one of the drawer runners. Pushing on the drawer simply caused the papers to crunch together.

"Dan and I opened the envelope and found pages of what looked like parchment paper. They were old and brittle and some of the ink was faded, but we could make out some of the words. I immediately realized that if anyone could do justice to these aged sheets, it would be you. We are putting them into this box along with this letter. I know you'll do the right thing."

The letter continued with a few personal anecdotes and then closed. I turned to Stan and asked to see the papers. He handed me a few, and I was immediately intrigued.

Each page, about the size of a newspaper sheet, was hand-lettered in elegant copperplate. The papers contained some line drawings, but many were so badly smeared that I couldn't figure out what they represented. The pages were unsigned. We had no idea who wrote them, though some historical references seemed to indicate they were written around 1780. The only clue to authorship was the appearance of three small triangles in the bottom-right corner of each page, like this: $\Delta\nabla\Delta$, so we have taken to calling them the *Triangular Manuscripts*. They all seemed to deal with inventions of various sorts, one per page, like a laboratory notebook.

The text had been processed through a fairly elaborate cipher, which Stan had figured out. The cipher key changes every few letters, so recovering the original text is a slow process. Stan deciphered one of the shorter pages on his own, and together we worked out two more.

Though our work is still new and results are few, I want to share the partial results of our investigations. With Stan's permission, excerpts from the papers appear below. I did only the most minor editing possible to make the text available to modern readers—I preserved the original spelling, grammar, opinions, and even errors in the interests of historical accuracy.

The Eufonious Insektothon

Wonderful Strange are Animals that Lyte of their own Akkord. The Fyre burns Inside them, causing those that are Airborne to Ryse through the

Heat of their Bodies, in akkordance with my Principle of Ethereal Transmutation. Such Lytening Bugges, or Fyreflys, are often to be seen late of an evening about Country-syde Manors. Their Purpose is as yet unklear to me, tho it seems more than likely they Promote the Development of Lytening from the Skye, seeing as they deposit small Bits of Fyre into the Air wheresoever they Travel. Such Fyre Bits, upon being Link'd, do cause a Chain of Luminous Flux, leading to the Jagg'd pattern of Bolts of Lyte such as on a Stormy Nyte. As do Farmers plant Seeds in the chill of Spring, so do Insekts plant Fyre in the Calm Air of a Summer's Nyte, only to grow to full Lytening Bolts in the midst of Storm.

But such Animals, tho direkt'd by their own Instinkts, may yet be harness'd for greater Good by Man. Much as we have trained Dogs, Cats, Monkeys, Elefants, Lemurs, and, if rumor be trusted, the mithikal Jirraff found only in Afrika, so may we train these Bugges of Illuminary Fluxion.

I propose that by means of a System adapted from that used for Horses, I teach a Collektion of these Bugges to fly through a Volumme of Space for a set Periode of Tyme. I shall use a set of Eufoniums to communikate Musikal Cues to the Fyre-making Capacities of the Creatures. Each small Insekt shall be train'd to fly, then to hover at an especial Pointe in Space. Then each shall be instrukted, by means of Chords both Major and Minor, to lyte at a Partikular Moment, and then douse. Thus do we make a Volumme of Space into a Cloude of Lytes, each glowing at the Proper Moment, and to the Proper Degree, such that they form a Pikture in that Space.

This Pikture may be originally design'd within a Frame, built from simple materials such as Wood and String, and Beads upon Strings, that forms a Volumme of Space within which the Colored Beads are Strung. By properly adjusting the Musikal Chords play'd to the Creatures, we do create the Pikture in Space. Thus do I call this my *Eufonious Insektothon,* and shall seek Patronship for the funding thereof.

Upon suksessful completion of the Insektothon, I envision a Colorized Version, in which the Fyre-making Abdomen of each Animal is dipp'd in a Gelle of Color'd Material, which does then cover and color the Fyre thereof. Thus when the Animal does glow, it appears with the Color plac'd upon it. Four Colors are Necessary, pertaining to Earth (Brown), Air (Clear), Fire (Red), and Water (Blue). From these Four Colors may all other Colors be made, as is self-evident by Mental Introspektion.

The Lunatick's Refuge

Of late I have been considering the sorry state of the Lunatick, or Madman, as he stumbles through the World. Robb'd of Sense and Manners by Harsh Birthing or Sorry Cirkumstance, he must imitate, as best he can, the Lyfe of Men not so Afflikt'd. Lest I sound harsh, I hasten to assure my unknown yet assuredly Gentle Reader that all Men are Mad as may they be, but learn by Tricks and Deceits various to disguise the Affirmity. Such

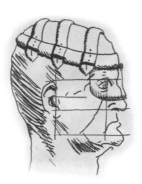

Men, which inklude myself, manage their way with only Miskonceptions, Errors, and Poor Judjment to plague their days. But those truly Mad must deal with a world lacking in Meaning and Reason, and this can only be pity'd.

Such Men, and to a frytening degree, Women as well, though their Fairer Sex protekts them from the most bitter enkounters with the World at large, must turn to Worlds of their own Devyce. Which is to say, they invent new Worlds to inhabit.

Such persons visit'd but mildly by Madness may yet make their way as Creators for others. Such Men may as like bekomme tellers of Stories, painters of Piktures, or those who shape Wood or Clay to ends Various, Ornamental, and by turns, even Useful. For such Madness should we be Gratefull, for our world is Illuminated by such Works when turned well on the Lathe of Insanity. But to those more sorrowfully Bestow'd, the true Lunatick, we can but be moved to pity, and to make his Lyfe full of as little Despair as Inventable.

Upon Reflektion on the matter, I foresee a Construktion for Lunaticks that will be created to soothe their urgent souls. This Devyce shall be affixed to the pitifull Madman's Head, and due to such attachement, shall move with his Head, Mirroring its every Motion. In such respekts it is but a Hat. But it is more, for the Lunatick's Hat shall enchant and divert him. It shall present him with Images and Sounds that will block those Aspekts of the World that serve only to strain the Lunatick's Faint Resources. Such Images and Sounds shall move, and even appear as Animated Figures, such that they seem to Replace the World that causes such Distress. They shall appear in front of the Madman, on a piece of the Hat that does cover his Eyes.

This Majikal Hat will be a Precious Devyce, power'd by many Attendants, who shall labor long to create Content to amuse the Madman in Pikture and Sound. The Madman shall be ty'd by the Attendants by a Chain of Power, which will hold him fast, close to the Source of the Illusionary World, and his Mobility will be Restrikted. And this shall be Good, for a Madman Confin'd is a Madman Safe. And thus shall the Madman be Sooth'd, and the Imaginary World will look and sound to the Madman as a Real World, and Restfullness will come to his Breast.

But the Madman, though his World be distorted through the Lens of Damaged Sentience, still knows the World As It Is. The World is not made of Ghosts and Vapors, and Beings that Float in the Air, Transparent as Glass. And thus shall the Hat be lacking. For the Piktures presented to the Madman shall appear in front of him, but yet not obskure the World, for such is the Way of Danger. Even the Insane are able to Step Asyde from the Kicking Horse, give Wide Berth to the Plummeting Can of Red Paint, and Dodge the Okkasional Flaming Man. All can do much Harm but are easily avoided with the fakulty of Vision and Sound. Thus the Majikal Hat must not truly Isolate the Madman, but rather allow the World As It Is to show through, and place the World As the Lunatick Wishes It To Be in front of the True World. Even the Lunatick's Attendants could never be so Cruel as to truly Isolate the Madman from the True World entirely when he Wears his Hat.

And thus the World of the Hat, presented to the Madman for to Soothe him, shall instead Drive him to Terror, and Deep Horror, for the world shall be filled with Transient Beings and Transparent Objekts not deriv'd of the World. The Madman will see his Majikal Hat as a source of Fear, and thus be Dis-Serviced.

Thus, have I developed *The Lunatick's Refuge*. This is a Majikal Hat refined with a sekond layer, also in front of the Eyes, but behind the first layer and before the World. Upon the first layer shall be the Images that soothe the Madman. In the World exist all the Perils that drive him Mad. In between is a layer that shall create an Opaque Place where the nearer layer creates Imaginary Objekts. Thus, when there is no Fantastickal Image on the first layer in front of the Lunatick, he sees the World As It Is, in its Terrifying Glory. When the first layer holds an Image Artifishal, the sekond layer is Opaque as the darkest Ink, so that the near objekt does not Float in the Air, but rather appears Part of the World. For all its Benefits, the Majickal Hat, both in Original and Improved Forms, must Not be Worn by the Sane, for it shall Surely turn them Mad as well.

I see these layers of Images and Opaque Places as thin Fishbowls. The near layer, two Panes of Glass held closely together, filled with Water, holds many Small Fishes that do Hover and Dart as needed to create the Image as diktated by the Lunatick's Assistants. How these Fishes shall be Train'd is a matter of importance, which I hope to diskover by way of Eksperiment. I believe they will be Amenable to Vibration, and shall investigate their control by Vibrating the Madman's Skull (by way of a Devyce attached to the Teeth). In the Opaque Layer, also Water between Panes, are Eels of the Blackest Color, train'd Similarly, and Kept between the first layer and the Outer World. I shall seek a Patron to support the Development of the Skull Vibrator and the Lunatick's Refuge.

The Millennial Extender

The Candle burns low upon my Desk. Tyme is visible in its every Flicker, each Dance of the Flame counts another Beat of my Heart. As must the Wick burn and shorten, so do the days of each Man. Due to my Principle of Wax Transmutation, we know that Wax Candles can neither be Created nor Destroy'd. The Illusion of Burning Wax is simply the failure of our Senses to perceive its Transformation into the Body of a Rhynoceros (in some Far-Off Place), whose Body is made of Wax. When the Rhynoceros dies, its Bones return to their basick Wax state, giving ryse to new Candles.

And as Candles burn, so do the days count down. To keep Tyme is to lock up Eternity, and this is the province of only Heaven Itself. But to mark Tyme, and rekord its Passing, is Noble and Good, for it allows us to plant at the Correct Moment, harvest when the Fruit is Rype, and stay Indoors to avoid the Noxious Gases of the Dekomposing Rhynoceri as they Transmute back into Wax.

Though Tyme can only be seen as it Passes, still we can mark the Passing. For many Years have I used my Cirkular Candelabra to mark the Moments. With this Cirkular Candelabra am I able to determine the Tyme of the Day to within a Minute. This is of great value to me in my Celestial Observations and cooking of Egges in a Hard-Boil'd Manner.

From Wyse Predecessors we have Inherited a great many Useful Devyces. The Self-Lyting Wood is of Great Value during long Winter's nytes. The Nose Hair Trimmer is of great value in the Toilette, for though this Domestikated Animal can indeed cause Serious Damage when neglekted, with Love and Attention it is usually Quite Safe. And Liquid Stone is indeed a Blessing for those tymes when one carves an Important Dokument in Granite and chisels the Wrongge Letter. Usually I find this the result of Insufficient Sleep, or Distraktion, most often traceable to Troubles in the Matter of Footwear.

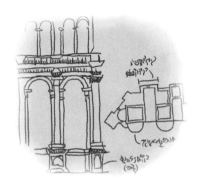

Perhaps the Most Useful of all such Devyces is the Crystal Chronograph. This wondrous Construktion allows us to track the Changes of the Days. The Crystal Chronograph in my Employ is Large as the Outside Wall of my Home, which faces the Square. But I am Glad to use the Space as it assures me of Fyner Hairkuts since my Hairdresser can no longer claim that she was not aware of the Date for our Regularly Skeduled Appointments.

The Crystal Chronograph has a Great Many other Uses, but I fear for its Long-Term Value. Perhaps the Desyners were not thinking as far as the Farthest Thinkers today think. Consider the Strukture of the Crystal Chronograph. There are six Tubes with Slits in their Sydes, and the Keeper of the Mekanism is responsible for placing the Korrekt Number of Crystals in each Tube. A glance at any Tube reveals how many Crystals are stacked insyde, from Zero to Nyne.

The two Leftmost Tubes, or Columns, indikate the Day of the Month. The middle Tubes rekord the Month of the Year. And the Rytemost Pair of

Tubes indikate the Year. Thus would the Fourth Day of the Sixth Month of the Nynety-Eighth Year be Represented as 04/06/98.

Clearly the Desyners did not expekt the Chronograph to last beyond the Fynal Day of December in the Nynety-Nynth Year of this Century. This is a Shocking and Unexpekted Flaw. I Suspekt that the Cause can only be Determin'd after Extensive Research on Tropikal Islands and propose to seek a Patron to Sponsor such Serious Work.

But the Problem Remains, that come the Last Day of the Century, we will Experience Terrible Problems, when those few who have been train'd to track Dates will suddenly make Many Errors. The Risks are Huge: Old Men will bekomme Children, and okkupy Clothing that is Many Syzes Too Large. Milk will bekomme Very, Very, Very, Very, Very Sour Overnyte. Ships will Cross Myty Oceans in Numerous Round Trips in the tyme Normally Requir'd to Wash a Shirt.

These Calamities must be Avoided. But the Makers of the Crystal Chronograph are not Numerous Enough to effekt all the Necessary Repairs in Tyme. We seem Poised for Trouble. If only we could Extend Tyme in some way, there myte be Tyme Enough to repair this and All Other Crystal Chronographs, or we could Invent something New that would not have these Problems.

Enter my *Millennial Extender.* Unlike my other Inventions, Creations, and Propositions, the Millennial Extender requires no Construktion. We merely need to Re-Interpret what we Already Have.

Consider that we now use the Leftmost Columns to represent the Numbers 01 to 31. This is Good and Sensible, since the Months have Days with these Values. But the Numbers 32 to 99 are Ignored, and this Wasted Potentshul can Weigh Heavily on the Sands of Tyme. Consider also the Months, represented by the center two Tubes, which are used to denote 01 to 12. The Wastage is Worse, since we have ignored months 13 to 99.

The Solution I propose is Simple. The Fynal Year of the Century is almost upon us. When it arryves, we mark the first day as 01/01/99, as Diktated by Convention. The Final Day of the First Month is of course 01/31/99. The Next Day would traditionally be counted as 02/01/99. To this I say No! Observe the Waste and the Tyme that is so casually Disregarded in such Cavalier Dismissal of the Missing Days.

Rather, the Next Day is Instead Marked in My New Rekkoning as 01/32/99. This continues, Counting the First Month as holding 100 Days. Then the Fynal Day of the First Month, 01/99/99 will Arryve, Nynety-Nyne Days after the first Day of the Month. Only Then do we move to the Next Month, 02/01/99. In This Way, we create a Year of 9801 Days (since Month 00 and Day 00 are Diffikult to Teach to the Assistants who Maintain the Chronograph). This is Just Less than 27 more Years in which to Address the Problems diskussed Above.

With this Simple Change, we easily gain 27 Years in which to Repair our Chronographs and Invent New Chronographs that are not Limited to Two-Digit Years. When the Last Day arrives, it shall be Demarked 99/99/99, and truly Tyme shall have been Fully Pack'd with Days.

Of course, I rekognize that this Problem is Stricktly a Result of Primitive Teknology and Embarrassing Lack of Foresyte by the Designers of the Crystal Chronograph. Surely no Future Civilyzation will make such a Mistake again. Should they do so, the Mass of Rhynoceros Flesh turning into Wax and Vyce Versa over the Course of a Few Short Hours will convince them never to make the Mistake again.

Concluding Remarks

I would like to thank Professor Stan Conversion for his assistance in deciphering the first three pages of the original manuscript and for his gracious permission in allowing me to present the excerpts above.

It is impossible to know where this archaeology project will take us. We have deciphered a few fragments on several other pages, and the ideas seem to interlock into some larger pattern. Stan and I have begun to develop some theories about what this bigger picture might be, but these pages and its contents are still pretty elusive. As our mysterious author might have said, it all seems Passing Strange.

Polygons under the Covers

ANDREW GLASSNER'S NOTEBOOK
January/February 1999

15

There are polygons everywhere. They're in our cereal, on our kitchen floors, and in the constellations in the skies. One place I didn't expect to see polygons is in the Fourier transform, but they're there as well.

The Fourier transform is an indispensable tool in signal processing. In computer graphics, it helps us understand and cure problems as diverse as jaggies on the edge of polygons, blocky-looking textures, and animated objects that appear to jump erratically as they move across the screen.

Alvy Ray Smith recently shared with me a memo of his that demonstrated a surprising interpretation of the mathematical functions known as the complex exponentials. He showed how in some circumstances these common expressions look like nothing more than regular polygons. Since these expressions are at the heart of the Fourier transform, I realized that this gave us a new interpretation of this important tool. This column is about that new interpretation.

I'll start off with a warm-up in using complex numbers to do geometry and then move on to the Fourier series, building up to a discussion of the new interpretation. If the Fourier series is new to you, don't worry—you'll see that it's actually pretty simple by the time we get there. And the payoff is worth the journey.

A Quick Refresher on Complex Numbers

The really cool results in this chapter depend on complex numbers. If you're familiar with this topic, you might want to just skim this section. Otherwise hang on and we'll cover the basics right now.

Complex numbers arose naturally as people thought about how to find some value of x that would satisfy $x^2 + 1 = 0$. It's a logical step in the sequence of trying to solve equations. To begin with, consider the equation $x + 3 = 5$. There is only one value of x that will work (that is, there is only one solution): $x = 2$. This x is an *integer*. Now consider $3x = 5$. The solution, $x = 5/3$, is a *real number* (that is, not an integer) and a *rational number*, which is specified as the ratio of two integers. Getting more ambitious, suppose we want to solve $x^2 = 3$. Now the only solution is $x = \sqrt{3}$, which is also real, but *irrational*. Mathematically, irrational doesn't mean emotionally unstable, but simply nonrational, that is, $\sqrt{3}$ cannot be expressed as the ratio of two integers. Some common irrational numbers are $\sqrt{2}$, $\sqrt{3}$, e, and π.

Back around 500 BCE, Pythagoras had developed a religion based on the mystic belief that the universe was based on integers. Everything could be explained with whole numbers and nothing but. He was willing to accommodate the idea of rational numbers, since they were themselves made of integers. Integer numbers, and their use to describe every aspect of the universe, were the fundamental starting points for his entire philosophy. But then he either invented or saw a proof that the length of the diagonal of a unit square was irrational. The proof is often taught in high school today—it's short, simple, and completely irrefutable. This was very, very bad news for Pythagoras, because it meant that his entire religion and philosophy were based on a mistake. Rather than reexamine his beliefs, Pythagoras decided to censor any discussion of the topic. He called irrational numbers *alogon*, which means "unutterable," and any mention of them was taboo.

Among his followers, known as the Pythagoreans, revealing the existence of irrational numbers was considered dangerously subversive. There are many fragmentary legends about those who revealed the existence of irrational numbers to the public. One story says that a man, perhaps named Hippasus of Metapontum, talked and was stabbed. Another story says that a group of publicizers was killed in a shipwreck under mysterious circumstances.

On a lighter note, consider the equation $x^2 + 1 = 0$. If we just grind out a solution, we find $x = \sqrt{-1}$. Whatever this may mean, it's been given the label i, so $i = \sqrt{-1}$ (engineers often use the symbol j for this; the right interpretation is usually clear from context). The question of just what $\sqrt{-1}$ "means" has been debated for a very long time, because it's a fascinating topic. But regardless of the philosophical interpretation, it's clearly a very convenient computational entity. We can combine a real and an imaginary number into a single new number z as $z = a + bi$, where a and b are real numbers (rational or irrational) and $i = \sqrt{-1}$. We say z is a *complex number.* Note that either part of z may be zero, so the complex numbers include all the pure reals and pure imaginaries.

What are the powers of i? Since anything raised to the 0 power is defined as 1, $i^0 = 1$, and anything to the first power is itself, so $i^1 = i$. By definition $i^2 = -1$. Building on these starting points, we find $i^3 = -i$, $i^4 = 1$, $i^5 = i$, $i^6 = -1$, and so on, the pattern repeating indefinitely.

Algebra with complex numbers is straightforward. To add, just add components. If $w = a + bi$ and $z = c + di$, then $w + z = (a + c) + (b + d)i$. To multiply, treat the complex numbers as factors: $(a + bi)(c + di) = ac + bci + adi + bdi^2 = (ac - bd) + (bc + ad)i$, using $i^2 = -1$. It's natural to try to get some kind of visual take on complex numbers. Since real numbers can be plotted along an axis, we can try to put them together with imaginary numbers along another axis. The plus sign in the complex number $a + bi$ seems to invite the idea of replacing it with a comma, giving the 2D point (a, b).

 In 1797 Caspar Wessel did just this. He placed the reals on the X axis of a normal 2D coordinate system and the purely imaginary numbers on the Y axis, creating what was later called an *Argand diagram.* The complex number $z = a + bi$ is represented by the point (a, b). A purely real number r sits on the X axis, and may be thought of as $r + 0i$. A purely imaginary number such as $0 + ri$ is on the Y axis. When a pair of axes is used this way, X identified with the reals and Y with the imaginaries, it is often referred to as the *complex plane.*

Interpreting complex numbers as points on the plane gives us some more ways to understand them. We can speak of the *magnitude* of a complex number $z = a + bi$, which is simply its Euclidean distance from the origin, $|z| = \sqrt{(a^2 + b^2)}$, and the *phase,* which is the angle it makes with the X axis, $\theta = \tan^{-1}(b/a)$.

A remarkable property of complex numbers is revealed when we compare the series expansions for sine and cosine with the series expansion of powers of e, Euler's constant. Many books derive these expansions. They work out to be

$$e^x = 1 + x + \frac{x^2}{2!} + \frac{x^3}{3!} + \frac{x^4}{4!} + \frac{x^5}{5!} + \frac{x^6}{6!} + \cdots$$

$$\cos x = 1 - \frac{x^2}{2!} + \frac{x^4}{4!} - \frac{x^6}{6!} + \frac{x^8}{8!} - \cdots$$

$$\sin x = x - \frac{x^3}{3!} + \frac{x^5}{5!} - \frac{x^7}{7!} + \frac{x^9}{9!} - \cdots$$

If we plug in i for x, we get the very useful identity

$$e^i = \cos 1 + i \sin 1$$

Combining this with de Moivre's theorem, a famous identity which tells us that $(\cos \theta + i \sin \theta) = (\cos 1 + i \sin 1)^\theta$, we find the important identity

$$e^{i\theta} = \cos \theta + i \sin \theta$$

which relates imaginary powers of e with complex numbers, or simply points on the complex plane. Notice that the magnitude of these points is 1, and the phase is simply θ. So if we know a complex number has magnitude r and phase θ, we may write it as $r(\cos \theta + i \sin \theta)$, or much more compactly as $re^{i\theta}$.

This expression, $r(\cos \theta + i \sin \theta)$, is called a *complex sinusoid*. If we plot its coordinates on the complex plane as θ moves from 0 to 2π, we get one complete circle of radius r. As θ grows beyond 2π, the sinusoid simply wraps around the circle again and again. Suppose we have two of these: $s_1 = e^{i\theta}$ and $s_3 = e^{i3\theta}$. Clearly s_3 spins around the unit circle three times faster than s_1. Just as Euclidean space is built on the idea that the X, Y, and Z axes are *orthogonal* (or at right angles) to one another, so does the Fourier transform makes use of the fact that these two functions are also orthogonal (though in a more abstract way).

Writing complex numbers as points in the complex plane gives us another way to see multiplication. If $z_1 = re^{i\theta}$ and $z_2 = se^{i\varphi}$, then $z_1 z_2 = (rs)e^{i(\theta + \varphi)}$. In words, this tells us that when two complex numbers are multiplied, we multiply their magnitudes and add their phases. If the magnitude of a complex number z is 1, then multiplying by z is equivalent to a rotation counterclockwise by the phase of z.

To wrap up with a bang, let's return to $e^{i\theta} = \cos\theta + i\sin\theta$, and set $\theta = \pi$. Then we arrive at one of the most remarkable expressions in all of mathematics:

$$e^{i\pi} + 1 = 0$$

This expresses a deep harmony among five fundamental constants representing number theory (0), arithmetic (1), algebra (i), trigonometry (π), and calculus (e).

Napoleon's Theorem

Now that we've covered complex numbers, let's begin with a lovely little theorem in elementary geometry:

> *Napoleon's Theorem:* Given any triangle $\triangle ABC$, erect equilateral triangles on each side (all facing inward or all facing outward) and connect the centroids of each of these triangles. The resulting triangle will itself be equilateral.

You may recall that the *centroid* of a triangle is the arithmetic average of the three vertices. Figure 15.1 shows an example of this theorem in action. I'll call the original three points $\mathbf{V} = (v_0, v_1, v_2)$, the three points at the tips of the new triangles $\mathbf{T}$, and the three points that make up the Napoleon triangle $\mathbf{N}$.

There are lots of ways to prove this theorem and, if you like working things out for yourself, you may want to take a shot at it yourself before reading on. I've seen proofs that are strictly geometric, strictly algebraic, and various combinations of the two. The approach I'll use here is based on representing each vertex of the triangle as a complex number. We'll see how to carry out

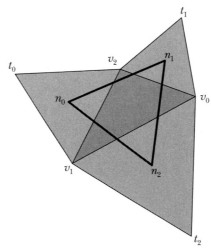

Figure 15.1
A demonstration of Napoleon's Theorem. The original triangle, **V,** shown in blue, is made of points (v_0, v_1, v_2). On each edge, we build an equilateral triangle facing outward; the new points, **T,** at the tip of these triangles are (t_0, t_1, t_2). The centroids of the three new triangles, (n_0, n_1, n_2), are joined with heavy black lines to form the Napoleon triangle, **N,** which is equilateral.

the construction with the complex interpretation, then prove that it's right.

Figure 15.2
Finding n_0 at the intersection of two medians.

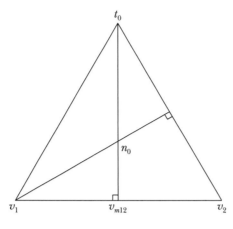

Figure 15.2 shows the edge formed by v_1 and v_2. I chose this edge at random; they all work the same way. The figure shows the geometry resulting from building an equilateral triangle on these points and then finding the centroid. We first find point t_0 at the apex of the triangle, then drop the median down from t_0 to v_{m12}, the midpoint of v_1 and v_2. Next we draw the median from v_1 to the midpoint of v_2 and t_0, and the intersection of these two medians is the centroid, marked by the complex point n_0. It doesn't matter which two medians we use in this construction, because all three meet at n_0.

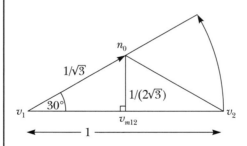

We can save time by observing that we don't have to actually make point t_0. Figure 15.3 shows the geometry of the equilateral triangle. Triangle $\Delta v_1 n_0 v_{m12}$ is a 30-60-90 triangle. If distance $\left|v_1 v_2\right| = 1$, then $\left|v_1 v_{m12}\right| = 1/2$ and $\left|v_1 n_0\right| = 1/\sqrt{3}$. So we can find n_0 simply by taking the vector $v_2 - v_1$, rotating it 30 degrees counterclockwise, scaling it by a factor of $1/\sqrt{3}$, and adding it back to point v_1.

This is exactly the sort of geometric thing that complex numbers are good at. If we multiply the vector $v_2 - v_1$ by a complex number $d = (1/\sqrt{3})e^{i\pi/6}$, then we're set. In symbols, $n_0 = v_1 + d(v_2 - v_1)$. This n_0 is one of the three points n_i making up the Napoleon triangle **N.**

To prove that Napoleon's Theorem is correct, we need to show that **N** is an equilateral triangle. To do that, I'll change our construction process a little (this will keep the algebra from getting too messy). We'll construct the Napoleon triangle in two steps. Starting with the original triangle **V,** we'll create the three points **T** at the vertices of the temporary construction triangles and then find the centroids of these triangles, which give us the points **N.**

To build the set of points **T,** we'll take each edge in turn as we did before, but rotate it by 60 degrees counterclockwise. To do this, we'll just multiply the edge vectors by a complex number $g = e^{i\pi/3}$ representing a counterclockwise rotation of 60 degrees and add back in the starting point. For example, $t_0 = v_1 + g(v_2 - v_1)$. The Napoleon points **N** are the average of the two points on each edge and the newly constructed point on **T.** For example, $n_0 = (t_0 + v_1 + v_2)/3$.

Now we're ready for the punch line. We'll prove that triangle **N** is equilateral by taking one of the edges, rotating it by 120 degrees clockwise, and showing that we land exactly on top of the adjacent edge. That is, we take **N** and rotate the whole thing by 120 degrees and get the very same triangle; only equilateral triangles satisfy this property.

For specificity, let's follow one edge in particular—say $n_0 n_2$. Looking at Figure 15.1, we expect that rotating this will land us on $n_2 n_1$. We already have g lying around, which rotates by 60 degrees, so if we apply it twice we'll get 120 degrees. Algebraically, we want to show that $g^2(n_0 - n_2) = n_2 - n_1$, or equivalently,

$$g^2(n_0 - n_2) - (n_2 - n_1) = 0$$

Plugging in the values we derived earlier for **N** (i.e., $n_0 = (t_0 + v_1 + v_2)/3$) and **T** (i.e., $t_0 = v_1 + g(v_2 - v_1)$) and simplifying, this becomes

$$(g^2 - g + 1)[(g - 1)v_0 - (1 + 2g)v_1 + (2 + g)v_2]/3 = 0$$

A moment's algebra shows that $g^2 - g + 1 = 0$, so the formula is true. We have confirmed that rotating this edge by 120 degrees gives us the previous edge. There was nothing special about our choice of edge, so all edges share this property. Ergo **N** is an equilateral triangle. Napoleon's Theorem is indeed true!

Figure 15.4 shows the development of the three triangles when they point inward, rather than outward, and the equilateral triangle they form. It's interesting to note that because of symmetry, we can tile the plane with Napoleon constructions. Figure 15.5 shows a tiling of the plane using the

Figure 15.4
Building the Napoleon
triangle with inward-
pointing triangles. The
original triangle, the
same as in Figure 15.1, is
shown in blue.
(a) The first triangle.
(b) The second triangle.
(c) The third triangle.
(d) The Napoleon tri-
angle formed from the
centroids of the three
triangles is shown in
thick black lines.

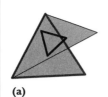 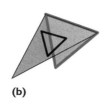  

(a)   (b)   (c)   (d)

triangles of Figure 15.1. In Figure 15.6 I've marked the equilateral triangles formed by the inward-pointing construction and the nonregular tiling
they create.

Napoleon's Theorem?

Wait a second. This construction is known far and wide as Napoleon's Theorem, but did Napoleon really come up with this? I mean the general, Napoleon Bonaparte?

Nobody seems to really know for sure, but it does seem rather well established that Napoleon was an avid amateur mathematician and a master of
the geometrical compass constructions due to Mascheroni. There's a famous story that in 1797 Napoleon was discussing geometry with the great
mathematicians Joseph-Louis Lagrange and Pierre-Simon Laplace. Appar-
ently during the conversation Napoleon was holding forth on his own dis-
coveries, prompting Laplace to remark, "We expected everything of you
except lessons in geometry." Some reports have Laplace saying this with respect and surprise, in acknowledgment of Napoleon's surprising mathematical ability. Other stories describe Laplace as somewhat snippy, saying this in dismissal of Napoleon's attempt to teach him his own subject.
Given that Napoleon later made Laplace a marquis, I think the former

Figure 15.5
Tiling with Napoleon
triangles.
(a) A tiling of the plane
using the original trian-
gle (yellow) and the
three outward-pointing
equilateral triangles built
upon it (red, green,
blue).
(b) The lattice created
by the Napoleon tri-
angles. The Napoleon
triangles are shown in
gray.

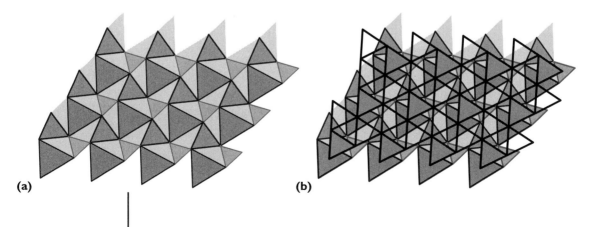

(a)   (b)

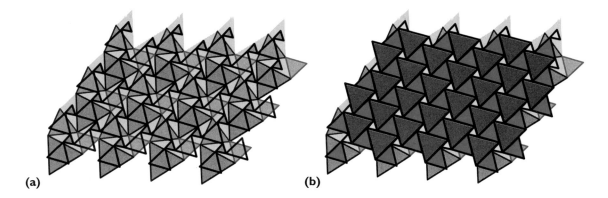

(a)

(b)

interpretation is probably more likely. He also made Lagrange a count, which seems a fitting title for a mathematician.

Napoleon's mathematical aptitude suggests that he might indeed have proposed this theorem, except that none of the historical record seems to back it up. Michael Deakin recently reported a search through the mathematical literature for anything of the form of Napoleon's Theorem. The first printed instance he could find was as a problem in issue 122 of a magazine called *Ladie's Diary,* printed in 1825. The problem was posed by Mr. W. Rutherford and made no mention of Napoleon. A proof by Mr. John Walker was printed in the following issue, and again the general was absent.

So where did the connection to Napoleon come from? The earliest printed attribution of this theorem to Napoleon seems to be in a book by A. Faifofer called *Elementi di Geometrica.* Many editions of this book were published, but Napoleon is not mentioned in association with this problem until the seventeenth edition, published in 1911. Curiously, Faifofer himself died in 1909. It's possible that Faifofer left instructions in his will to make this change, or that he reached out from his grave and adjusted the manuscript with a ghostly hand. I suspect that the attribution was added in a more conventional way, probably by an unknown editor.

Lighting Design the Hard Way

The Fourier transform is an important tool for understanding signals of all sorts, and of great value in computer graphics. If you're already familiar with it, you might want to just skim this section and the next.

Let's start off with an analogy. Suppose you're the director of a new off-off-Broadway play. You don't have much money, so you've only bought nine

Figure 15.6
The same lattice as in Figure 15.5, but using the Napoleon triangle built from inward-pointing triangles.
(a) The lattice created by the triangles. The Napoleon triangles are shown in gray.
(b) A colored version of the complete lattice.

identical lights for your theater. Since you can't afford gels, all of the lights project the same off-yellow color. The show opens next week, but you're still unhappy with the lighting for the important midnight picnic scene.

Theatrical lights contain a built-in slot in front of the lens that is designed to hold a thin, etched metal plate. When the light shines through the holes in the plate, a pattern of light and dark is projected onto the stage. For example, one plate might project a shadow pattern like that of moonlight through a tree's leaves. You bought nine different plates, and they've already been inserted in front of the nine lights. The lights have been aimed properly, but you're unhappy with the way they mix. Looking at the set, you know that some lights need to be brighter and others need to be dimmer. This is controlled at the lighting board, which contains a series of sliders, one per lamp. Push the slider up, and the corresponding lamp gets brighter (incidentally, both the lights and the plates go by a variety of names in different countries and industries; in American stage and television the lights are called *instruments* or *luminaires,* and the shadowing plates are called *gobos* or *cookies).*

It's late at night, and everyone else has gone home. You're sitting alone in the theatre staring at the set, trying to imagine which lights need to be brighter and which dimmer, when you hear a terrible crash behind you. Jerking around in your seat, you see that a great load of junk has fallen off a shelf and collapsed onto the lighting board, screwing up all the settings. But it's your lucky day, because a glance at the stage reveals that the lighting is now perfect! There are only two problems: you can't see the sliders on the board because the junk is obscuring them, and you can tell that there's no way to get the junk off without knocking all the sliders into new positions. Somehow you need to determine the positions of the sliders just from the lights themselves.

Perhaps you can eyeball their intensities. You climb up on the stage and look up at the lights, but that's hopeless: they're all much too bright to look at directly. You look at the pattern of light falling on the stage itself, but the complicated shadows cast by the lights makes it impossible to visually distinguish how much each light is contributing. You call your friend Jackie, who advises you to do something strange: go through the props, get out nine napkins, and arrange them in a big 3-by-3 grid that covers the stage. She then advises you to use your handy light meter to measure and record how much light is falling on each napkin. With those measurements safely written down, she tells you that you can now clean off the lighting board without fear, since she can recover the slider settings from knowledge of the gobos in the lights and the nine readings you took.

How could she possibly untangle the contributions of each of the nine lights given only nine readings throughout the stage? This is exactly the sort of job that the Fourier transform does. We change the language a bit, but the idea is the same.

The new bits of language are the complex sinusoid (remember this from the first section), and the idea of a *signal*. For our discussion here, a signal may be considered to be nothing more than an indexed list of numbers. Whether they're real, imaginary, or complex makes no difference. We'll write the signal itself in lowercase bold letters, like **x**, and the elements of the signal indexed with either brackets or subscripts: $x[n]$ and x_n both refer to the nth element of the signal **x.** Signals can arise in an infinite number of ways; two of the most common are by sampling a given function (e.g., $x[n] = n + 2$ for $n = [0, 5]$) or by direct assignment (e.g., **x** is the temperature at noon over eight successive days in May).

So in our story, the nine light readings at the napkins create a nine-element signal. We're interested in matching the lighting with the sum of nine scaled lights. In a Fourier problem, we want to match a signal with the sum of nine scaled complex sinusoids. In the story, the goal was to find the slider value for each light. In a Fourier transform, we want to find the scaling coefficient for each sinusoid.

The Fourier Transform

In the one-dimensional Fourier transform, we take a set of complex sinusoids, scale them, and add them together to create a signal. If we already have a signal to start with, then we use the Fourier transform to *analyze* the signal and find the contribution of each sinusoid. The inverse Fourier transform turns the process around and *synthesizes* the signal by adding up scaled sinusoids. Figure 15.7 shows an example. It's a big subject that I'll cover in only the briefest way; the Further Reading section points to some books where you can learn more.

There are actually a few different types of Fourier transform. In this chapter I'll be exclusively concerned with the *discrete-time Fourier series* (DTFS). This takes as input a series of complex samples of a signal **x**. The result is **a,** the set of coefficients that describe the amplitude of complex sine waves of increasing frequency. By convention the elements of **x** are written $x[n]$,

Figure 15.7
The left column shows four sine waves. From the top, they plot sin(x), sin(2x), sin(3x), and sin(4x). The middle column shows those waves after scaling by a real constant. On the right, I show the result of adding them together to build a composite real signal. The Fourier transform uses complex sinusoids, so in addition to these sine waves it includes corresponding imaginary cosine waves.

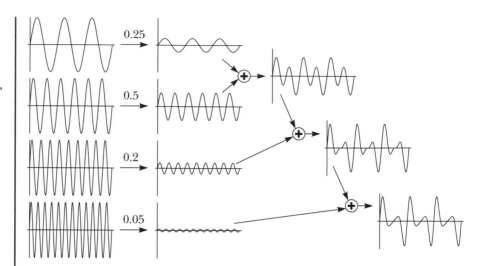

while the elements of **a** are written a_k. We'll assume that we have N values of the signal **x,** and thus also N coefficients at our disposal in **a** to match **x.** The sine waves that are used to match **x** are called the *basis functions* for the decomposition of **x.**

A discussion of why complex sinusoids are good basis functions would take us very far afield; I recommend consulting one of the books in the Further Reading section if this question interests you.

Now that we've set the stage, let's look at the specifics of the transform. We know that a convenient way to write the complex sine wave $\cos(\theta)$ + $i\sin(\theta)$ is $e^{i\theta}$. Our list of sine waves begins with $\theta = 0$; that is, the first complex sine wave is $e^{i0} = 1$. This is often called the DC (direct current) value; it's not really much of a sine wave, since it's just the constant 1. We can scale this wave to add a global offset to the entire synthesized signal. The remaining waves used by the Fourier process are the complex sinusoids that have a frequency given by integer multiples of $2\pi/N$. These are $e^{i(2\pi/N)}$, $e^{i2(2\pi/N)}$, $e^{i3(2\pi/N)}$, and so on, up to $e^{i(N-1)(N-1)(2\pi/N)}$. The left column of Figure 15.7 shows the first few of these.

The complex coefficients a_n tell us how strongly to weight each of these waves to reconstruct the original signal **x.** The complete *synthesis equation* for element $x[n]$ is

$$x[n] = \frac{1}{\sqrt{N}} \sum_{k \in [0, N)} a_k \, e^{-ik(2\pi/N)n}$$

If this is new to you, don't let all the superscripts and subscripts throw you. Remember, all we're doing is adding up values of complex sinusoids to come up with a single number. In words, to find the value for element $x[n]$, we add up N different sine waves. For each wave, indexed by k that runs from 0 to $N - 1$, we take the basic frequency $(2\pi/N)n$, multiply it by k, call this θ, evaluate $\cos(\theta) + i \sin(\theta)$, and then scale the resulting complex number by a_k. The factor of $1/\sqrt{N}$ at the start is a necessary normalization factor, which I won't get into here.

The matching *analysis equation* turns the process around and computes the a_k from the signal **x**:

$$a_k = \frac{1}{\sqrt{N}} \sum_{n \in [0, N)} x[n] e^{-ik(2\pi/N)n}$$

The only difference here (besides the swap of the a's and x's and their indices k and n) is that the exponent has a minus sign. In words, to find the kth coefficient, we step through the sine waves (this time indexed by n), take the basic frequency $-k(2\pi/N)$, multiply it by n, call this θ, evaluate $\cos(\theta) + i \sin(\theta)$, and scale this by $x[n]$.

These two equations are a matched pair. If you start with a signal **x**, analyze it to compute the vector **a**, and synthesize a new signal **x′** from that, you'll get back what you started with.

The bottom line is that the DTFS lets us take a list of complex values **x** and convert them into a list of complex coefficients **a**, and vice versa. Whether we want to think of our signal as a set of values, or as a set of coefficients of complex sine waves, or both at once, makes no difference, because they both describe exactly the same information. Sometimes the set of values $x[n]$ is referred to as the *signal space* representation of the signal, and the set of coefficients a_k is referred to as the *frequency space* representation.

The DTFS (and the other variants of the Fourier transform) are useful because many operations are more convenient or meaningful on one space or the other. These two equations tell us how to easily go back and forth between the two equivalent representations. The important thing to remember is that both the values of x and the coefficients a may be complex.

Basis Polygons

What the heck has all this Fourier stuff got to do with Napoleon's Theorem? Here we were happily doing geometry on the complex plane and talking about historical figures, and suddenly we were talking about signals and sine waves. The connection, of course, is their common use of complex numbers. The point of visiting Napoleon's Theorem was to get comfortable using complex numbers to represent points in the plane and multiplying by $e^{i\theta}$ to represent a rotation by θ. The interesting thing is that this viewpoint leads to a really nice interpretation of the Fourier transform.

The DTFS discussed above is a one-dimensional kind of beast: the signal values are indexed by a single number and the coefficients are as well. Fourier transforms have been applied to two, three, and higher numbers of dimensions, and those are all useful. Usually in graphics we think of a 2D Fourier transform as operating on an image: we start with a collection of real numbers representing pixel intensities, transform those into complex amplitudes (this time of two-dimensional complex sinusoids), and back again.

But let's reconsider the input to the DTFS. But the DTFS actually operates in complex space, and it's completely appropriate to use complex numbers for the signal $x[n]$. If we think this way, then we can consider the complex sinusoids that form the heart of the transform as complex numbers themselves. In the discussion of Napoleon's Theorem, we saw that multiplication by a complex number $se^{i\theta}$ causes a scaling by s and a counterclockwise rotation by θ. This is called a *spiral dilation*. Well, these are precisely the terms in the heart of the Fourier transform.

Let's write out the synthesis equation for the DTFS in matrix form. The reconstructed signal vector $\mathbf{x}$ is given by the product of a matrix $\mathbf{F}$ and the coefficient vector $\mathbf{a}$, or in symbols, $\mathbf{x} = \mathbf{Fa}$. A little shorthand will be convenient; we'll write $\gamma = i2\pi/N$. Then the tableau form of the synthesis equation may be written as

$$
\begin{bmatrix} x_0 \\ x_1 \\ x_2 \\ \vdots \\ x_{N-1} \end{bmatrix} = \frac{1}{\sqrt{N}} \begin{bmatrix} e^0 & e^0 & e^0 & \cdots & e^0 \\ e^0 & e^{\gamma} & e^{2\gamma} & \cdots & e^{(N-1)\gamma} \\ e^0 & e^{2\gamma} & e^{4\gamma} & \cdots & e^{2(N-1)\gamma} \\ \vdots & \vdots & \vdots & & \vdots \\ e^0 & e^{(N-1)\gamma} & e^{2(N-1)\gamma} & \cdots & e^{(N-1)(N-1)\gamma} \end{bmatrix} \begin{bmatrix} a_0 \\ a_1 \\ a_2 \\ \vdots \\ a_{N-1} \end{bmatrix}
$$

Recall that $e^0 = 1$, so the top row and left column are all 1's. Notice that this matrix is symmetrical; the rows and columns can be transposed. Now we're almost ready for the trick.

Every element of **F** is simply the complex number $\cos\theta + i\sin\theta$ for some value of θ. But each entry in the matrix also represents a point on the complex plane. And when multiplied with another complex number, it causes a spiral dilation. In fact, because the magnitude of each element of **F** is 1, they're simply rotations. And not just any rotations, but rotations of integer multiples of the angle $2\pi/N$. Now, what do you get if you place points around the circumference of a circle, each separated by an angle $2\pi/N$? It's just a regular polygon with N sides! If $N = 3$, you get an equilateral triangle, if $N = 4$ you get a square, and so on.

Now we're ready for the big climax! The insight we've been building up to can be expressed in two different, but equivalent, ways:

1 The rows and columns of the Fourier matrix are regular polygons in the complex plane.

2 Any N-sided polygon may be described as a weighted sum of N regular polygons.

Let's see why these statements are true, and why they're so cool.

We'll start by looking at the columns of **F**, and plot them in the complex plane as a sequence of points. For specificity, I'll select $N = 8$, so $\gamma = i2\pi/8 = i\pi/4$ and multiplication by e^γ is a counterclockwise rotation of 45 degrees.

The leftmost column of **F** is simply the complex point $(1, 0)$ repeated eight times. It will be helpful to think of this as a really degenerate octagon, where all the vertices are coincident. Figure 15.8a shows the results.

The second column is the sequence of points $[e^0, e^{i\pi/4}, e^{i2\pi/4}, e^{i3\pi/4}, e^{i4\pi/4}, e^{i5\pi/4}, e^{i6\pi/4}, e^{i7\pi/4}]$. If we plot these, as in Figure 15.8b, we get a regular octagon inscribed in a circle of radius 1. The octagon starts at $(1, 0)$ and proceeds counterclockwise.

The third column doubles the angles, giving us the points $[e^0, e^{i2\pi/4}, e^{i4\pi/4}, e^{i6\pi/4}, e^{i8\pi/4}, e^{i10\pi/4}, e^{i12\pi/4}, e^{i14\pi/4}]$. If we remember that $e^{in\pi} = 1$ for any integer n, then these points are $[e^0, e^{i\pi/2}, e^{i\pi}, e^{i3\pi/2}, e^{i2\pi}, e^{i\pi/2}, e^{i\pi}, e^{i3\pi/2}]$. In words, the eight points form a square (or diamond) that wraps around itself twice, as in Figure 15.8c. This is still a octagon, but a very strange one. One way of

Figure 15.8
The eight basis polygons, plotted in the unit circle. The points are numbered in the order they are visited.
(a) The degenerate octagon, where all eight points land on (1, 0).
(b) The counter-clockwise octagon.
(c) The octagon is made of points that form two overlapping diamonds.
(d) An eight-pointed star.
(e) The octagon is made of alternating visits to (1, 0) and (-1, 0).
(f) The octagon in 15.8d traversed clockwise.
(g) The octagon in 15.8c traversed clockwise.
(h) The octagon in 15.8b traversed clockwise.

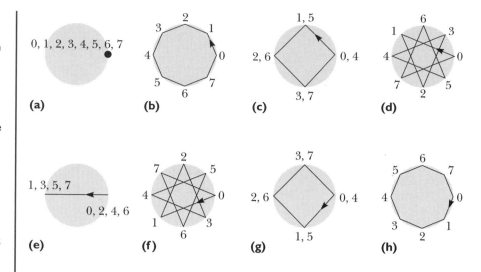

thinking about this is that we're going around the octagon, but skipping one point each time we move.

Following the pattern, the fourth column yields a star octagon, as in Figure 15.8d. You can think of this as our original octagon, except we skip over two points on each move. It's still an octagon, but it's a pretty twisted one.

The fifth column simplifies to the two points (1, 0) and (−1, 0) in alternation. Figure 15.8e plots this sequence of points. Though it looks like a line, this is again a distorted octagon.

The remaining polygons are repeats of their predecessors, taken in the opposite order and thus traversed in the opposite direction. The sixth column yields Figure 15.8f, where we have a star octagon that looks like Figure 15.9d, but is visited clockwise rather than counterclockwise. The remaining two columns repeat the diamond and regular octagon, except these two are also traversed clockwise.

Another way of writing the matrix tableau then is as in Figure 15.9, where each column is indicated as a series of points around the indicated polygon.

Recall that we spoke of the Fourier transform as decomposing an input signal into a sum of basis functions, which were complex sinusoids. In the new interpretation, we can say that the Fourier transform decomposes a polygon into a sum of *basis polygons,* themselves simply regular polygons (though some are degenerate). Then the vector **a** represents the version of

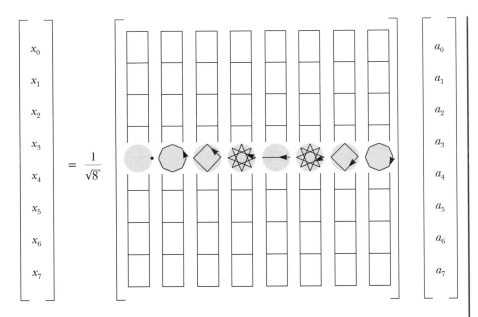

$$\begin{bmatrix} x_0 \\ x_1 \\ x_2 \\ x_3 \\ x_4 \\ x_5 \\ x_6 \\ x_7 \end{bmatrix} = \frac{1}{\sqrt{8}}$$

Figure 15.9
A tableau form of the Fourier transform. Each basis octagon is represented by a column of the matrix.

the input polygon in *basis space*. Converting **a** back to **x** means simply weighting the basis polygons and adding them back together again.

To see this in action, consider how $x[2]$ is computed. We form the dot product of the column vector **a** and row 3 of the matrix. This row represents the third vertex of each basis polygon. Thus the position of each vertex in the output polygon is found as a weighted sum of the corresponding vertices in the basis polygons.

To see how symmetrical this all is, Figure 15.10 shows the analysis form that computes **a** from **x.** Notice that the only change in the matrix is that now the basis polygons are traversed in the opposite order.

Figure 15.11 shows an example of applying this interpretation. Here I've made a little cat's head out of eight points. The pieces of the figure show what happens when I break the figure into its basis polygons, crank up the diamond component, and then resynthesize the figure. In Figure 15.11b, I scaled up the diamond by 1.5, and later figures show higher amplitudes. You can clearly see the cat's head being pulled toward the double-wrapped diamond as that component of the shape dominates.

Note that Figure 15.11 isn't a morph. In that technique, you have two line drawings representing the start and end states, and you move the points in some way from their start locations to the end locations. Rather, I have only

Figure 15.10
A tableau form of
the inverse Fourier
transform. Each ba-
sis octagon is rep-
resented by a col-
umn of the matrix.

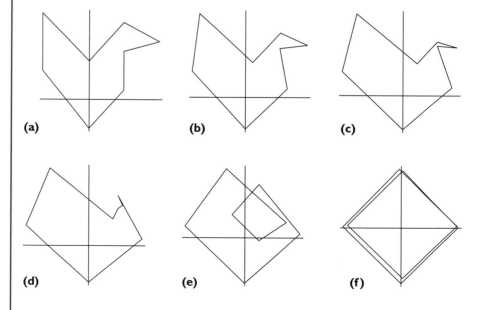

$$\begin{bmatrix} a_0 \\ a_1 \\ a_2 \\ a_3 \\ a_4 \\ a_5 \\ a_6 \\ a_7 \end{bmatrix} = \frac{1}{\sqrt{8}} \begin{bmatrix} \ \end{bmatrix} \begin{bmatrix} x_0 \\ x_1 \\ x_2 \\ x_3 \\ x_4 \\ x_5 \\ x_6 \\ x_7 \end{bmatrix}$$

Figure 15.11
The transformation
of a cat. (If you use
your imagination,
the octagon in
15.11a is something
like a cat's head.)
Each figure shows
the result of ampli-
fying the counter-
clockwise "dia-
mond" component
of the Fourier
transform (as
shown in Figure
15.8c), and leaving
other components
unchanged.
(a) The original
cat's head.
(b) Amplification
of the diamond
component by 1.5.
(c) Amplification
by 2.
(d) Amplification
by 3.
(e) Amplification
by 8.
(f) Amplification
by 100.

one shape throughout, and that's the cat's head. All that's happening is
that the diamond-shaped component of the Fourier transform is being
scaled up with respect to the other components, so that when I reconstruct
the shape the diamond predominates. In other words, the cat's head had a
diamond shape already in it (as do most octagons). All I've done here is
emphasize its diamond nature over its other constituent shapes.

I think that this is a wonderful way to look at polygons. The fact that it's the Fourier representation that makes this all work out is natural, and like all the best insights, obvious in retrospect.

Further Reading

My main inspiration for this chapter was Alvy Ray Smith's "Eigenpolygon Decomposition of Polygons" (Technical Memo 19, Microsoft Research), where I first saw the idea of basis polygons. Alvy describes the basis polygons as the eigenvectors of a matrix of rotations operating on polygons in the complex plane.

A very nice discussion of Napoleon's Theorem, operators, and related ideas appears in *Over and Over Again* by G. Chang and T. W. Sederberg (Mathematical Association of America, 1997). There are some nice discussions of Napoleon's Theorem on some of the online math sites. I adapted the proof given by Alexander Bogomolny (*http://cut-the-knot.com/proofs /napoleon_complex.html*) for this chapter; Scott Brodie gives a couple of other proofs (*http://mirrors.org.sg./mathi/proofs/napoleon.html*). There are also some interactive gadgets around for playing with the construction (*http://www.saltire.com/applets/advanced_geometry/napoleon_executable /napoleon.htm*). Some of the historical information on Napoleon's Theorem came from a mail thread on the Internet, where primary sources were Mike Deakin and Julio Gonzalez Cabillon. To read the mail thread, go to *http://forum.swarthmore.edu/discussions/epi-search/all.html* and search for "napoleon."

The section developing complex numbers was based on the discussion in *Introduction to Geometry* (2nd Edition) by H. S. M. Coxeter (Wiley & Sons, 1969). I also found some material online. The stories of the Pythagoreans and irrational numbers were based on information in "The Origin of Geometry" by Michael Serres (*http://acnet.pratt.edu/~arch543p/readings /origin_of_geometry.html*), "Early Greek Science: Thales to Plato" by Michael Fowler (*http://landau1.phys.virginia.edu/classes/109/lectures/thales.html*), and "A Brief History of the Pythagorean Theorem" by Chad Schmidt (*http:// www.schools.edina.k12.mn.us/SouthView/Sview/chad/histofpy.htm*).

There are lots of places to learn about Fourier transforms. If you don't mind learning from a textbook, *Digital Signal Processing* by Oppenheim, Willsky, and Young (Prentice Hall, 1983) is a good book to teach yourself from. I also like *Signals and Linear Systems* (2nd Edition) by Gabel and Roberts (J. Wiley, 1980). For a treatment of signal processing and Fourier transforms specifically targeted to the computer graphics community, I humbly offer my own book, *Principles of Digital Image Synthesis* (Morgan Kaufmann, 1995).

String Crossings

ANDREW GLASSNER'S NOTEBOOK
March/April 1999

16

When I was about 10 years old, my local high school held a summer crafts class. Each day we were given something new to do: hammering ashtrays out of round metal, weaving lanyards, or filling bottles with layers of colored sand. One of the projects involved driving little brass nails into a piece of wood so that they were equally spaced around a circle and then winding shiny metal wire between every pair of nails. Figure 16.1 shows the idea. The result was a shiny spider's web of wire that each kid proudly took home as a piece of art.

I don't know what the parents did with those creations, but I do know that the cool pattern stayed in my mind. I didn't know it at the time, but I'd learned an algorithm for making an aesthetic visual piece. Years later when I started to learn computer graphics, I programmed up these string-art creations on vector storage tubes and plotters, mixing colors and changing line widths and generally having a fine time.

I hadn't thought about these designs for years, until recently my artist friend Dan Robbins mentioned that he was planning a sculpture that involved a similar kind of design (discussed in the next section). Part of his sculpture involved placing objects at the intersections of pairs of strings. He wanted to plan part of the sculpture in advance and asked me if

Figure 16.1
String art from a
16-sided regular
polygon.

there was a way to determine how many strings were necessary to get a desired number of intersections.

This chapter starts with an answer to Dan's question, then explores some other questions derived from these simple but elegant string-art patterns. I discovered that these lovely little geometric patterns lead to numerical patterns every bit as elegant and aesthetically pleasing.

The Right Angle

Let's begin with the simplest example of the approach. We take two line segments and place them at right angles to each other. We divide each one into $N + 1$ equal pieces, then run strings from the internal divisions on one line to those on the other. If we number the divisions $1, \ldots, N$ from the common point in the lower left, then from any nail i on the vertical

Figure 16.2
The right-angle
string-art patterns
for $N = 1$ through
$N = 6$.

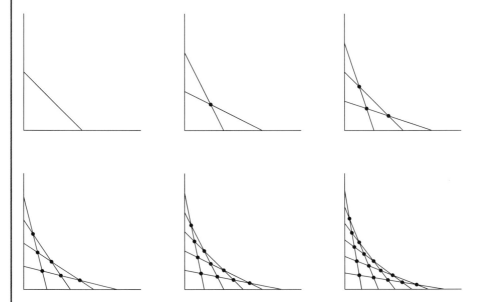

piece we'll run a string to nail $N - i - 1$ on the horizontal, for a total of N strings. Figure 16.2 shows the progression for the first few values of N.

Now let's take a precise form of Dan's questions: How many crossings k are there for a given value of N? We'll write this number as $k(N)$. We can see from Figure 16.2 that that when $N = 1$ we have only one string, so clearly $k(1) = 0$, and when $N = 2$ we have only two strings, so $k(2) = 1$. The general pattern may be clear to you from examination. Take any of the patterns and consider the string running from the highest point on the vertical axis to the leftmost point on the horizontal axis. That string crosses over all the other strings. Since there are N total, and this string is one of them, that yields $N - 1$ crossings. Now the next string also crosses them all, but we've already accounted for one of the strings, so there are $N - 2$ new crossings. And so it goes, until the last string adds just one new crossing, and we're done.

So if there are N segments and $N - 1$ lines, then the number of crossings is given by $(N - 1) + (N - 2) + \ldots + 2 + 1$. There's a nice closed-form solution for this sort of summation, rumored to have been discovered by Karl Friedrich Gauss as a child. The story goes that a math teacher came to class unprepared one day and decided to fill the class time by telling the students to add up all the numbers from 1 to 100. Most of the students sat down and dutifully added $1 + 2$, then added 3 to the result, then 4 to that, and so on. But in only a few seconds Gauss announced to the teacher that the answer was 5050. The teacher assumed that this young child had simply learned this result as a piece of trivia and set him about the more time-consuming task of adding the numbers from 1 to 500. After only a moment's paperwork, Gauss announced the answer was 125,250. The teacher, of course, was stunned.

Apocryphal or not, the way to repeat this kind of performance is to note that in a summation from 1 to N, the outermost pair of numbers add up to $1 + N$. Working inward, the next pair add up to $2 + (N - 1) = 1 + N$. The next pair is $3 + (N - 2) = 1 + N$, and so on. If N is even, then there are exactly $N/2$ of these pairs. If N is odd, then there are $N/2$ pairs, plus one extra number left alone in the middle: $N/2$ itself. Thus, regardless of whether N is even or odd, we can write

$$\sum_{i=1}^{N} i = \frac{N}{2}(N + 1)$$

Table 16.1 The number of crossings for a given number of wires in a right-angle pattern.

Number of wires	Number of crossings
2	1
3	3
4	6
5	10
6	15
7	21
8	28
9	36
10	45
11	55
12	66
13	78
14	91
15	105
16	120
17	136
18	153
19	171
20	190

This elegant summation formula is just what we need for our crossing problem. Here we count from 1 to $N - 1$, so the sum is

$$k(N) = \sum_{i=1}^{N-1} i - \frac{N-1}{2} N$$

which is a nice little answer. Table 16.1 gives the value of $k(N)$ for a range of N's, which are plotted in Figure 16.3. It's no surprise that the curve is a parabola, since $k(N)$ is a quadratic in N.

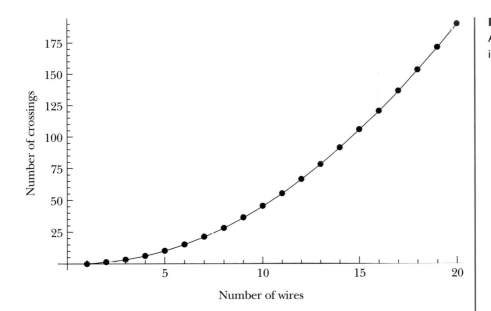

Figure 16.3
A plot of the data
in Table 16.1.

If we want to create a piece of art with a particular number of crossings, then we can simply solve for N given k using the quadratic formula and take the positive root:

$$N = \frac{1}{2}(1 + \sqrt{1 + 8k})$$

Most of the values of N that result from this process are not integers. I don't really know how to interpret a fractional result here, since I don't know how to create a fractional nail or fractional lines.

I wondered how much string is consumed by this process. Let's assume that the lengths of the two sides are each 1. Then we can write any line as joining coordinate α along one axis with $(1 - \alpha)$ along the other. The length of that line is then simply

$$\sqrt{\alpha^2 + (1 - \alpha)^2} = \sqrt{\left(\alpha\sqrt{2} - \frac{1}{\sqrt{2}}\right)^2 + \frac{1}{2}}$$

To find the total amount of string, we march an index i from 1 to $N - 1$, compute $\alpha = i/N$, and add up the lengths:

$$\sum_{i=1}^{N-1} \sqrt{\left(\frac{i\sqrt{2}}{N} - \frac{1}{\sqrt{2}}\right)^2 + \frac{1}{2}}$$

Figure 16.4
A plot of the total amount of string required as a function of the number of individual pieces used.

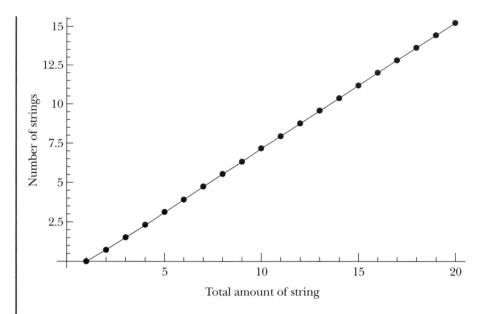

The resulting values are plotted in Figure 16.4. I was surprised to find that the result looks linear: each time you add a new string, you shorten the others by just the right amount so that the total amount of new string appears to be a constant. I don't understand why this should be so.

A Closer Angle

Figure 16.5
An acute string pattern.

Let's now close up the 90-degree angle into something smaller, as in Figure 16.5. Clearly the topology of the diagram hasn't changed—the way the lines cross each other is the same, so $k(N)$ is the same as for the 90-degree case. But how about the lengths? A point $(0, \alpha)$ on the vertical axis is connected to point $((1 - \alpha)\cos\theta, (1 - \alpha)\sin\theta)$ on the diagonal axis. The length between them is

$$\sqrt{[(1-\alpha)\cos\theta]^2 + [\alpha - ((1-\alpha)\sin\theta)^2]} = \sqrt{1 - 2\alpha + 2\alpha^2 + 2(\alpha - 1)\alpha\sin\theta}$$

Summing this up as before over $N - 1$ strings, we get the result shown in Figure 16.6, which again seems to be linear. This little figure lends itself to all sorts of nice designs; a few examples are shown in Figure 16.7.

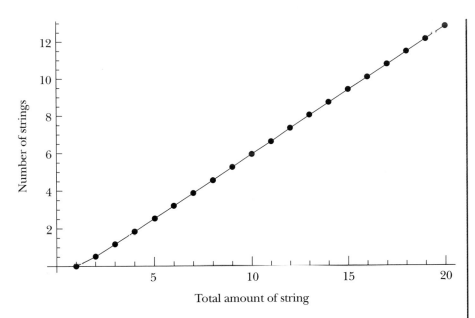

Figure 16.6
A plot of the total amount of string required for a 30-degree acute string pattern as a function of the number of individual pieces used.

The y-axis is labeled "Number of strings" with values 2, 4, 6, 8, 10, 12.
The x-axis is labeled "Total amount of string" with values 5, 10, 15, 20.

The Regular Complete Graph

Let's now return to the nails-and-wire construction of Figure 16.1. I call this a *regular complete graph*, because it is a complete graph (that is, a graph where every vertex is connected by an edge to every other vertex) and it is based on a regular polygon. The natural question to ask now is, how many crossings are there in this graph? There's a bit of a subtlety in the question that needs to be refined. I'll describe the problem, then restate the question.

We'll need to establish a couple of conventions, which I'll do by example. Clearly the smallest polygon that has any internal edges is the square. Figure 16.8a shows the regular complete graph for $N = 4$. We can see that there is only one crossing: $k = 1$. This shows my first convention—I won't count lines that come together at a vertex as a crossing.

Figure 16.7
Some designs made with acute string patterns.

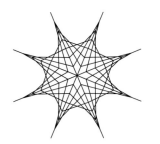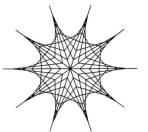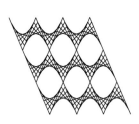

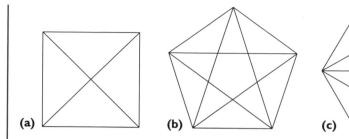

(a)　　　　　(b)　　　　　(c)

Figure 16.8b shows the pentagon associated with $N = 5$. It's easy enough to just count the crossings and find that $k = 5$. Figure 16.8c shows the hexagon associated with $N = 6$, and things are starting to get complicated. The important thing to note in the hexagon is what's happening in the very center: three "diagonals" are crossing each other at the same point. I've marked this with a red dot. Let's call this a third-order crossing, so we could also say this crossing has order 3. Until now, all the crossings have been of order 2. How do we count crossings of order greater than 2? This is the problem I alluded to before when we simply wanted to "count the crossings."

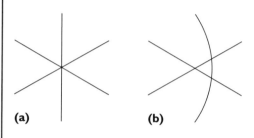

(a)　　　　　(b)

Here's my other convention: we will "explode" all such crossings into a collection of crossings of order 2. We'll do this by jiggling the lines around as needed, bending them to one side or the other of the common point so that each crossing has only two lines. Figure 16.9 shows what happens for a third-order crossing: we get three second-order crossings. It doesn't matter which line you jiggle or how you jiggle it; the result is always the same. Thus I will count that single point in the center of Figure 16.8c as the equivalent of three second-order crossings. I've found it helpful to sometimes redraw the graphs with wiggly lines rather than straight ones until there are only second-order crossings, as in Figure 16.10 for the hexagon. Happily, this kind of cosmetic distortion can't change the number of second-order crossings unless you actually distort the topology (that is, you start crossing over

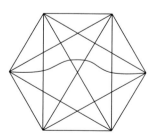

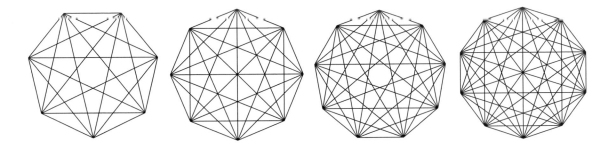

lines that you weren't crossing over before you exploded the higher-order crossings).

From now on, I'll use the term *crosses* to refer to a second-order crossing. So here's our improved problem statement: how many crosses C are contained in a regular complete graph of N vertices? If we just count up the crosses in Figure 16.10c, you'll find that there are 15 of them. Figure 16.11 shows a few more complete graphs. By manually counting them several times, I confirmed that for $N = 4$ through $N = 11$ the sequence of cross numbers is $\{1, 5, 15, 35, 70, 126, 210, 330\}$. There is a nice little formula for the number of crosses, which I'll show at the end. In this chapter, I'll take the scenic route toward that goal. The resulting formulas for the crossing number $C(N)$ are equivalent.

I'd like to define one more term before we get rolling. Consider any vertex of a regular complete graph of N vertices. There are $N - 1$ other vertices, and since there's a line to each one, there are $N - 1$ lines radiating from each vertex. Two of those lines are part of the perimeter of the graph and are never involved in any crosses. I call the $N - 3$ remaining lines the *fan* associated with that vertex. Figure 16.12 shows a couple of examples. Every vertex in the graph has a fan of $N - 3$ radiating lines, though of course some might deviate from a straight edge to avoid crossings of order 3 or higher.

Now that we have our conventions established and terms defined, let's find an expression for $C(N)$. It turns out to be a surprisingly pleasant journey.

One Vertex at a Time

I'm going to describe a way of counting crosses that leads to an expression for $C(N)$. I'm not going to

Figure 16.11
The complete regular graphs for $N = 7, 8, 9, 10$. Notice that the graphs for $N = 8$ and $N = 10$ require exploding to avoid crossings of order more than 2. The cross numbers for these graphs are 35, 70, 126, 210.

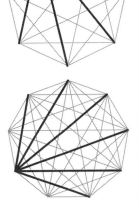

Figure 16.12
Fans (marked in red) for $N = 7$ and $N = 9$.

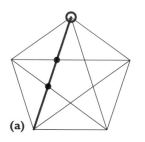
(a)

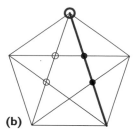
(b)

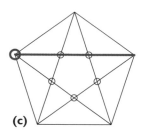
(c)

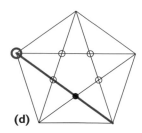
(d)

Figure 16.13
Counting intersections for N = 5.
(a) Select a vertex (outlined in red), and follow its fan from one end (the line in red). There are two crosses (solid black dots).
(b) The second line of the fan. There are two new crosses (solid black dots).
(c) The next vertex counterclockwise, shown in blue. Select one end of the fan (the blue line). There are no new crosses.
(d) The next line of the fan, and the last new cross. The sequence for the first vertex is {2, 2} and the second vertex is {1}; the total sequence is {{2, 2}, {1}}.

present a proof, because I don't have one, and this wouldn't be the right place for the rigor of a proof anyway. But it's a rather straightforward argument. I hope to convince your intuition that this is a sound approach, and you could write a proof if you were sufficiently motivated.

We'll take two steps to counting the total number of crosses. In this section, we'll first focus on what happens when we add one more vertex to a graph we've already counted. In the next section we'll use this result to count up all the crosses.

So let's return to the simple case of N = 5. Let's pick one particular vertex and follow the fan of lines coming out of that vertex. We'll start at one end of the fan and count all the crosses, then move to the adjacent fan, count those, and so on.

In Figure 16.13a I've selected one vertex and marked it with a red circle. I've selected one end of the fan and drawn that line in red. That line accounts for two crosses. Then in 16.13b I've marked the next line of the fan from that same vertex, and it picks up two more crosses. This vertex has the sequence {2, 2}. In Figure 16.13c I repeat the process by moving to the next vertex counterclockwise from the one we just looked at and marking it in blue. The first line of the fan doesn't pick up any new crosses. In Figure 16.13d we see that the second line of the fan does create one new cross. Because that completes the fan for that vertex, I'll write its sequence as simply {1}. The rest of the vertices don't pick up any new crosses, so the complete description of this cross-counting procedure for N = 5 is {{2, 2}, {1}}.

As a thought experiment, you might want to convince yourself that the sequence for N = 4 is simply {{1}}.

Now let's look at N = 6, shown in exploded form in Figure 16.14. The first vertex has a sequence {3, 4, 3}, shown in Figures 16.14a, b, and c. The next vertex, marked in blue, has a sequence {2, 2}, shown in Figure 16.14d, e,

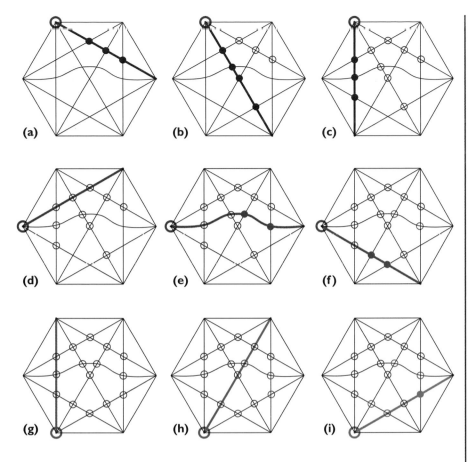

Figure 16.14
Finding crosses for
$N = 6$.
(a, b, c) The fan
for the first vertex,
resulting in se-
quence {3, 4, 3}.
(d, e, f) The sec-
ond fan, resulting in
{2, 2}.
(g, h, i) The third
fan with sequence
{1}. The total se-
quence for $N = 6$
is thus {{3, 4, 3},
{2, 2}, {1}}.

and f. And the vertex after that, in green in Figure 16.14g, h, and i, is simply {1}. Thus the sequence for $N = 6$ is {{3, 4, 3}, {2, 2}, {1}}.

You may notice something interesting is going on with these sequences. If
not, take a look at Figure 16.15, where I've marked the results for $N = 7$.
The sequence for $N = 7$ is {{4, 6, 6, 4}, {3, 4, 3}, {2, 2}, {1}}. The pattern
that's emerged is that the sequence for a graph with N vertices is made up

Figure 16.15
Finding crosses for
$N = 7$.
(a) The first vertex
is {4, 6, 6, 4}.
(b) The second
vertex is {3, 4, 3}.
(c) The third ver-
tex is {2, 2}.
(d) The fourth ver-
tex is {1}. The to-
tal sequence for
$N = 7$ is thus
{{4, 6, 6, 4},
{3, 4, 3}, {2, 2}, {1}}.

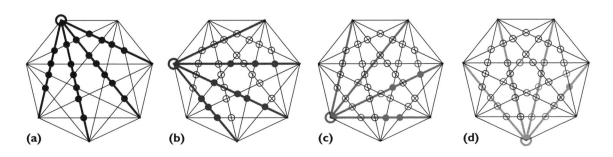

Table 16.2 The sequences for graphs $N = 4$ through $N = 10$.

N	Sequence for crosses in the regular complete graph of size N
4	$\{\{1\}\}$
5	$\{\{2, 2\}, \{1\}\}$
6	$\{\{3, 4, 3\}, \{2, 2\}, \{1\}\}$
7	$\{\{4, 6, 6, 4\}, \{3, 4, 3\}, \{2, 2\}, \{1\}\}$
8	$\{\{5, 8, 9, 8, 5\}, \{4, 6, 6, 4\}, \{3, 4, 3\}, \{2, 2\}, \{1\}\}$
9	$\{\{6, 10, 12, 12, 10, 6\}, \{5, 8, 9, 8, 5\}, \{4, 6, 6, 4\}, \{3, 4, 3\}, \{2, 2\}, \{1\}\}$
10	$\{\{7, 12, 15, 16, 15, 12, 7\}, \{6, 10, 12, 12, 10, 6\}, \{5, 8, 9, 8, 5\}, \{4, 6, 6, 4\}, \{3, 4, 3\}, \{2, 2\}, \{1\}\}$

first of a sequence introduced by that graph, followed by the sequence for the graph with $N - 1$ vertices. Table 16.2 shows the progression of sequences for a few more values of N, where the pattern comes out pretty clearly.

What's going on here? One way to look at this is to realize that each graph with N vertices can be broken into two pieces: a graph with $N - 1$ vertices, and everything left over. The subgraph of $N - 1$ vertices is responsible for contributing everything but the first subsequence for a graph. How can we characterize what's due to just the "new" part of the graph?

Figure 16.16
(a) The graph $N = 7$.
(b) The graph $N = 8$. The new vertex and edges are in red. The graph is distorted to remove all crossings of degree three and higher.

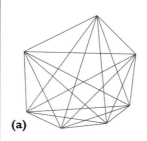
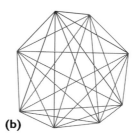

(a) (b)

In Figure 16.16 I've taken $N = 8$, and split it into two pieces. The $N = 7$ subgraph is in black, while the "new" parts are drawn in red. In Figure 16.17 I've emphasized one of the outermost lines of the fan coming out of the new, red vertex with a heavy red line.

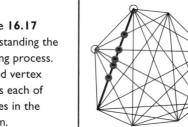

Consider the vertex that is counterclockwise to the red vertex. In Figure 16.17 I've marked this vertex and its fan in blue. It's clear that the heavy red line cuts across the entire blue fan; I've marked all five of these crosses by a red dot with a blue outline. Since in a graph with N vertices, each vertex has a fan of $N - 3$ vertices and obviously the sequences

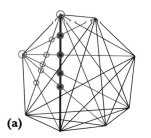 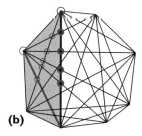

(a) **(b)**

Figure 16.18
(a) Moving on
from Figure 16.17,
the next line in the
red fan crosses all
but one of the lines
in the blue fan.
(b) The blue fan
line that is missed
and the region of
the graph that isn't
seen by the heavy
red line.

are all symmetrical, we'd expect the first and last numbers in the "new" sequence to be the fan size in the "old" polygon $((N-1)-3)$ plus the one new edge, or $N-1-3+1 = N-3$. As a quick sanity check, for $N = 8$, we'd expect the sequence to start and end with 5. It does. A quick scan of Table 16.2 suggests that this pattern continues as N grows.

As far as this particular line goes, we don't have to bother checking the fans of the other vertices, because it's clear that the thick red line can't cross any of their fans. So the sequence for this vertex is so far just {5, . . .], and we can move on to the next line in the red fan.

The thick red line in Figure 16.18a marks the next step across the red fan. The trick to counting up its crosses is to compare it to the line of Figure 16.17. The empty circles are the crosses we found in Figure 16.17, and the filled-in circles are the new crosses with the blue fan. The interesting thing to observe is that we've "lost" one cross, due to one of the outermost lines of the blue fan. That's because the red line we're focusing on excludes the little subgraph that contains that line. Figure 16.18b emphasizes this omitted line and shades in the excluded region of the graph. So instead of crosses with all $N-3$ lines of the blue fan, we only cross $N-3-1 = N-4$ lines.

This line can intersect the fan of the next vertex going counterclockwise, marked in green in Figure 16.19 (note that one of the lines of the green fan overlaps with a line of the red fan; we can dismiss this shared line as a source of a cross). It's the same story again: the thick red line forms a cross with all $N-3$ lines of the green fan, except the shared one that's excluded. So the total number of crosses that are due to the heavy red line are $(N-4) + (N-4) = 2N-8$. For $N = 8$, that's eight crosses, and Table 16.2 gives the value for other values of N. We've now

Figure 16.19
Now we add in the
crosses formed by
the thick red line
and the green
vertex.

completely accounted for this red line with eight crosses, so our sequence for the red vertex is now {5, 8, . . .}.

The next line of the red fan is emphasized in Figure 16.20. The pattern continues: we lose one more cross from both the blue fan and the yellow fan, leaving us with $N - 5$ from each of those. We pick up crosses with the fan of a new vertex, marked in green. But two of its lines have already been

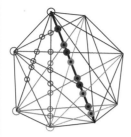

Figure 16.20
The nine crosses due to the thick red line and the blue, green, and yellow vertices.

taken, leaving us with $N - 5$ crosses from there. So we have a total of $3(N - 5)$ crosses, or nine in total. Again, Table 16.2 bears out the pattern in general. The remaining lines of the fan are symmetrical.

So the pattern for the "new" fan is $\{\{N - 3\}, \{2(N - 4)\}, \{3(N - 5)\}, \{2(N - 4)\}, \{N - 3\}\} = \{5, 8, 9, 8, 5\}$. I certainly haven't proven anything, but I hope that you'll agree with me that this was a pretty general argument. We can summarize this formally, though because the counting depends on whether N is even or odd we have to specify two different ways of counting up the elements. Defining

$$c(N, i) = i(N - 2 - i)$$

we can now say

$$S(N) = \begin{cases} N \text{ odd:} \{c(N, i)\}, \ i = (1, 2, \ldots, \lfloor N/2 \rfloor - 1, \lfloor N/2 \rfloor - 1, \ldots, 2, 1) \\ N \text{ even:} \{c(N, i)\}, \ i = (1, 2, \ldots, (N/2) - 1, N/2, (N/2) - 1, \ldots, 2, 1) \end{cases}$$

If you're unfamiliar with the notation $\lfloor N/2 \rfloor$ in the odd section, it means the *floor* of $N/2$, which in this case means simply its integer component. For example, $\lfloor 7 \rfloor = 3$, $\lfloor 8 \rfloor = 4$, and $\lfloor 9 \rfloor = 4$. This technique pops up all the time in situations where you're dealing with even and odd versions of sequences.

Now we know the sequence that's created when we add a new vertex to a graph. In the next section, we'll see a nice way to add up all the crosses.

Total Summation

In the last section, we saw that if we knew how many crosses were in a graph with N vertices, we could find the sequence that told us how many new crosses were introduced by adding a vertex to the graph. This suggests a nice way to find the total number of crosses. If we write $S^+(8)$ to mean the sum of all the elements in the sequence N (so from the above, $S(8) = \{5, 8, 9, 8, 5\}$, so $S^+(8) = 35$), then $C(N)$, the total number of crosses in the graph, is

$$C(N) = \sum_{i=4}^{N} S^+(N)$$

where we can use the formula for $S(N)$ given in the last section.

Well, this would work, and we could stop here, but it's not very satisfying. First of all, finding $S(N)$ itself looks messy, and then summing up its elements to get $S^+(N)$ is yet another step. It would be nice to come up with a simpler formula that gives us $S^+(N)$ directly without depending on $S(N)$; then we can use it immediately to find $C(N)$. In this section, I'll derive that formula. Again, I won't offer a proof, but I hope I'll show you that the pattern is pretty simple and would be amenable to a proof if you cared to work it through.

Let's look at the various sequences generated by counting crosses along the way. Refer to Table 16.2 for a summary of the sequences. To start the process, consider $N = 6$. The hexagon introduces the sequence $S(6) = \{3, 4, 3\}$. Is there a simple way to write the sum $S^+(6) = 3 + 4 + 3$? Well, we could look at this as $3 + 4 + 3 = (3 + 3 + 3) + 1 = 3^2 + 1$. Does this do us any good? Consider $S(7) = \{4, 6, 6, 4\}$. Then $S^+(7)$ has got four counts of 4 and two counts of 2, or $4^2 + 2^2$. Similarly, given $S(8) = \{5, 8, 9, 8, 5\}$, then $S^+(8) = 5^2 + 3^2 + 1$. Maybe you're starting to see the pattern. I'll write the trailing 1 as 1^2 so that it fits in with the other squares.

This nice pattern is a result of the construction of the sequences $S(N)$. It's all thanks to that little helper function $c(N, i)$ in the last section. What's happening is that throughout each even sequence $S(N)$, all $N - 3$ are greater than or equal to $N - 3$. When we take those out, we have $N - 5$ elements greater than or equal to $N - 5$. And so on, giving us $(N - 3)^2 + (N - 5)^2 + \ldots + 1^2$. The odd sequences work their way down to 2 rather than 1. Table 16.3 summarizes this pattern for $N = 4$ to $N = 11$ in tabular form, and Figure 16.21 plots it.

Table 16.3 Finding the total number of crosses in each fan. Values from $N = 4$ to $N = 11$.

N	Fan sequence S(N)	Sum $S^+(N)$
4	{1}	1^2
5	{2, 2}	2^2
6	{3, 4, 3}	$3^2 + 1$
7	{4, 6, 6, 4}	$4^2 + 2^2$
8	{5, 8, 9, 8, 5}	$5^2 + 3^2 + 1$
9	{6, 10, 12, 12, 10, 6}	$6^2 + 4^2 + 2^2$
10	{7, 12, 15, 16, 15, 12, 7}	$7^2 + 5^2 + 3^2 + 1$
11	{8, 14, 18, 20, 20, 18, 14, 8}	$8^2 + 6^2 + 4^2 + 2^2$

Well, this is nice. We're at our goal for this section, which is a simple formula for $S^+(N)$:

$$S^+(N) = \sum_{i=0}^{\lfloor N/2 \rfloor -2}(N - 3 - 2i)^2$$

This is really a step forward, since now we don't have to mess with $S(N)$ at all—we have a way to get $S^+(N)$ directly. We can now find $C(N)$ by just adding up these elements of $S^+(N)$, as in the summation formula at the start

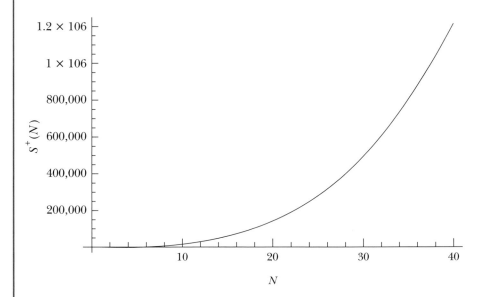

Figure 16.21
A plot of the function $S^+(N)$ from $N = 1$ to $N = 40$.

of this section. But it turns out that we can repeat almost the same trick again and get a simple little expression for $C(N)$ itself.

The Payoff

So far, to find $C(N)$ we sum a series of values $S^+(N)$. Each of those, in turn, is the result of a summation. It would be nice to get rid of one of those steps, just as we managed to find $S^+(N)$ without running through all the $S(N)$ summations. As I've advertised, that's just what we'll do now.

The insight is that each instance of $S^+(N)$ is just a sequence of squares, counting down by 2's, as shown in the last equation and in Table 16.4. When we combine these sums of squares, we still get a very nice pattern made up of lots of sums of squares.

Compare $S^+(9) = 6^2 + 4^2 + 2^2$ with $S^+(7) = 4^2 + 2^2$. You're probably way ahead of me, and you've already noticed that that $S^+(9) = 6^2 + S^+(7)$. The same thing is true for the even values. Let's follow the sequence from the start, and the pattern will become pretty clear. Remember that the total number of crosses $C(N)$ for a graph of size N is found from the number of crosses for a graph of size $N - 1$ plus the number of new ones added in by the new vertex: $C(N) = S^+(N) + C(N - 1)$.

We could apply this little recurrence formula directly and be done. But we can also write $C(N)$ without relying on its previous values. The easy case is $N = 4$. Here, $S(4) = S^+(4) = 1$. The total number of all crosses for $N = 4$ is $C(4) = 1$. Now $S^+(5) = 2^2$, so $C(5) = S^+(5) + C(4) = 2^2 + 1$. As before, I'm going to write that last term as 1^2, so that everything in sight is being

Table 16.4 A running sum of the rightmost column of Table 16.3 gives the total cross number $C(N)$.

N	C(N) expressed as sum of squares
4	1^2
5	$2^2 + 1^2$
6	$3^2 + 2^2 + 2(1^2)$
7	$4^2 + 3^2 + 2(2^2) + 2(1^2)$
8	$5^2 + 4^2 + 2(3^2) + 2(2^2) + 3(1^2)$
9	$6^2 + 5^2 + 2(4^2) + 2(3^2) + 3(2^2) + 3(1^2)$
10	$7^2 + 6^2 + 2(5^2) + 2(4^2) + 3(3^2) + 3(2^2) + 4(1^2)$
11	$8^2 + 7^2 + 2(6^2) + 2(5^2) + 3(4^2) + 3(3^2) + 4(2^2) + 4(1^2)$

squared. Things start to get interesting with $N = 6$. We know that $S^+(6) = 3^2 + 1^2$. So $C(6) = S^+(6) + C(5) = (3^2 + 1^2) + (2^2 + 1^2)$, or $3^2 + 2^2 + 2(1^2)$. Moving on to $N = 7$, we find $S^+(7) = 4^2 + 2^2$. Adding this to $C(6)$, we get $4^2 + 2^2 + 3^2 + 2^2 + 2(1^2) = 4^2 + 3^2 + 2(2^2) + 2(1^2)$.

Table 16.4 summarizes this way of writing $C(N)$. In words, we simply count down from $N - 3$. The first two numbers are squared, the next two are squared and doubled, the next two are squared and tripled, and so on down the line until you reach 1 (which we square as well for consistency).

Table 16.4 holds the clue to the big payoff! We only need to write this pattern in the form of an equation. That's easily done. And the really nice thing is that there's no need for special cases for even and odd values of N. Drumroll, please, for the formula for $C(N)$, the total number of crosses in a regular complete graph with N vertices:

$$C(N) = \sum_{i=0}^{N-4} \left(\left\lfloor \frac{i}{2} \right\rfloor + 1 \right)(N - 3 - i)^2$$

A tabulation of $C(N)$ from $N = 1$ to 50 in steps of 5 is shown in Table 16.5. A plot of these values is shown in Figure 16.22. The graph goes up pretty steeply—a regular complete graph of $N = 200{,}000$ has about 6.6×10^{19} crossings.

Table 16.5 Values of $C(N)$ from 1 to 50 in steps of 5.

N	C(N)
5	5
10	210
15	1,365
20	4,845
25	12,650
30	27,405
35	52,360
40	91,390
45	148,995
50	230,300

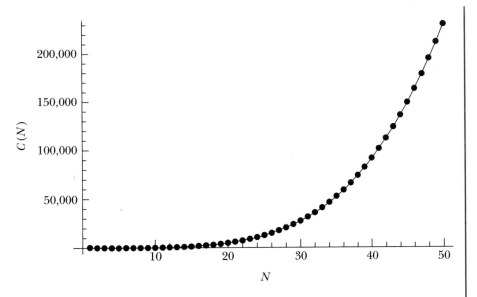

Figure 16.22
A plot of C(N)
from N = 1 to
N = 50.

Earlier in this chapter, I said that there was another, simpler way to compute the number of crosses. When this chapter was first published, several readers wrote to me and suggested this simpler approach. It makes a nice comparison with what we've seen so far—basically a single observation and a standard formula are all that's needed. If the previous discussion was the scenic route, then this is the highway.

Let's revisit our physical motivation. We have N nails at the vertices of a regular N-gon. Each cross is the result of two strings, and each string is created from two nails. So each cross is the result of a set of four nails, joined in pairs. Figure 16.23 shows four arbitrary nails on the graph N = 9, which I've labeled A, B, C, and D going around the graph counterclockwise.

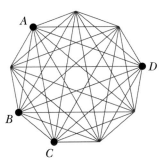

Figure 16.23
Four points on the
graph N = 9.

Looking at these, we can cluster them into three pairs, as shown in Figure 16.24: *AB/CD*, *AC/BD*, and *AD/BC*. The first and third pairings don't cross each other; only the middle one does. This will be true for any set of four points taken around a regular N-gon. Basically, if we think of each set of four nails as a little graph with four vertices, then only one pairing will create lines that cross. So for each set of four points that we pick on the graph,

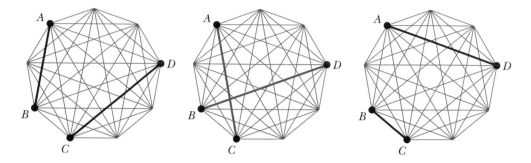

we get exactly one cross. If we can find out how many sets of four nails there are in a graph of *N* nails, we'll also have the number of crosses.

The answer to this question is given by a standard formula from combinatorics, the field of mathematics that studies how objects can be grouped and combined. The formula we want is written $C(m, r)$. The C is for "combinations," and the formula itself is usually pronounced "m choose r." This formula counts the number of unique combinations of r different items that can be drawn from a pool of m items. The general formula is

$$C(m, r) = \frac{m!}{r!(m - r)!}$$

In our case, we want to count the number of ways to draw four things from a pool of *N*, so this can be written as

$$C(N) = \frac{N!}{24(N - 4)!}$$

We can simplify this a little by noticing that when $N!$ is divided by $(N - 4)!$, only the four largest values in the numerator remain. So we can get rid of the factorials altogether, and here's our new, simplified shortcut version of $C(N)$:

$$C(N) = \frac{(N)(N - 1)(N - 2)(N - 3)}{24}$$

It's possible to prove that both this $C(N)$ and the one I gave earlier result in the same values, but because it's a rather complicated and unenlightening calculation, I won't go through the details here.

Chapter Sixteen

It's nice to have such a simple, closed-form solution, though I also enjoyed discovering all the patterns hiding inside the more scenic approach we took earlier.

Wrapping Up

There's something really pleasing about discovering graceful patterns. In this chapter we started with a simple but attractive pattern of lines and moved through a sequence of attractive patterns of numbers. We found the number of crosses in a regular complete graph by a series of relatively simple steps, which were then pretty easy to combine because their patterns were so clear.

Discovering unexpected and graceful patterns in art and mathematics is a real joy. And when the math and pictures complement each other, it's particularly delightful to enjoy these two different and beautiful aspects of the same idea.

Index

H

half-angle substitution, 129

half-turn rotational symmetry, 27

harlequin strut units, 48–50
  defined, 49
  illustrated, 49
  tightening, 50
  See also cube; unit origami

hexagonal envelope,
    225–226
  cutter diagram, 225
  flap geometry, 225
  illustrated, 226

hollow die cutting, 224

horizontal reflection
    symmetry
  defined, 26
  repeated twice, 28

I

icosadodecahedron, 63–64
  defined, 63
  illustrated, 63
  little turtle unit, 63–64

icosahedron, 54–57
  assembling, 56–57
  defined, 54
  nested, 63
  net, 113
  from triangle face units,
    54
  See also Platonic solids

image maps, 212

implicit functions, plotting,
    79–85

index of refraction, 14–15
  computing, 14
  ice reference data, 15

inflation
  dart, 200
  defined, 200
  finite number of, 203
  kite, 200
  kite and dart, with triangles, 211
  pattern, 211
  thick rhomb, 207
  thin rhomb, 207

inscribed angle, 154–155
  central angle and, 155
  cyclic quadrilateral, 171,
    172
  defined, 154
  illustrated, 155
  vertex, 156
  See also angle(s)

inscribed quadrilateral, 179

inscribed triangles, 156, 161
  illustrated, 157
  reflected, 162
  See also triangles

interlocking tiles, 33–35
  defined, 33–35
  rules for building, 35

interpolating normals,
    94–97
  length, 95
  using component interpolation, 95

interpolation
  equal-angle, 95–96
  methods, 95

intersections
  of ray/circle, 168
  string, 271–272, 280
  of two lines, 151
  of two medians, 254

inverse Fourier transform
  defined, 259

tableau form of, 266
  See also Fourier transform

inversion, 173–174
  defined, 173
  formula, 175–176

isometries, 26, 27
  combining, 27–30, 32
  defined, 25
  identity, 27
  period band pattern with,
    30

isosceles triangles, 186

K

kaleidocycles, 118–120
  constructing, 119
  decorating, 119, 120
  defined, 118
  illustrated, 118, 119
  net, 118
  partially open, 118
  tiles, 120
  triangles, 118

kite and dart tiles, 198–201
  aperiodic bead sequence,
    199
  atlas, 201
  converting rhombs into,
    208
  dart inflation, 200
  decoration, 198, 213–214
  defined, 198
  deflation, 200
  geometry, 198
  inflation with triangles,
    211
  kite inflation, 200
  pattern, 199
  symmetrical decoration,
    214
  See also Penrose tiles

Andrew Glassner's Notebook *was typeset in Baskerville, with display lines in Gill Sans. Baskerville was created by John Baskerville around 1754. Eric Gill designed his namesake font in 1928. The book was printed on 70# Opus Web Gloss, 588 ppi.*